I0821044

To:

From:

Date:

The 3-Minute Prayer Jar Devotional

WANDA E. BRUNSTETTER

with DONNA K. MALTESE
and JANICE THOMPSON

Print ISBN 979-8-89151-174-3

Cover design by Greg Jackson, Thinkpen Design

Published by Barbour Publishing, Inc., 1810 Barbour Drive, Uhrichsville, Ohio 44683, www.barbourbooks.com

Our mission is to inspire the world with the life-changing message of the Bible.

Printed in China.

Hope, Healing & Forgiveness. . .
for Your Lovely Soul

These devotions were written especially for when you need a little reminder that every day can be covered in prayer. Just three short minutes is all you'll need to refresh and revitalize your spirit.

- Minute 1: Read the day's Bible verse and reflect on its meaning.
- Minute 2: Read the devotional and think about its application for your life.
- Minute 3: Pray.

Although these devotions aren't meant as a tool for deep Bible study, they can be a touch point to keep you grounded and focused on God, the giver of hope, healing, forgiveness, and so much more. May every moment you spend with the *3-Minute Prayer Jar Devotional* be a blessing!

WHAT IS A PRAYER JAR?

One of the most important things we can do to keep hope alive is pray. The Bible tells us in James 4:8 that if we want to draw closer to God, we are to reach out to Him. By going to God in prayer, we can offer our adoration, petitions, intercession, and thanks to Him. One thing we can do to remind ourselves to pray often is make a prayer jar and place it where we will see it every day. Each time we look at the jar, we will think of who and what we want to pray for. A prayer jar can deepen our relationship with God and strengthen our faith.

A prayer jar can be something as simple as a canning jar. It can be left plain or decorated with ribbon, stickers, buttons, sequins, feathers, or glitter. The one I use is an antique canning jar, which I've left plain. I write my prayer requests, verses of scripture, or notes of thanks to God on small pieces of paper. After praying about the request or reflecting on the Bible verse, I fold the paper in half and place it in the prayer jar. From time to time, I take out one or more of the prayers—and if that prayer has been answered, I thank the Lord for answered prayer and then write down the date. If my prayer request has not yet been answered, it goes back into the jar. Do you have a special prayer request today? If so, consider creating your own prayer jar.

Day 1

SWEET SLEEP

If you lie down, you will not be afraid;
when you lie down, your sleep will be sweet.

Proverbs 3:24 esv

Have you ever wondered why God created humans to need sleep?

The body is a wonderful thing. It self-heals as we sleep. Here are some important functions that take place while you're snoozing: Your tissues repair and grow. Your immune system receives the support it needs. Your memory is "consolidated" (meaning, the storage of memories takes place). Your hormones are regulated. Energy is restored. Body temperatures are regulated. And, most important of all, you're emotionally and physically restored.

Now you see why it's so important to get the rest you need! If you don't slow down to allow your immune system to receive support, what happens? If you plow forward and don't let your memory "consolidate," then what? If you don't receive emotional and physical restoration, how can you possibly handle the issues that crop up today?

Slow down and crawl under the covers for some much-needed zzz's!

Thank You for the reminder that I need rest, Jesus! Amen.

PRAYER JAR INSPIRATION:

I will treat rest as a friend.

Day 2

FORGIVING THE FORGIVER

I am a woman of a sorrowful spirit. . . . I was pouring out my soul before the Lord. . . . Out of my great complaint and bitter provocation I have been speaking.

1 Samuel 1:15–16 ampc

There may come a time when you have some difficulty forgiving God Himself—for prayers that weren't answered the way you expected, for the tragic death of a loved one, for failed plans you thought God was backing, for not being able to rein in the world's cruelty, for a miracle that never came. . .

When a believer is unable to "forgive God" for what she's suffered, chances are good that she'll leave the church or, even worse, badmouth God to believers and nonbelievers alike!

The Bible is filled with examples of people who were disappointed and angry with God—including David, the apple of God's eye (2 Samuel 6:1–8); Jonah (3:10–4:4); Jeremiah (15:18); and Moses (Numbers 11:10–15).

Fortunately, God understands. He knows our emotions can wreak havoc on our thoughts. During these times, we need to vent our feelings, pour out our hearts, and ask God to help us restore our relationship with Him.

Lord, I offer my heart, sore and heavy.

PRAYER JAR INSPIRATION:

Hear my prayer, O Lord! Help!

Day 3

CALLED FOR

On the day I called, You answered me; and You made me bold and confident with [renewed] strength in my life.

Psalm 138:3 amp

Day after day goes by, and still you cannot seem to find the strength to do what your heart truly desires: to fulfill the plans God has set before you. What's a woman to do?

Pray. Go to God. Sit, kneel, prostrate yourself before Him. Push from your mind all the ifs, ands, or buts that stand between you and the goals God has planted in your heart. Allow yourself to be filled with the Spirit's presence. Focus on your breath, allowing it to match the endless rhythm of God's heartbeat. And when you sense God within and without, call on Him. Make your request known. If you cannot put it into words, present your groans and moans, knowing the Spirit will translate your petition, knowing that God will answer your request or change it so that your desire matches His will.

Lord, I call on You for strength to realize my dream.

PRAYER JAR INSPIRATION:

God of all living, renew my strength; embolden my heart.

Day 4

REST IS CRITICAL

"Come to me, all you who are weary and burdened, and I will give you rest."

MATTHEW 11:28 NIV

Rest feels counterproductive at times, especially if you're goal oriented. No doubt you would prefer to race toward the goal and feel accomplished at the end. But when it comes to recovery from emotional, spiritual, and psychological trauma, there are no clear-cut goals.

Some people would say, "Trust the process," but it's better to say, "Trust the God of the process." What you can't see, He can. What you can't predict, He can. He knows how and when you'll finally reach that invisible goal, and you really can trust Him at every step along the way.

It's important to note that Jesus Himself is the one who said, "Come to me, all you who are weary and burdened, and I will give you rest." He is the ultimate rest giver. So the key to finding rest is to spend time with Him.

I will come to you to find rest, Jesus. Amen.

PRAYER JAR INSPIRATION:

Jesus is my resting place.

Day 5

PASSING IT ON

All praise goes to God, Father of our Lord Jesus, the Anointed One. He is the Father of compassion, the God of all comfort. He consoles us as we endure the pain and hardship of life so that we may draw from His comfort and share it with others in their own struggles.

2 Corinthians 1:3–4 voice

In every calamity we suffer—every trouble that trips us up—we receive God's comfort, compassion, and consolation. As soon as He sees a tear fall from our eyes or hears the deep sigh of a heavy heart, He rushes to our side and offers all the love and comfort we need. And He does this so that we can offer the same mercy, comfort, and compassion to others.

When others bring us heartache, God sends His comfort. So why not offer the comfort of our forgiveness and mercy to the ones who wound us? Why not extend what God has extended to us?

The next time you experience God's compassion, pass it on to one who may not expect yours. Take in the comfort you've received from heaven and give it to someone else.

Thank You, Lord, for being a source of comfort when I'm wounded. Help me pass that comfort on by not only forgiving my offenders but loving them and lifting their pain.

PRAYER JAR INSPIRATION:

The compassion and comfort God gives to me is what I aim to pass on to others.

Day 6

ALWAYS FOUND

God is our refuge and strength, a helper who is always found in times of trouble. Therefore we will not be afraid.

Psalm 46:1–2 hcsb

The world is constantly changing. Things we never imagined would ever happen are becoming the norm.

Fortunately, we have God in our lives. We have a Savior, an eternal helper, who has proved in the past and the present that He's always there for us. In Him we can put all our hope and find our refuge and strength amid troubled times. "Therefore we will not be afraid, though the earth trembles and the mountains topple into the depths of the seas, though its waters roar and foam and the mountains quake with its turmoil" (Psalm 46:2–3 hcsb).

Woman of God, you never need to fear or feel too weak to find your footing in the flood or to secure a safe place behind the flames of fire. God will always be there for you to give you strength.

Holy Refuge and Strength, thank You for always being there when trouble comes. Because of Your constant presence amid flood, wind, and fire, I will find the strength when I need it.

PRAYER JAR INSPIRATION:

God of strength, be my constant refuge in this time. Help me keep my eyes on You.

Day 7

ALLOW THE WORD TO SPEAK

All Scripture is God-breathed and is useful for teaching, rebuking, correcting and training in righteousness.

2 Timothy 3:16 niv

How's your Bible time going?

There are times when you read a verse and it doesn't settle deep in your spirit. Then there are other times when you read that same verse and it strikes you like a bolt of spiritual lightning.

When you take the time to slow down to heal, don't forget to include Bible time. Words of wisdom in those pages will help you through every single transition in the healing process. And remember, the Bible is alive and active (see Hebrews 4:12). It didn't die out with the last apostle.

The truths in God's Word hold as much power today as they ever did. And when you take the time to apply them properly, they can also be a healing balm in time of need. So, what are you waiting for? Grab that Bible and start reading!

I'm so grateful for Your Word, Lord! Where would I be without it? I'm thankful that I'll never have to know. Amen.

PRAYER JAR INSPIRATION:

The Word of God is alive and active!

Day 8

ADORNED IN LOVE

Clothe yourselves with tenderhearted mercy, kindness, humility, gentleness, and patience. Make allowance for each other's faults, and forgive anyone who offends you. Remember, the Lord forgave you, so you must forgive others. Above all, clothe yourselves with love, which binds us all together in perfect harmony.

Colossians 3:12–14 NLT

So many people are focused on taking care of their own and letting the rest of the world take care of itself. But Jesus asks you to adopt a different attitude—the one He wore. This attitude means clothing yourself with mercy, kindness, humility, gentleness, and patience. It means not only making allowances for each other's faults (for nobody is perfect) but forgiving anyone who offends you, just as you've been forgiven by God. Better yet, it means adorning yourself in love, allowing it to emanate from you, touching every person you meet!

Imagine what kind of a world we'd have if everyone shared all things, forgave, and loved one another. That is what you, through Christ's strength, are called to do today.

Remind me each day, Lord, to clothe myself in love—to forgive as You forgive me.

PRAYER JAR INSPIRATION:

I dress myself today as Jesus dressed Himself—adorned in love!

Day 9

REMADE

After you have suffered for a little while, the God of all grace [who imparts His blessing and favor], who called you to His own eternal glory in Christ, will Himself complete, confirm, strengthen, and establish you [making you what you ought to be].

1 Peter 5:10 amp

Life can be difficult. But even though you may experience some suffering now and then, you are not to lose hope. Instead, remember that the Lord of all creation—the one who fashioned you for a special purpose that only *you* can live out—may allow some trouble to come your way so that you become the woman He created you to be.

When God saw Gideon cowering in a corner, He addressed him as a mighty warrior! How could this man in hiding—the one whose family was the weakest in his tribe and who was the youngest in his family—be a warrior? By going in the strength he had, knowing God was with him (Judges 6:11–14).

So, woman of God, go in the strength you have. Be the woman the Lord already knows you are. And do so without fear, knowing He goes with you.

Thank You, Lord, for making me complete in Your eyes.

PRAYER JAR INSPIRATION:

God remakes me in His strength and presence.

Day 10

INTENTIONAL

Would not God discover this? For he knows the secrets of the heart.

Psalm 44:21 esv

When you do something intentionally, it means you're doing it on purpose. You've put thought into it. People use the phrase "be intentional" when they talk about things like starting diets or healing broken marriages.

People who struggle in specific areas must be intentional as well. For example, hoarders must be intentional when tackling their homes. Addicts must be intentional when dealing with alcohol or drugs.

You get the idea. Intentional means work.

Sometimes we must be intentional about slowing down. We have to treat our busyness as an addict would treat that bottle of alcohol. It's not our friend, and we have to stop inviting it to dwell with us.

Be intentional about your quiet times with God and with simple things like rest. Sleep. Stillness. When you make up your mind to do a thing, it's more likely you will actually do it.

I want to make up my mind, Lord. I want to be more intentional. Help me keep my focus so that I can do this in the areas that matter most. Amen.

PRAYER JAR INSPIRATION:

Intentional = purposeful

Day 11

ADMISSIONS

When I refused to admit my wrongs, I was miserable, moaning and complaining all day long so that even my bones felt brittle. Day and night, Your hand kept pressing on me. My strength dried up like water in the summer heat; You wore me down.

Psalm 32:3–4 voice

Let's face it: When we mess up and try to hide our wrongs—or simply refuse to admit that we've erred—we begin to suffer. We become so miserable that we can barely breathe, so heavy is the sin that presses down upon us.

The Holy Spirit keeps reminding us of what we'd like to forget. But suppressing our misdeeds instead of confessing them wears us down emotionally, mentally, spiritually, and physically. John 16:8 tells us that the Holy Spirit convicts us of sin—and that God's forgiveness is the only remedy for the pain.

Today, do a wellness check on yourself. Ask the Spirit to bring to light any misdeeds that need God's remedy. And do so knowing His remedy always brings relief.

Look me over, Spirit. See if there's anything within me that I need to fess up to God. Then, fill me with the sweet relief found in Your forgiveness.

PRAYER JAR INSPIRATION:

When I admit my wrongs, God assists with His relief!

Day 12

PEP TALK

"No man will [be able to] stand before you [to oppose you] as long as you live. Just as I was [present] with Moses, so will I be with you; I will not fail you or abandon you. Be strong and confident and courageous."

JOSHUA 1:5–6 AMP

After Moses died, God gave Joshua a good pep talk. He told him that just as He had been with Moses—guiding him, giving him encouragement and strength—He would be with Joshua. He would never fail him nor leave him. It was these words that gave Joshua the power to go on with the grand plan God had outlined for him as an individual and for the people he would lead.

God has a grand plan for you as well. And even though you may at times feel alone on the road He has set before you, He is walking right beside you. He will neither fail nor abandon you. Knowing that will give you all the strength, confidence, and courage you need to see things through.

Thank You, Lord, for this pep talk. I needed it so much right now. Knowing that You are walking at my side and will never abandon me gives me the strength and courage to do whatever You would have me do. In Jesus' name, amen.

PRAYER JAR INSPIRATION:

God forever walks by my side, enabling me to do what He has called me to do.

Day 13

WIPED OUT

"Come to Me, all who are weary and burdened, and I will give you rest. Take My yoke upon you and learn from Me, for I am gentle and humble in heart, and you will find rest for your souls. For My yoke is comfortable, and My burden is light."

MATTHEW 11:28–30 NASB

It's possible you're exhausted and don't even realize it. Some of the symptoms of exhaustion include chronic tiredness, headache, achy muscles, moodiness, frustration, slowed reflexes, and impaired decision-making.

If you're experiencing any of those things, you might be blaming them on something else when you're really just worn out.

The human body wasn't built to go, go, go. God designed you to need rest so that you could think more clearly, feel good, be in an upbeat mood, and have normal, healthy reflexes. These are all important things for day-to-day living.

The only way to heal an exhausted body is to deliberately hit the PAUSE button. When you do. . .aah! Sweet rest makes all things better.

I will pause from my labors, Lord! Amen.

PRAYER JAR INSPIRATION:

Just because I'm a doer doesn't mean I have to be an overdoer.

Day 14

PRAYERS AND PROMISES

Then Jacob prayed. . . . Rescue me now, please, from the hand of my brother, from the grip of Esau. I am afraid that he may come and crush us all. . . . And Jacob prayed on.

Genesis 32:9, 11–12 voice

Afraid that an angry Esau would destroy him and his family rather than receive his gifts, a restless Jacob did the only thing he could do: pray.

When we're up against the wall, unsure of how the future might play out and afraid that all our wrongs will come back to bite us, going to God in prayer is the best strategy.

Through humble prayer, we can review all the promises God has made on our behalf. We can remind ourselves that we are "not worthy of even a little of all of the loyal love and faithfulness You have shown to me, Your servant" (Genesis 32:10 voice). We can rehearse in our minds and hearts the fact that all our blessings have come from God and that it is He alone who can rescue us from our fears and anxieties.

If fear is preventing you from asking for forgiveness, pray to God for pcacc of mind and heart.

Lord, I humbly request courage and rescue as I endeavor to seek another's forgiveness.

PRAYER JAR INSPIRATION:

Through prayer, I'm assured of God's promises, protection, and peace.

Day 15

A STRONG TOWER

The name of the Lord is a strong tower; the righteous runs to it and is safe and set on high [far above evil].

Proverbs 18:10 AMP

When the world is crumbling down around you, when the load on you is so heavy you can barely breathe, when you are feeling weaker than weak, there is a place you can go. To Yahweh, the Lord. His name is a strong tower. To Him you can run and find safety from all that bedevils and bewilders you. In His name you can rise above every evil that threatens you. As you look down from His tower, all the troubles of this world become mere flotsam floating by, drifting way below you and out to an endless sea.

For the Lord's name is faithfulness, power, mercy, compassion, love, protection, safety, grace, goodness, and wisdom. All those things—all that He is—surround you when you reside in the tower of His strength.

Lord, my Mercy and Strength, to You I run.

PRAYER JAR INSPIRATION:

I find hope, shelter, and strength in the name of my Lord.

Day 16

WRUNG OUT

There is a river whose streams make glad the city of God,
the holy place where the Most High dwells.

PSALM 46:4 NIV

I can't. I'm too tired.

Maybe you've used those words a time or two of late. You're not physically ill. You don't have any real symptoms to speak of. But you just can't.

Think about that phrase for a moment. Back in the olden days, women would wash the laundry, then hang it on the line to dry. But sometimes clothes were too wet to dry in a timely fashion, so the ladies would wring them by hand first to get the excess water out. That way they stood a better chance of drying on the line.

When you're wrung out, it's as if life has taken you and twisted you in its hands, draining every last drop of energy. Now you're hanging out on the line, all dried out, and feeling completely useless.

The only way to fix this problem is with the kind of saturation that comes from rest and time with the Lord.

You are the stream I long to drink from, Lord! Amen.

PRAYER JAR INSPIRATION:

I can rest and refresh my soul at the river of life.

Day 17

NOTHING IS IMPOSSIBLE

For with God nothing is ever impossible and no word from God shall be without power or impossible of fulfillment.

Luke 1:37 AMPC

Sometimes, the harm others do to us seems irreparable. It feels impossible to forgive—much less forget. In these times, we must remember that everything is possible with God. That with His help and guidance, we should be able to accomplish whatever He commands us to do.

God has called us to forgive, so we must believe He will give us the power to do so. Perhaps that power will come from our prayers. Perhaps it will come from a greater understanding of Him and of the healing power in His Word. Perhaps it will come from a sermon or the wisdom of a friend.

God will find a way to reach you, teach you, help you, heal you, and get you to a point where you can forgive and heal. All you need to do is open yourself to His help. . .and believe you will receive it.

Help me, Lord, to forgive and heal. I open myself up to Your Word and will, knowing You will respond and lead me where You want me to go.

PRAYER JAR INSPIRATION:

Thank God that with Him, nothing is impossible!

Day 18

CONTINUALLY LOOKING

Search for the LORD and for his strength; continually seek him. Remember the wonders he has performed. . . . Honor and majesty surround him; strength and joy fill his dwelling.

1 CHRONICLES 16:11–12, 27 NLT

Every day a woman has her full list of chores before her—if not on paper, then on the screen of her mind. With such a long list of have-to-dos or want-to-dos, she can easily get caught up in the busyness of her day and rarely take a moment to think about God, maybe forgetting Him entirely. Before she knows it, the sun has set and she's too weak to do anything but flop into bed.

Yet that's not what God has envisioned for His Eves. He wants them to be continually looking for His presence and His strength. To be seeking Him every moment of every day. God wants His daughters to remind themselves of the wonders He has done and is doing and will do in the future. For only in the Lord will His girls find all the strength and joy they hope for at the beginning, middle, and end of each day.

Help me, Lord, to keep my mind and eyes looking for You in every moment of my day.

PRAYER JAR INSPIRATION:

I'll be looking for You, Lord, around every corner!

Day 19

THINGS ABOVE

Set your minds on things above, not on earthly things.

COLOSSIANS 3:2 NIV

Set your mind on things above. Sounds tricky, doesn't it? But if you've spent years giving in to negative mind chatter, it can be hard to break free.

The biblical solution is to set your mind on things above. Every time you're tempted to allow negativity to ruin your day, switch your thinking to the Lord. Come up with an easy phrase like "What would Jesus do?" It might seem silly to repeat an old phrase like this, but it forces you to refocus your attention on Him and away from your problems.

So, what would Jesus do about the situation you're walking through? How would He heal the problem you're facing? Are you more hopeful now that you've included Him in the story?

Cast your vision on Christ today. He has all the answers you need.

Healing can come when I cast my gaze on You, Lord! Amen.

PRAYER JAR INSPIRATION:
It's possible to shift my focus to things above.

Day 20

SPIRITUAL LAW

If you don't want to be judged, don't judge. If you don't want to be condemned, don't condemn. If you want to be forgiven, forgive. Don't hold back—give freely, and you'll have plenty poured back into your lap—a good measure, pressed down, shaken together, brimming over. You'll receive in the same measure you give.

Luke 6:37–38 voice

There is a spiritual law—one that often goes unrecognized in everyday life—that says whatever you do will come back around. If you judge others, you too will be judged. If you condemn others, you too will be condemned. And if you don't forgive others, you won't be forgiven either. Why? Because whatever you do (or don't do) will be done (or not done) to you. And it will be done (or not done) *to the same extent* that you do it (or don't do it).

So today, think about how you are treating those who have transgressed against you or who owe you in some way. Taking this spiritual law into account, consider what you might need to do to make things right with them. Then, do it.

Help me, Lord, to treat others as I would like to be treated by them—and by You.

PRAYER JAR INSPIRATION:

Lord, show me how to treat others the way You treat me!

Day 21

STRENGTH IN WEAKNESS

He has said to me, "My grace is sufficient for you [My lovingkindness and My mercy are more than enough—always available—regardless of the situation]; for [My] power is being perfected [and is completed and shows itself most effectively] in [your] weakness."

2 Corinthians 12:9 AMP

What do you do with your hope when you've prayed and prayed and prayed and still gotten no relief from God for your physical, mental, or emotional trouble? Do you give up on Him, or do you turn to Him even more?

The apostle Paul had a "thorn in the flesh" (2 Corinthians 12:7) that tormented him. Three times he asked the Lord to take it away from him. But Jesus told him that His grace, His abundant and continual supply of love and mercy, was enough to carry Paul through his trouble. That *His* strength and power were going to work best through Paul's weakness.

So don't lean into the enemy's whispers that God has abandoned you. Instead, tap into the abundant grace and power that Christ is pouring into you. Then you too will find the joy of Christ's strength dwelling in and enfolding you even in moments of weakness.

Enfold me, Lord, in Your power and strength.

PRAYER JAR INSPIRATION:

My hope in Christ lives on!

Day 22

WORDS MATTER

Therefore, as God's chosen people, holy and dearly loved, clothe yourselves with compassion, kindness, humility, gentleness and patience.

COLOSSIANS 3:12 NIV

Here's the truth: Any negative words spoken to you as a child, the ones that wounded you and shaped your mindset? You don't have to be a slave to them any longer. Perhaps those thoughts became your reality because you didn't know any better, but now you do. Now you realize that God has so much more in mind for you.

You're beautiful. You have the mind of Christ. You'll amount to everything God has planned for you. You're an amazing child of God, loved and adored.

It's time to heal from the ugly words. The lies. The manipulation. The mean-spirited phrases that were meant to wound. Give those phrases to God. Write down on a piece of paper: "I am beautiful to my Lord. I have His mindset, His thoughts. I will go far with His help." You will, you know. Those words from yesterday can't hold you back now!

Nothing can hold me back now, Lord! Amen.

PRAYER JAR INSPIRATION:

Words can bring hurt or healing.

Day 23

MAKING PEACE

Do not retaliate with evil, regardless of the evil brought against you. Try to do what is good and right and honorable as agreed upon by all people. If it is within your power, make peace with all people.

Romans 12:17–18 voice

When we're insulted, maligned, or injured—physically, mentally, emotionally—our flesh would like nothing better than to reach out and hurt the other person. But if we're to live by the Spirit, we must take the higher road.

We are to fight evil with good. To make peace with those who injure and insult us. This is what separates the godly from the ungodly.

This idea of not retaliating was first laid out by Jesus, who said we are to offer our left cheek if someone strikes our right. To give up our coat if someone takes our shirt (Matthew 5:39–40).

Not retaliating is the harder path to take. But it's all part of the forgiveness journey that God expects us not to forsake. If you know someone with whom you need to make peace, do everything within your power to make that happen. And let the rest go.

Give me, Lord, the strength I need to not just forgive but repay evil with good and be at peace with all.

PRAYER JAR INSPIRATION:

God will help me, peace by peace.

Day 24

ULTIMATE PROVIDER

Riches and honor come from You, and You are the ruler of everything. Power and might are in Your hand, and it is in Your hand to make great and to give strength to all. Now therefore, our God, we give You thanks and praise Your glorious name.

1 Chronicles 29:12–13 HCSB

Everything we have comes from God. Not one thing is our own creation. He is the true source of all we desire, all we need. Yet how often do we give Him the thanks He deserves? How much of His bounty do we take for granted?

Today, remember that God is your ultimate and abundant Creator and Provider of everything you desire and need to live, to breathe, and to walk His Way. Get down on your knees and thank Him for the hope and strength He equips and inspires you with. Then use those blessings to live out His plan for you. Dream with the ultimate dreamer. Walk in step with the grand planner. And you will find all you need and hope for.

Everything I am and have, Lord, has come from Your loving hand. For this I thank, honor, and worship You. Help me use Your blessings to further Your kingdom. In Jesus' name, amen.

PRAYER JAR INSPIRATION:

My hope and strength are gifts from my Lord. To Him I give all my thanks.

Day 25

NO MORE MIND GAMES

I have been crucified with Christ and I no longer live, but Christ lives in me. The life I now live in the body, I live by faith in the Son of God, who loved me and gave himself for me.

Galatians 2:20 NIV

The enemy loves nothing more than to play mind games with you. He whispers negative words into your ear, and (despite your best attempts) you begin to believe them. He tells you you're unlovable. He tells you you're not as good as others. He whispers, "You'll never fit in. Why even try?"

Many of these cruel whispers have been playing on repeat since childhood. You're not sure when they started, but they're familiar. And you've been believing them for so long that changing your mindset seems impossible.

But it's not impossible. With God *all things* are possible. Even a radical change of thinking. Give your mind chatter to Him. And while you're at it, tell the enemy to get lost! He has no business messing with a child of the King, after all!

Today I give my mind chatter to You, Lord! I won't give myself over to negative thoughts anymore. Amen.

PRAYER JAR INSPIRATION:

The enemy is a liar. God is the truth-teller.

Day 26

LOVING WELL

Love others well, and don't hide behind a mask; love authentically. Despise evil; pursue what is good as if your life depends on it. Live in true devotion to one another, loving each other as sisters and brothers.

Romans 12:9–10 voice

Jesus made sure His followers knew the commandments that encompass all the laws of Moses and the prophets. The first and most important one is "You shall love the Lord your God with all your heart and with all your soul and with all your mind (intellect)" (Matthew 22:37 AMPC). The second "is like it: You shall love your neighbor as [you do] yourself" (Matthew 22:39 AMPC).

In other words, you are to love God and others well. And to love well, you must look past the ways others have wronged you. Your love and forgiveness must be real, just like God's is to you.

The greater the evil someone has committed against you, the harder it becomes to love and forgive. Yet that's exactly what God asks you to do. And He never gives you a challenge you can't handle.

Help me, Lord, to love others authentically, just as You love all people. My aim is to follow Your commands.

PRAYER JAR INSPIRATION:

May I love and forgive well!

Day 27

MOUNTAIN-MOVING MAMA

"I assure you and most solemnly say to you, if you have [living] faith the size of a mustard seed, you will say to this mountain, 'Move from here to there,' and [if it is God's will] it will move; and nothing will be impossible for you."

MATTHEW 17:20 AMP

Some days you may feel as if everything is against you—as if all you do is spend your time trying to overcome one obstacle after another. At the end of the day, you feel not only weak and exhausted but a bit disgusted with yourself and the world.

That's when you need to remember the power that is yours if you will only take it and go deep. Jesus promises that with even the littlest bit of trust and confidence in Him, you can say to any mountainous obstacle you face, "Get out of my way," and if God wills it, it will disintegrate. Whenever you dig deep in your faith, nothing will be impossible for you.

Lord, when I feel weak, when I can no longer overcome the obstacles before me, please remind me that I can move mountains. That with You in my life, nothing will be impossible for me. In Your name, amen.

PRAYER JAR INSPIRATION:

With Jesus by my side, I hang on to the hope that I can and will do the impossible.

Day 28

CONFUSION MUST GO!

God is not a God of confusion but a God of peace.

1 Corinthians 14:33 ncv

To be confused means you can't decide which is the better of the two (or three or four) choices in front of you. Confusion says, "It might be this one. Or it might be that one." Then an argument ensues in your mind as you try to reason it out.

God is not the author of confusion. The enemy is! He wants to offer you too many options, too many choices, so that your thoughts are never still.

Why does Satan want to keep you preoccupied? Because he knows that you'll never truly heal if you don't take the time to get beyond the voices in your head that tell you to do this thing or that thing.

Today, speak to that confusion in Jesus' name. Tell it to go. And in its place, God will provide supernatural peace to help you make the right choices. His choices. Healthy choices. The ones that lead to life and healing.

Thank You for giving me direction, Lord. I don't need to live in confusion. I can follow hard after You. Amen.

PRAYER JAR INSPIRATION:

Confusion must go in Jesus' name!

Day 29

GOING DEEPER

For if you forgive people their trespasses [their reckless and willful sins, leaving them, letting them go, and giving up resentment], your heavenly Father will also forgive you. But if you do not forgive others their trespasses [their reckless and willful sins, leaving them, letting them go, and giving up resentment], neither will your Father forgive you your trespasses.

MATTHEW 6:14–15 AMPC

After giving His disciples a model for prayer, Jesus explained the forgiveness part more fully. (And the Amplified Bible, Classic Edition helps us better understand what this forgiveness may entail.)

While our mouth might say we forgive someone, we may still hold on to some anger. In such cases, we haven't yet truly forgiven that individual.

Consider how you would feel if God didn't fully forgive you—if He just couldn't let go of something you did. Thankfully, God doesn't do things halfway. When He forgives, He does so fully. And that's what sets us free!

Whom might you need to forgive more fully?

Lord, give me the strength to go deeper, to let go of all grudges and resentments so that I—and the person who has done me wrong—can be totally free.

PRAYER JAR INSPIRATION:

I forgive others as God forgives me!

Day 30

ALL YOU NEED

My God in His [steadfast] lovingkindness will meet me. . . . I will sing of Your mighty strength and power; yes, I will sing joyfully of Your lovingkindness in the morning; for You have been my stronghold and a refuge in the day of my distress.

PSALM 59:10, 16 AMP

Before you even know what you need, your loving God has His ample supply of provisions ready to meet you. That's because He sees everything that's going on in your life. He knows all your thoughts, your feelings, your dreams, your hopes, and your requirements. And He knows exactly what you will encounter every day, way before you have an inkling of what's ahead.

So don't just hope that God will be there with His strength, love, and courage when you need it. *Know* He will be there with whatever you need to do whatever you need to do for Him.

Thank You, Lord, for having all I need just when I need it!

PRAYER JAR INSPIRATION:

Each day, I hope for and will sing of God's endless blessings ready and waiting just for me.

Day 31

DON'T BELIEVE THE LIES

Do not lie to one another, seeing that you have put off the old self with its practices and have put on the new self, which is being renewed in knowledge after the image of its creator.

Colossians 3:9–10 esv

Have you ever believed a lie for so long that it felt like the truth? Think of the little girl who is told she's stupid. She begins to live out that message, opting to slack off in school. If people already think she's stupid, she might as well become a self-fulfilling prophecy, right?

It happens all the time. People begin to believe the lies spoken over them and live them out as truths.

But they're not.

We've been taught not to lie, but we're not taught to avoid believing lies. It's time to realize they're both equally dangerous.

Have you been living out any lies in your life? What negative words have had an impact on the way you view yourself and others? It's not too late to turn those messages around. God is speaking life over you today. He's speaking hope. He's saying, "Believe the truth of my Word: You are a beloved child of the King!"

Lord, please give me the ability to tell the truth from a lie so I'm not deceived. Amen.

PRAYER JAR INSPIRATION:

Lies have no authority over me!

Day 32

ALL RIGHT

For everyone has sinned; we all fall short of God's glorious standard. Yet God, in his grace, freely makes us right in his sight. He did this through Christ Jesus when he freed us from the penalty for our sins.

Romans 3:23–24 NLT

If you have sinned, don't think you're alone. It's a part of the human condition. There's no way we can always get things right. We've all fallen *way* short of the standard God set in Moses' law.

But then came Jesus. Now we are right in God's eyes. Because the man who knew no sin died for us, we can live in God again!

So never allow yourself to think Jesus hasn't forgiven you for that time you spilled a friend's secrets. Or for those things you said to your husband—things you want to take back even though you're certain he was wrong. Whatever sin you're nursing because you're not sure you were ever forgiven, take it to Jesus. Confess it again and believe that you've been forgiven and freed.

You're all right in God's eyes!

I know I often fall short, Lord. Nevertheless, I know You've forgiven me. Help that truth sink into my heart.

PRAYER JAR INSPIRATION:

Thank God for His grace!

Day 33

STANDING BY

At my first trial no one supported me [as an advocate] or stood with me, but they all deserted me. May it not be counted against them [by God]. But the Lord stood by me and strengthened and empowered me, so that through me the [gospel] message might be fully proclaimed, and that all the Gentiles might hear it; and I was rescued from the mouth of the lion.

2 TIMOTHY 4:16–17 AMP

When Paul stood before the Roman tribunal, facing a death sentence, all his friends and coworkers deserted him. But the Lord didn't. He not only stood by Paul but gave him divine strength and power so that he could escape being beaten by those who stood against him.

If at any point you are in dire need of support or some sort of defense, take heart. Remember that just as the Lord stood by Paul, He stands by you. He is the best and greatest defense and strengthener you could ever ask for. He'll make sure that when all is said and done, you, like Daniel, have not one mark of a lion's tooth or claw on you (Daniel 6:23).

Thank You, Lord, for being the one support and strengthener I can truly count on.

PRAYER JAR INSPIRATION:

I live in the hope and knowledge that God stands beside me, giving me the strength and power I need to do His will.

Day 34

THINK ON THESE THINGS

Finally, brothers and sisters, whatever is true,
whatever is noble, whatever is right, whatever is pure,
whatever is lovely, whatever is admirable—if anything is
excellent or praiseworthy—think about such things.

PHILIPPIANS 4:8 NIV

The Bible gives the perfect tool for unclogging the spiritual and mental pipes: good thoughts. Good thoughts will purge bad ones every time. And you can prepare yourself for these attacks before they even happen.

What would it be like if you made a list (in advance) of "true" things. Noble things. Pure things. Lovely things. Admirable things. Excellent things. Praiseworthy things. What if you had an actual list to refer to whenever the enemy clogs the pipes with negativity? What if you reached for that page and began to speak aloud the goodness of God in your life?

Talk about a quick flush! That negativity would have to go when confronted with the powerful plunging truth of God's goodness in your life!

Help me guard my thoughts, Jesus. I don't want to give way
to the enemy by dwelling on impure things. Amen.

PRAYER JAR INSPIRATION:

I will think on "true" things—good things!—today.

Day 35

THROUGH THIS MAN

So let it be clearly known and understood by you, brethren, that through this Man forgiveness and removal of sins is now proclaimed to you; and that through Him everyone who believes [who acknowledges Jesus as his Savior and devotes himself to Him] is absolved (cleared and freed) from every charge from which he could not be justified and freed by the Law of Moses and given right standing with God.

Acts 13:38–39 AMPC

Jesus has thrown you a lifeline. He is the one man whose death cleansed you of sins. If you believe in Him, acknowledge Him as your Savior, and dedicate your life to Him, you will be cleared of any misdeeds that have stained your record.

There's no way anyone can get through this life without erring. But whether your misstep was intentional or unintentional, God will forgive you through Jesus. No ifs, ands, or buts about it.

Whenever your thoughts spiral out of control, head to Jesus or dive into His Word. Take to heart the fact that you are a free woman who's been cleared of all charges against her. Then offer your praise to God!

Thank You, Lord, for removing my sins—for absolving me of every charge!

PRAYER JAR INSPIRATION:

In Jesus, I am free indeed!

Day 36

GOD IS LOVE

God is love. . . . And we have come to know and to believe the love that God has for us. God is love, and the one who remains in love remains in God, and God remains in him.

1 John 4:8, 16 HCSB

Here we have a few very powerful and amazing truths. The first is that God is love. The second is that He has an amazing amount of love for us.

Yet that's not all! John tells us that because God is love, the woman who abides in love, who lives it out in her life, abides in God—and God abides in her! The Creator and sustainer of the entire planet, solar system, and universe—the one who holds all the power and people of this earth in His hand—this God, this Person, this Spirit is love. And if we dwell in that love, not only do we live in Him, He also lives in us!

In those moments when you feel unlovable, unloved, and unable to love, remember the hope you have in the God who is love.

Thank You, Lord, for allowing me to experience Your love.

PRAYER JAR INSPIRATION:

I hope in the God of love.

Day 37

EXPOSURE

Have nothing to do with the fruitless deeds of darkness, but rather expose them.

Ephesians 5:11 niv

Why do you suppose God took the time during creation to separate light from darkness? He drew a very clear line between the two. In that one swift move, He was teaching us that there are two worlds and that we must choose one or the other. (Hint: He's hoping we'll choose the kingdom of light!)

God is still drawing a line between the two. Take a closer look at today's verse: "Have nothing to do with fruitless deeds of darkness, but rather expose them."

God is in the exposing business. There are no shifting shadows with Him. He wants the light of His Word, His Son, His salvation message, to shine bright over all the dark places.

When you hover too closely to people who are living in darkness, you pull yourself into the shadows.

Step out of the shadows. Healing only comes in the light, and you'll need to take strong, definitive steps in the direction of that light to dispel the darkness.

I'm so glad I've chosen to live in the kingdom of light, Jesus!
Thank You for always shining bright in my life. Amen.

PRAYER JAR INSPIRATION:

I can expose evil deeds of darkness by shining my light.

Day 38

BELIEVING PRAYER

Are you hurting? Pray. Do you feel great? Sing. Are you sick? Call the church leaders together to pray and anoint you with oil in the name of the Master. Believing-prayer will heal you, and Jesus will put you on your feet. And if you've sinned, you'll be forgiven—healed inside and out.

James 5:13–15 msg

God's Word reminds us that, sometimes, it's best to pray for ourselves in a group setting, not alone. The more believing hearts that are gathered together the better.

We're encouraged to pray when we're hurting and to sing praises when we're feeling great. In times of illness, it may be the anxiety of an unconfessed sin that's keeping us down. Perhaps we want to get a few things off our chest so that we can feel the peace of God's forgiveness inside and out. Or maybe we've confessed to God but, for some reason, don't feel as if we've been forgiven.

Whichever scenario applies to you, take your faith to fellow believers. Ask them to pray with you. Then do so, knowing you'll be forgiven.

Increase my faith, Lord, as I pray with fellow believers, seeking Your forgiveness.

PRAYER JAR INSPIRATION:

Believing prayer brings results—praise God!

Day 39

CONSTANT LOVE

He heals the brokenhearted and binds up their wounds. . . . The Lord takes pleasure in those who fear him, in those who hope in his steadfast love.

Psalm 147:3, 11 esv

We all have those days when we feel as if no one loves us. . .when disappointment after disappointment cracks our foundation of strength. . .when we feel exhausted, as if we have been trying in vain to swim against a strong current. . .when absolutely nothing is going our way.

Take heart in the fact that God loves you. He is cognizant of all that is going on in your life. He gathers to Him those cast out. He heals those with broken hearts. He binds up the wounds of those crushed in spirit and lifts those who are humble.

Go to God, the one who loves you more than you could ever know. Tell Him all your troubles, hurts, wounds, and challenges. Allow Him to love you, to give you peace, and to comfort you with His words.

I come to You, Lord, seeking Your face, love, peace, and understanding.

PRAYER JAR INSPIRATION:

God's immense love for me never wavers.

Day 40

A SPECIAL GIFT

"Let us discern for ourselves what is right; let us learn together what is good."

Job 34:4 NIV

Did you know that the Holy Spirit can give you the supernatural ability to tell the truth from a lie? If you ask for that, He will surely give it. And this special gift is really going to come in handy if you're living with (or working with) someone prone to manipulation.

With the help of the Spirit of God, you can be set free. Shackles can fall. And while you might not physically be able to walk away from a person who is attempting to manipulate you, you can most certainly learn healthy ways to deal with them.

Today, take a few minutes and ask God to endow you with the ability to discern good from evil, the truth from a lie. If a child asks his father for bread, will the father give him a stone? No. If you ask for discernment, then discernment you will surely receive.

I need discernment desperately, Lord! Sometimes it's really hard to tell the truth from a lie. I need that ability. I don't ever want to be confused or to listen to the wrong voices. Amen.

PRAYER JAR INSPIRATION:

With God's help, I can discern what is good.

Day 41

MOVING FORWARD IN GOD

If God hadn't been there for me, I never would have made it. The minute I said, "I'm slipping, I'm falling," your love, God, took hold and held me fast. When I was upset and beside myself, you calmed me down and cheered me up.

Psalm 94:17–19 msg

There may be days when you doubt God has truly forgiven you. That's when you need to look into His Word once more. His truth will keep you from slipping back into your old ways—the one direction God doesn't want you to go.

Perhaps there's a certain sin for which you're not sure God has forgiven you. . .

These are all lies, planted in your mind by the father of lies. So have confidence. Know that God does forgive and that He's always waiting to steer you back onto His track. Remember that God has a hold on you—and He'll never, ever let you go. Why? Because He loves you more than you can ever imagine. You have a place in His plan.

Today, know God is always there for you. His love will keep you close and calm.

You know what I've done, Lord. Help me move forward in a new way!

PRAYER JAR INSPIRATION:

In God, I trust that I can (and will) move forward.

Day 42

DEVELOPING HOPE

Hope [in God's promises] never disappoints us,
because God's love has been abundantly poured out within
our hearts through the Holy Spirit who was given to us.

Romans 5:5 AMP

Let's face it. This is a fallen world. And we will continue to have our share of problems here on earth. Yet still, even in those trials, we're never to forget that God does love us and that we still have His grace on us. Those things remain true. It's just that God allows troubles because He wants us to become more and more like His Son. And just as He did with Jesus, God will use our trials for our good—*if* we trust Him to do so, *if* we continue to hope in His promises.

So today, even in your trials, remember God's great love for you. Know that whatever is happening will come to some good. All you need to do is trust. To hope.

God, I hope not in man nor beast nor money nor
success but in You and Your great love!

PRAYER JAR INSPIRATION:

I can rejoice in all days, in all ways, for God
loves me. And I hope in His promises!

Day 43

UPSIDE-DOWN PLAN

"You are of your father the devil, and your will is to do your father's desires. He was a murderer from the beginning, and does not stand in the truth, because there is no truth in him. When he lies, he speaks out of his own character, for he is a liar and the father of lies."

John 8:44 ESV

Have you ever noticed that the enemy's lies are often the polar opposite of the Word of God? The Bible says, "Greater is He that is in me!" The devil whispers in your ear, "God doesn't care."

The Bible says, "You can be victorious!" The enemy says, "You're such a failure."

The Word of God is clear: "You are a beloved child of God!" The devil taunts you with "No one cares about you. You're not lovable."

It's always the opposite. Satan's upside-down plan is to attack you with lies so far-fetched that they clearly don't line up with God's promises.

And you've fallen for a few of those lies through the years, haven't you?

But no more. Once you see the enemy's schemes and tactics, you can create a battle plan. You can say, "I see what you're up to, Satan, and I'm not having it!"

Thank You for the reminder that the lies of the enemy don't have to take me down, Lord! Amen.

PRAYER JAR INSPIRATION:

I will create a plan to battle the enemy's lies.

Day 44

ROOM FOR CHANGE

Change your life, not just your clothes. Come back to God, your God. And here's why: God is kind and merciful. He takes a deep breath, puts up with a lot, this most patient God, extravagant in love, always ready to cancel catastrophe. Who knows? Maybe he'll do it now, maybe he'll turn around and show pity. Maybe, when all's said and done, there'll be blessings full and robust for your God!

Joel 2:13 MSG

As we've seen with Saul the persecutor who became Paul the preacher, God goes to great lengths to forgive us and help us become what He originally designed us to be. But with that forgiveness must come a change of heart.

Saul's change was so drastic that he began to preach Jesus at the same place he'd planned to persecute Christians!

Your God is very patient with you. He puts up with a lot. So don't be afraid to tell Him all that's going on in your life. No matter how much you've transgressed His command to love Him and others, He will not only forgive you but find a way to change your situation into a blessing—just as He did for Saul.

Lord, I need to get a few things off my chest. . .

PRAYER JAR INSPIRATION:

God, strengthen me as I accept Your forgiveness. Help me find room for change!

Day 45

A CONDUIT OF LOVE

If I speak with the tongues of men and of angels, but have not love [for others growing out of God's love for me], then I have become only a noisy gong or a clanging cymbal [just an annoying distraction].

1 Corinthians 13:1 AMP

Do you really believe God loves you? Do you believe in that love with all your heart, spirit, soul, and mind? Because if you don't believe in that superabundant love God has for you, you're going to have a difficult time loving others.

Perhaps you feel as if love is a hopeless idea. Perhaps you were deprived of love or lost a loved one in the early years of your life. Perhaps you loved another and your love wasn't returned. The pain of that experience has put you off of love.

If any of these possibilities rings true, remember who you are: God's creation. The person He wants to have an intimate relationship with. The person He loved, even before you became aware of Him.

Lord, give me love for others.

PRAYER JAR INSPIRATION:

I am a conduit of God's great love.

Day 46

THE ILLUSION

Abstain from every form of evil.

1 Thessalonians 5:22 ESV

Satan is the master of all magicians. He excels in the art of illusion and performs tricks that make magic shows look tame. And humans believe him. They buy into the lies.

Satan isn't content just to whisper in your ear. He sends his manipulations and lies out through social media, movies, and even the mainstream media. He gets people stirred up and convinces whole groups that something is good when, in fact, it's really bad (contrary to the Word of God).

Satan has some skills. And that's why you must have skills too. You have spiritual discernment, the holy ability to tell the truth from a lie. And it's not limited to face-to-face conversations. You can hear something online and, instead of being swept in, know in your knower that it's not true. That's how powerful spiritual discernment can be.

Thank You for the gift of discernment, Lord! Amen.

PRAYER JAR INSPIRATION:

I will not be swept into the world's tricks and deceit.

Day 47

PETER'S WEAKNESS

This very night, before the cock crows in the morning, you will deny Me three times.

MATTHEW 26:34 VOICE

During the Last Supper, Peter told Jesus, "Lord, maybe everyone else will trip and fall tonight, but I will not. I'll be beside You. I won't falter" (Matthew 26:33 VOICE). Jesus disagreed. . .and said so.

Later that night, Jesus went with the disciples to the garden of Gethsemane. He told them to sit down while He went to pray. Taking with Him Peter, James, and John, Jesus told the trio to stay awake while He went a little farther.

In great agony, Jesus met with God in prayer. And every time He went back to see how the three were doing, He noticed Peter had fallen asleep. Jesus told him, "The spirit is willing, but the body is weak" (Matthew 26:41 VOICE).

Just like Jesus knew Peter's weakness, He knows yours. And just as He forgave Peter, He forgives you. Your job is to simply accept His forgiveness—and to stay awake so that you too are not pulled into sin.

Thank You, Lord, for Your continuous compassion and understanding.

PRAYER JAR INSPIRATION:

Lord, help me to stay alert and prayerful so that I will be strong amid testing.

Day 48

DARING TO HOPE

Yet I still dare to hope when I remember this: The faithful love of the Lord never ends! His mercies never cease. Great is his faithfulness; his mercies begin afresh each morning.

Lamentations 3:21–23 NLT

It's not easy being a godly human. So many times and in so many areas of our lives we find ourselves tripping up, doing or saying the wrong thing. Or, in our struggle to support ourselves and our loved ones, we may find ourselves putting our work, our need to earn money, or our desire to attain the good life above our faith, families, and friends. Soon we realize how little we've done for God, how often we've ignored our families, and how many of our friendships have fallen by the wayside.

Yet we can hang on to the hope that God's love is never ending. His loving-kindness never wanes. His faithfulness to us is immense, immeasurable, infinite. His mercies are new every morning. Every day we have a fresh start.

Make that day today!

Thank You, Lord, for Your abundant love, mercy, and faithfulness!

PRAYER JAR INSPIRATION:

Today I will make a new start at ____________________.

Day 49

RAISE THE STANDARD!

So shall they fear the name of the Lord from the west, and his glory from the rising of the sun. When the enemy shall come in like a flood, the Spirit of the Lord shall lift up a standard against him.

Isaiah 59:19 kjv

It's hard to focus when you're in a crowded (or loud) room, isn't it? You wouldn't choose a public restaurant or a ball game as a place to spend your quiet time with the Lord.

But now let's think about that idea in reverse. If the enemy is shouting loud, negative thoughts into your heart and mind, one way to counter-balance is through good noise on your end like reading scriptures aloud or singing praise songs at the top of your lungs.

The noise of truth can drown out the noise of negative mind chatter. It might seem like a momentary distraction, but distractions are good when the lies of the enemy come in like a flood.

In those moments when he's chasing hard after you, you can—with the Spirit's help—raise up a standard against the enemy.

I understand that the enemy will attempt to overtake me, Lord; but with You on my side, I can't lose! Amen.

PRAYER JAR INSPIRATION:

God is greater and His voice is louder than the enemy's!

Day 50

WHO HAS NOT SINNED?

Jesus: *Let the first stone be thrown by the one among you who has not sinned.*

JOHN 8:7 VOICE

Deciding to test Jesus, the scribes and Pharisees brought a woman before Him who'd been caught in the act of adultery. Under the law of Moses, such a woman was to be killed by stoning.

Jesus started writing something in the dirt, and then He stood up and said, "Let the first stone be thrown by the one among you who has not sinned" (John 8:7 VOICE).

At first, the Pharisees just stood there. Then, one by one, they began to leave.

Jesus wants you to know you're not the only one who sins. That sounds obvious, but when we're plagued by guilt, we sometimes need this reminder. Not that we should be cavalier about our sins or God's forgiveness—that wouldn't be healthy for anyone. But sometimes, we do need to remember that what God has washed away will stay washed away. There's no need to keep worrying if you've been forgiven or not. You have. Now it's time to move on to a brighter future!

Thank You, Lord, for Your forgiveness. Help me accept it and move on.

PRAYER JAR INSPIRATION:

All sin. But all who ask are forgiven. Thank You, Lord!

Day 51

SUPPORTED BY LOVE

Unless the Lord had helped me, I would soon have settled in the silence of the grave. I cried out, "I am slipping!" but your unfailing love, O Lord, supported me. When doubts filled my mind, your comfort gave me renewed hope and cheer.

Psalm 94:17–19 NLT

In this material world, it's easy to get lost in the minutiae of life—to find yourself not living your dream but dreaming your life. And then something happens. As you come up against real and unexpected trouble, your heart skips a beat. You suddenly find yourself crying out to God, "Lord, I'm slipping! Catch me! Hold me up! Help me stand!"

And in that moment, God will respond. He will reach out with that unfailing love of His in which you've set much of your hope. That love will lift you up, keep you from going down into the abyss.

When you begin to doubt not just God's love but His very existence, cry out to Him again. When you do, He will comfort you, hold you, sit with you until your hope and cheer are restored.

Hold me up, Lord, with Your unceasing and unfailing love!

PRAYER JAR INSPIRATION:

God is always there to support me with His love, to renew my hope!

Day 52

LIE DOWN AND SLEEP

In peace I will both lie down and sleep;
for you alone, O Lord, make me dwell in safety.

Psalm 4:8 ESV

All you need is a good night's sleep, and everything will be better tomorrow. You're sure of it.

But you can't sleep. Your mind tumbles through half a dozen conversations you had today. Regrets sweep over you as you realize you could have—*should have*—done things differently. You plan a strategy for tomorrow for how you'll make things better.

Before long, an hour has passed and you're still wide awake. Then another hour. Then you find yourself turning on the light and reaching for your phone to scroll through social media.

Mind chatter is especially difficult in the wee hours of the night. It's hard to flip the switch to turn off the day, especially if it was a troubling day. But God wants you to leave those things in His (very capable) hands. Part of trusting Him is releasing yesterday, today, and tomorrow to Him. As best as you're able, do that today.

I will rest, Lord! I will get as much sleep as I can because I know
I will need that energy to face a brand-new day. Amen.

PRAYER JAR INSPIRATION:
I will sleep in peace when I release yesterday,
today, and tomorrow to God.

Day 53

RELEASING THE ENTIRE BURDEN

Cast your burden on the Lord [releasing the weight of it] and He will sustain you; He will never allow the [consistently] righteous to be moved (made to slip, fall, or fail). . . . I will trust in, lean on, and confidently rely on You.

Psalm 55:22–23 ampc

You've asked God for forgiveness, and you believe He has given it to you. But some questions remain.

This is when you want to spend some quality time with God, asking Him to help you get to the root of the matter. For until you confess all, totally unburdening your mind and heart to God, you won't have the confidence to press on. And when you're not spiritually strong, you're more likely to fail again.

So find some time to spend with God—time beyond your daily devotions. Ask Him to sustain you and to help you release your entire burden. Once all is off your chest and forgiven, nothing in the world can shake you!

Lord, help me cast all of my burden upon You,
confident that You will forgive all.

PRAYER JAR INSPIRATION:
God can bear the weight of my sin—and forgive it!

Day 54

STIRRING UP LOVE AND BLESSINGS

The mouth of the righteous is a fountain of life and his words of wisdom are a source of blessing, but the mouth of the wicked conceals violence and evil. Hatred stirs up strife, but love covers and overwhelms all transgressions [forgiving and overlooking another's faults].

PROVERBS 10:11–12 AMP

Words carry great power. The words that come out of our mouths can either bless or curse, build up or cut down, stir up love within hearts or suffocate others with hatred. Where do your words fall on this spectrum?

Today, keep watch over the things you say. Consider the effect they have on others. Ask God to help you stop before you speak. To pause and, if needed, turn what would have been a curse into a blessing. Speak words of love and encouragement. Doing so will change not only the lives of others but your own as well.

Help me pause before I prattle, Lord. To speak words alive with life. To send out blessings and curtail curses. To love well and, in doing so, to forgive and overlook the faults of others. In Jesus' name, amen.

PRAYER JAR INSPIRATION:

Lord of all, make my mouth a fountain of wisdom, blessing, and love.

Day 55

RUN WITH PERSEVERANCE

Therefore, since we are surrounded by such a great cloud of witnesses, let us throw off everything that hinders and the sin that so easily entangles. And let us run with perseverance the race marked out for us, fixing our eyes on Jesus, the pioneer and perfecter of faith. For the joy set before him he endured the cross, scorning its shame, and sat down at the right hand of the throne of God.

HEBREWS 12:1–2 NIV

No runner enters a race to lose. He sees himself crossing the finish line near the top of the pack. All marathon runners set out to finish well. Otherwise, why bother?

God wants you to finish well in every area of your life. You might not start off on the best footing, but you really can finish well by making good choices along the way.

Your thought life is very much like a marathon. This battle to clean up your thoughts won't be won in an instant. You're in this for the duration, and you have to go the distance, one errant thought at a time. But if you don't give up, if you strive every day to keep your thoughts and heart in alignment with the Word of God, you'll finish the race stronger than ever before.

I want to be a person who finishes well, Lord. Give me the tenacity to keep going even when I don't feel like it. Amen.

PRAYER JAR INSPIRATION:

God wants me to finish well.

Day 56

DARK HEART

"The heart is hopelessly dark and deceitful, a puzzle that no one can figure out. But I, God, search the heart and examine the mind. I get to the heart of the human. I get to the root of things. I treat them as they really are, not as they pretend to be."

Jeremiah 17:9–10 msg

You've asked God for forgiveness. You've read all the Bible passages, talked to some other Christian friends, and even consulted with your pastor. And still your heart is sending you false signals, trying to convince you there must be something else you must say, some deed you must perform before you can be fully forgiven.

This is when you need to stop listening to your heart and start believing God's Word. Instead of letting your heart boss you around, go to God. Tell Him you're struggling with accepting His forgiveness. Ask Him to get to the root of the problem. Allow Him to search your heart and examine your mind—to heal you where you need healing, to search your inner darkness, and to bring out the light.

God will help you find the truth.

Lord, search my heart. Examine my mind.
Bring me the light of Your forgiveness.

PRAYER JAR INSPIRATION:

My God is my beacon of light.

Day 57

WORTHY LOVE

"When he came to his senses, he said, 'How many of my father's hired hands have more than enough food, and here I am dying of hunger! I'll get up, go to my father, and say to him, Father, I have sinned against heaven and in your sight. I'm no longer worthy to be called your son.'"

LUKE 15:17–19 HCSB

The son who had squandered the inheritance from his father found himself in dire straits. Realizing what he had done, he decided to go back home and humbly apologize to his dad.

"But while the son was still a long way off, his father saw him and was filled with compassion. He ran, threw his arms around his neck, and kissed him" (Luke 15:20 HCSB). Before the son could even get his entire apology out, his father called for his servants to put the best robe on the boy, to slip a ring on his finger, and to shod his feed with sandals.

Just as the prodigal's father loved, forgave, and had compassion on his son, your Father God loves, forgives, and has compassion on you. If you've strayed, remember that God's love for you never dies.

Thank You, Father God, for loving me no matter how unworthy I feel myself to be.

PRAYER JAR INSPIRATION:

Lord, help me not squander my inheritance of love.

Day 58

ONLY ONE SAVIOR

"From this man's descendants God has brought to Israel the Savior Jesus, as he promised."

ACTS 13:23 NIV

Codependent people can't seem to function on their own. They see you as a savior figure, someone who will sweep in and save the day when they end up in a jam.

The problem is, you're no savior. (You know it's true!) Despite your best attempts, you simply don't have what it takes to save another human being. From anger. From alcohol. From drugs. From pain.

Only Jesus can save. But He won't intervene in tough situations if you're standing in the way, playing His role in the story. Healing will never come to that other person if you've given yourself the lead role.

Move yourself to a secondary character part and let Jesus have His rightful place. When you do that, healing will come—to the other person and even to you.

I'm tired of playing the role of savior, Jesus. It's not a role I was ever meant to play. I hand the reins back to You today. Amen.

PRAYER JAR INSPIRATION:

There's only one Savior—JESUS!

Day 59

HUMBLE PRAYERS

He also told this parable to some people who trusted in themselves and were confident that they were righteous [that they were upright and in right standing with God] and scorned and made nothing of all the rest of men.

Luke 18:9 AMPC

Some people are so pleased with themselves that they don't think they need forgiveness.

Jesus addressed this issue with a parable about two men—one a Pharisee, the other a tax collector—who went to the temple to pray.

The Pharisee stood up and declared, "I thank you, God, that I am not like other people—cheaters, sinners, adulterers. I'm certainly not like that tax collector! I fast twice a week, and I give you a tenth of my income" (Luke 18:11–12 NLT). The tax collector, however, "stood at a distance and dared not even lift his eyes to heaven. . . . Instead, he beat his chest in sorrow, saying, 'O God, be merciful to me, for I am a sinner'" (Luke 18:13 NLT).

Jesus then said, "This sinner, not the Pharisee, returned home justified before God. For those who exalt themselves will be humbled, and those who humble themselves will be exalted" (Luke 18:14 NLT).

Which of "those" are you?

Mercy, God! I come asking Your forgiveness.

PRAYER JAR INSPIRATION:

May I pray each day with a humble heart!

Day 60

SHADOW OF UNFORGIVENESS

"Whenever you stand praying, if you have anything against anyone, forgive him [drop the issue, let it go], so that your Father who is in heaven will also forgive you your transgressions and wrongdoings [against Him and others]."

Mark 11:25 amp

Have you ever gone to God in prayer but found yourself stumbling for the right words? Or perhaps you didn't exactly feel like praying, so you just sent up an SOS prayer (a short and sweet plea for help) and went on your way?

If you're struggling to find the words to pray to God or you just don't feel you're in the mood to speak with Him, chances are there's a barrier between you and God. And that barrier could be the fact that there's someone in your life you have not forgiven.

So today, before you pray, take stock of what is in your heart. If there is any shade obscuring God's light, consider who you may need to forgive. Then do so. And you too will receive full forgiveness.

Help me, Lord, to forgive others so that You may forgive me.

PRAYER JAR INSPIRATION:

I hope and pray God's light would lead me to full forgiveness.

Day 61

GIVE AND TAKE

The fear of man lays a snare, but whoever trusts in the Lord is safe.

Proverbs 29:25 ESV

In many relationships, there's a taker and a giver. Attachments are formed that can turn unhealthy in a hurry, especially if the emotional and physical needs of one zap the other. Can you relate?

Maybe you've been in more than one friendship or romantic relationship where you found yourself on the "giver" side, rarely receiving anything in return. Those codependent relationships are draining, and they're wholly unfair.

There's no room for healing in situations like that. The Lord can move only if you stop fixing the problem for the other person. It's time to rediscover boundaries. They can protect you from overgiving.

Or overtaking. If you've been the one zapping your friend or spouse, it's time to give them a break. Let God do what only God can do. He wants to bring healing.

It's been all give and no take in some of these relationships, Jesus. Help me find balance. Amen.

PRAYER JAR INSPIRATION:

I will make room in my relationships to let God do what only He can do.

Day 62

MAKING THINGS RIGHT

***Eternal One** (to Moses): Tell the Israelites that sinning against each other is just like abandoning Me.*

NUMBERS 5:6 VOICE

God teaches that when His people commit a wrong against someone else, they are abandoning all God stands for. In other words, the perpetrators are committing a wrong against God Himself!

In Leviticus 19:18 (VOICE), God told His followers to "love your neighbor as you love yourself." Why? "For I am the Eternal One." In other words, God is saying, "Do this because I told you so. I'm in charge!" Thus, when you do someone wrong, a big part of your confession and apology must go not only to the party you've injured but to the Big Guy Himself! And there's no expiration date to this edict. God wants you to make things right in whatever way you can.

Today, think about someone who needs an apology from you. Consider how you might try to make things right. Then, start by seeking God and confessing it to Him in prayer.

I confess, Lord, that I have done wrong. Hear my prayer.

PRAYER JAR INSPIRATION:

God, help me make things right.

Day 63

NOBODY'S PERFECT

*We are made right with God by placing our faith in Jesus Christ.
And this is true for everyone who believes, no matter who we are.
For everyone has sinned; we all fall short of God's glorious standard.*

Romans 3:22–23 NLT

Before Jesus came, people did their best to follow the laws God made. But they fell short. Continually. Very short. Consider David, the apple of God's eye. Even as close as he was to God, he slept with a married woman. Then, when he learned she was pregnant, he set things up so that her husband would be killed in battle and he could claim her for his own!

When we look at ourselves, at how much we fall short in God's eyes, it makes it easier to forgive those who have fallen short in our eyes. Today, humbly forgive those who have disappointed or wronged you in some way, reminding yourself that no one but Jesus is perfect.

*I ask for Your forgiveness, Lord, as I forgive others,
knowing we all fall short in Your eyes.*

PRAYER JAR INSPIRATION:
My own imperfections urge me to forgive those in others.

Day 64

ENOUGH

On the contrary, we speak as those approved by God to be entrusted with the gospel. We are not trying to please people but God, who tests our hearts.

1 Thessalonians 2:4 NIV

Co- is a funny little prefix. Usually *co-* attempts to bring people together. But sometimes this naughty little prefix goes a bit too far.

To be codependent on someone means you can't function on your own. And, while it's great to live in community, God never intended for you not to be able to do most of life's most basic things on your own.

Co- tries to convince the dependent one that she can't possibly survive without the other's help. It whispers, "You're not enough." Or even, "God in you isn't enough."

But in Christ, you are enough. You don't need to place all your dependence on another human being when the Creator of the universe stands ready to intervene on your behalf with just a word.

Is it time to show *co-* the door? It might just be time to step back a few feet and try to tackle some challenges on your own. With God's help, you can. With God's help, you *will*!

I need to learn boundaries and healthy relationships.
Release me from codependency, Lord, I pray. Amen.

PRAYER JAR INSPIRATION:

With God's help. . .I can!

Day 65

COVERED BY GOD

The Lord God made clothing out of skins for Adam and his wife, and He clothed them.

Genesis 3:21 HCSB

Despite Adam and Eve's disobedience, God still showed them His love and care. In doing so, He revealed His forgiving nature. To protect His children from the heat and cold, God killed some animals and used their skins to tenderly cover the humans' nakedness. Perhaps the animal skins would remind His children of their fall into sin.

In their nakedness, Adam and Eve had been innocent and honorable. Now, to cover their shame and allay their fears, death entered paradise.

This killing to cover the couple's sins foreshadowed what Jesus would one day do to cover ours. Adam and Eve's fig leaves were not an adequate covering. But in His grace, mercy, love, and kindness, God made the pair long and durable coats of skin to protect them from the elements. This reminds us that God provides forgiveness for deeds past, present, and future.

Thank You, Lord, for always taking such good care of me—for Your love, gentleness, mercy, grace, and kindness. You alone allay my fears. You alone wipe away my tears. To You alone I sing my praise!

PRAYER JAR INSPIRATION:

Thank You, God, for always being there for me.

Day 66

PLEASING THE SPIRIT

Do not bring sorrow to God's Holy Spirit by the way you live. Remember, he has identified you as his own, guaranteeing that you will be saved on the day of redemption. . . . Instead, be kind to each other, tenderhearted, forgiving one another, just as God through Christ has forgiven you.

Ephesians 4:30, 32 NLT

When you become a follower of Christ, you are to change some of your ways and embark on a new life. Every day, Jesus gives you the opportunity to "throw off your old sinful nature and your former way of life" (Ephesians 4:22 NLT) and to "put on your new nature, created to be like God" (Ephesians 4:24 NLT).

That means you need to stop telling lies and letting anger control you. Your words are to be words of encouragement, not abuse. And even more than that, you're not to grieve the Spirit. Instead, you're to be a woman of compassion and forgiveness.

Today, make God and His Spirit happy. Be nice, gentle, compassionate, and forgiving to others, just as God is to you.

Lord, make me a woman pleasing to You, Your Spirit, and others, being kind, gentle, compassionate, and forgiving.

PRAYER JAR INSPIRATION:

My hope lies in gladdening God, just as He gladdens me!

Day 67

NEEDY?

Do all you can to live a peaceful life. Take care of your own business, and do your own work as we have already told you. If you do, then people who are not believers will respect you, and you will not have to depend on others for what you need.

1 Thessalonians 4:11–12 NCV

Perhaps you're the one who's always tugging at others to help you. You've convinced yourself you can't possibly make it on your own, so you cling tightly to the ones who offer the most moral support. This is good. . .to a point.

If your neediness surpasses what's normal and healthy, your friend(s) might be ready to pull away. And let's face it: It's not healthy for you either. God wants you to learn to stand, not on your own two feet but with your hand firmly clasped in His.

Today, decide to be healed from whatever it is that has held you bound to people who are currently playing a Godlike role in your life. These folks aren't your savior. There's only one, and He already paid the ultimate price so that you could live in total freedom. Today is the day you can finally take steps in that direction by admitting your need to Him.

With Your help, I don't have to become dependent on others, Lord. Please guard my heart and give me wisdom. Amen.

PRAYER JAR INSPIRATION:

Jesus is my only Savior.

Day 68

HOW BADLY DO YOU WANT IT?

Heal me, Lord, and I will be healed; save me and I will be saved, for you are the one I praise.

Jeremiah 17:14 niv

How badly do you want to be healed?

There are some great stories in the New Testament about people who wanted healing. First, we discover a story about a woman with an issue of blood. She had struggled for years with this problem, which caused her to be ostracized from society and looked on as unclean. She was so desperate for healing that she decided to work her way through the crowd to touch the hem of Jesus' garment. When she did, she was instantly healed!

Another story of similar desperation is found in Luke 5. The friends of a sick man cut a hole in the roof of a house to drop their sick friend down inside so that Jesus would take notice of him. Jesus healed that man when He saw the faith of his friends.

These stories raise a legitimate question: How badly do you want it? Today, run straight to Jesus, the one who has healing in His wings.

You're right there, Jesus, just waiting for me to reach out and touch the hem of Your garment! Thank You for being my healer. Amen.

PRAYER JAR INSPIRATION:

I want healing. I really, really want it!

Day 69

PATIENCE AND TOLERANCE

The servant of the Lord must not participate in quarrels, but must be kind to everyone [even-tempered, preserving peace, and he must be], skilled in teaching, patient and tolerant when wronged. He must correct those who are in opposition with courtesy and gentleness in the hope that God may grant that they will repent and be led to the knowledge of the truth [accurately understanding and welcoming it].

2 Timothy 2:24–25 AMP

You are not just a daughter of God but a servant of the Lord. And as such, you are to walk as He walked, talk as He talked.

So, you're not to be quarrelsome. Instead, find a way to be kind to everyone. Teach them where the truth of a particular matter lies. And overall, be patient with people, even those who are difficult and have wronged you in some way. In doing so, you will not only be keeping and promoting peace but hopefully providing some much-needed space for God to change people's hearts.

Remember how gentle and kind, loving and patient your Savior is. Then go and do the same.

God, please gift me with more tolerance and patience around difficult people. Help me promote Your peace and love.

PRAYER JAR INSPIRATION:

My hope of patience and tolerance lies in God's abundant and available supply!

Day 70

WAYMAKER

No temptation has overtaken you that is not common to man. God is faithful, and he will not let you be tempted beyond your ability, but with the temptation he will also provide the way of escape, that you may be able to endure it.

1 Corinthians 10:13 esv

The Bible tells us that God makes a way where there seems to be no way. This was certainly true of the Israelites as they made the journey out of Egypt (bondage) into the Promised Land. They faced all sorts of obstacles along the way, including the ultimate one as the Egyptian army chased them into the Red Sea; but God miraculously parted the waters, and they came through on dry land. The Egyptians weren't so fortunate.

God provides for His own. He makes a way, even in seemingly impossible situations. If you've been feeling trapped, if you think there's no way out of your circumstances, look to the waymaker.

He made a way for Paul and Silas out of a prison cell.

He made a way for the woman with the issue of blood.

He made a way for the thief on the cross.

And He will make a way for you too.

I can't depend on others to save me, Jesus, but I know that You already have! May I always put my trust in You. Amen.

PRAYER JAR INSPIRATION:

Jesus is the waymaker.

Day 71

INSENSITIVE

Love does no wrong to a neighbor; therefore love is the fulfilling of the law.

Romans 13:10 esv

Not everyone is wired the same. If someone has hurt you with their insensitivity to your problem, don't get worked up for too long. Remember, they might not have the same depth of feeling or emotion as you do.

Some people simply aren't empaths. Even some believers struggle in this area. They're not deliberately trying to hurt you with their insensitivity. They're just oblivious or approaching it from a completely different angle.

One of the joys of understanding the different personality types is that it helps you guard your heart when you bump up against friends who have a radically different take on things.

And here's another great lesson to glean from insensitive people: You can demonstrate the opposite spirit. You can become even more sensitive to the needs of others so that you can better minister to them when they're hurting.

Guard my heart, Jesus. I don't want to overreact when people aren't as sensitive as I hope they'll be. Help me deepen my sensitivity to others so I can show them Your love during hard seasons. Amen.

PRAYER JAR INSPIRATION:

I will be more sensitive to the needs of others.

Day 72

CLOTHED WITH JOY

You have turned my mourning into joyful dancing. You have taken away my clothes of mourning and clothed me with joy, that I might sing praises to you and not be silent. O Lord my God, I will give you thanks forever!

Psalm 30:11–12 nlt

In this life, there will be some rough spots, some trials we have to endure. But those trials are what draw us ever closer to God and help us become more like His Son.

The way to endure those trials is by focusing on the fact that God is with us through them. We may have to face some enemies, but God will not let them triumph over us. We may get sick, but when we call out to God, He will restore us. We may keep falling into a pit of despair, but God will lift us out. We may have eyes full of tears tonight, but God will bring us joy, just as He brings the morning.

No matter how far down you might go, remember that God will bring you back up. Just trust in Him.

Deliver me from this pit of despair, Lord, and lift me into Your joy!

PRAYER JAR INSPIRATION:

Even in despair, I have hope in the joy of God's deliverance.

Day 73

OUT OF THE RUBBLE

Then I said to them, "You see the trouble we are in: Jerusalem lies in ruins, and its gates have been burned with fire. Come, let us rebuild the wall of Jerusalem, and we will no longer be in disgrace."

NEHEMIAH 2:17 NIV

You never saw it coming. The tragedy hit from out of nowhere, almost wrecking you. Now you're standing in the rubble, looking at the shattered remains of what used to be, and wondering how to move forward from here.

This might be a good time to do a deep dive into the story of Nehemiah. He came back to Jerusalem to discover his beloved hometown in ruins. The walls were torn down and the city was reduced to rubble. For a while, all he could do was weep.

Then Nehemiah got busy concocting a plan. In his mind's eye, he saw those walls rising again. And this man of God rose to the task, gathered the troops, and began the arduous process of rebuilding.

That's what it's going to take in your life too. It will take work. It will take courage. But you can heal, even after the most traumatizing event imaginable.

Lord, the walls of my life have crumbled, but I'm trusting You with the rebuilding process! Heal me, I pray.

PRAYER JAR INSPIRATION:

No matter how massive the pile of rubble, God is bigger still.

Day 74

A JOYFUL HEART

A cheerful heart is good medicine, but a broken spirit saps a person's strength.

PROVERBS 17:22 NLT

When you've been sick with an infection for more than a couple of days, visiting the doctor is inevitable. And once she writes that prescription, you can almost feel yourself getting better, even before you've swallowed that first tablet. The promise of medication gives you hope, even before it takes effect.

The Bible has a prescription that works wonders on a broken heart or troubled spirit: joy. When you apply joy—as you would swallow that antibiotic—you feel better. Much better. And here's the good news: Joy works even faster than medication, which must get into your system before it begins to have an effect. Joy offers an instantaneous lift!

No matter what you're struggling with today, pray for joy. When it floods over you, you're going to feel much, much better.

I love the joy-filled people You've placed in my life, Lord. I want to be more like that. Fill me to overflowing so that I can spill over onto those I love. Amen.

PRAYER JAR INSPIRATION:

My goal is to radiate the joy of Jesus around my friends.

Day 75

OVERFLOWING JOY

"I have loved you even as the Father has loved me. Remain in my love. When you obey my commandments, you remain in my love, just as I obey my Father's commandments and remain in his love. I have told you these things so that you will be filled with my joy. Yes, your joy will overflow!"

John 15:9–11 NLT

Jesus presents a somewhat easy formula for finding joy in this life: Simply obey His commandments and remain in His love. And what are Jesus' commandments? To "love and unselfishly seek the best for one another, just as I have loved you" (John 15:12 AMP).

Take a moment to think about it. Imagine what this world would be like if everyone loved each other. If each man, woman, and child unselfishly sought the best for others. The joy wouldn't just be overflowing. It would be surging!

Yet you may be asking yourself, *I am just one person. How can I even begin to make this a remote possibility?* Begin with you. Love others—the people around you, here and now. Begin with your world today!

Help me, Lord, to begin where I can on the road to a life overflowing with joy: by loving all those whose lives touch my own.

PRAYER JAR INSPIRATION:

My hope of joy, Lord, rests in remaining in Your love.

Day 76

LOOK UP

I lift up my eyes to the hills. From where does my help come?
My help comes from the Lord, who made heaven and earth.

Psalm 121:1–2 ESV

A cancer diagnosis. A divorce you never saw coming. These shockers are enough to send you reeling, careening down a cliff.

If you're like most people, you barrel through the crises, smiling bravely and thinking, *I just need to get through this.* But that's not true. "Getting through it" isn't enough. You'll need time to deal with the pain. The grief. The trauma. You'll need plenty of time to heal your heart, your mind, and your soul.

But you're not inclined to think like that. So you plow forward, doing all the things you know to do, then dive right back into your work. It's a lovely distraction from the pain, right?

Wrong. God wants you to stop. To lift your head and your heart to search for Him. You can't fix this problem on your own, but He can. So lift your eyes to the hills. Your help comes from the Lord.

I won't look to myself for answers, especially during a hard recovery, Lord. I will look only to You, my Healer. Amen.

PRAYER JAR INSPIRATION:

I can lift my eyes from my circumstances and up to Jesus today!

Day 77

SUNLIGHT

But if we walk in the light, as he is in the light, we have fellowship with one another, and the blood of Jesus his Son cleanses us from all sin.

1 John 1:7 ESV

If you've lived in a dank, dark prison cell for any length of time, the sunlight can be blinding. You squint and put your hand over your eyes to protect them from the glare. And for a moment—just a moment—you contemplate running back into that cell to avoid the pain of adjusting.

But you forge ahead, allowing your eyes time to adjust.

The same is true when your spirit is first coming alive to the truth of the gospel message. Some of it might seem a little too glaring. You squint and squirm, wondering if you've made the right decision.

But once your eyes are fully opened to the truth, shackles fall. You see clearly, and it all makes sense. And before long the light becomes your friend, not a hindrance. In fact, you can't wait to share it with others who are enduring their own dark prison cells.

Walk free in the light, friend!

You are the light, Jesus. So, if I stick close to You, I will always walk in the light. Thank You for the freedom that Your light brings. Amen.

PRAYER JAR INSPIRATION:
My spiritual eyes can (and will) adjust to the truth of God's Word.

Day 78

SOUL TALK

Why are you in despair, O my soul? And why have you become restless and disturbed within me? Hope in God and wait expectantly for Him, for I shall again praise Him for the help of His presence.

PSALM 42:5 AMP

Here, in today's verse, we overhear the psalmist talking to himself. He asks his soul, his innermost self, why it is so hopeless, restless, and anxious. Then he reminds his soul to hope in God and to wait for Him with the expectation that God *will turn things around* in a good way. When his Lord's presence provides the help the psalmist needs, his joy within and his praise without will return!

Take a cue from this psalmist. When your soul is down, when the inner woman is wearing a frown due to fear, hopelessness, restlessness, or anxiety, have a talk with her. Remind her that she can put her hope in God. He will come through in His time. He will turn things around. And she will be praising Him with all joy!

Don't despair, dear soul. God will help us.
We will be lifting our praise of Him in joy!

PRAYER JAR INSPIRATION:
My hope in God brings my soul joy!

Day 79

FROZEN

I sought the Lord, and he answered me; he delivered me from all my fears.

Psalm 34:4 NIV

In the deep winter, life slows down. Things freeze over. If you live in a place where you face particularly harsh winters, it's likely you face a lot of snow and ice days, where you're stuck at home, unable to go anywhere.

Those "frozen in" days are like what you go through after a period of shock. When startling (and deeply disturbing) things happen, it's as if you're locked down. Frozen.

During those frozen seasons, it's hard to envision springtime coming. But it will. The ice will melt. The situation will change. You will see the sun again.

In the meantime, allow God to hover close. He's with you, even in the dead of winter. If you seek Him, you will surely find Him, even in the middle of the trauma. And when you do, your worries and fears will begin to thaw in a way that could only be described as supernatural.

I need supernatural intervention, Lord!
I'm tired of living in frozen spaces! Amen.

PRAYER JAR INSPIRATION:
What areas of my life need thawing today?

Day 80

A HEALING PLACE

Yet we know that a person is put right with God only through faith in Jesus Christ, never by doing what the Law requires. We, too, have believed in Christ Jesus in order to be put right with God through our faith in Christ, and not by doing what the Law requires. For no one is put right with God by doing what the Law requires.

GALATIANS 2:16 GNT

Were you raised in church? If so, what "brand" was it? Some churches are thriving bodies, perfect for raising kids. Others are slightly off-balance, pushing works above grace (or even the other way around, condoning all sorts of sinful lifestyle choices while claiming the Bible isn't relevant for today).

Where we've come from can affect where we are. And let's face it—churches are sometimes a hotbed for strife and confusion if they veer from the intent of the Word of God.

If you were raised in a church that contributed to your brokenness instead of seeking to fix it, there's time to turn things around. You can make sure your children are raised in a healing place. It's possible to bring them up in an environment where the Bible has top priority but grace is displayed in all situations as well.

Balance is key.

I love Your Word, Lord. And I want my behavior to reflect that. But I don't want to be bound by legalism. Show me how to live by faith and display Your love to this hungry world. Amen.

PRAYER JAR INSPIRATION:

Authentic faith leads to good works.

Day 81

CHOOSE!

Though the fig tree does not blossom and there is no fruit on the vines, though the yield of the olive fails and the fields produce no food, though the flock is cut off from the fold and there are no cattle in the stalls, yet I will [choose to] rejoice in the LORD*; I will [choose to] shout in exultation in the [victorious] God of my salvation!*

HABAKKUK 3:17–18 AMP

It's easy to be happy when everything is going well—when your pay is good, your tasks rewarding, your dwelling secure, your church prospering, your kids on the right track, and your body in tip-top shape. The challenge comes when something (or everything) is going off the rails—when your pay is lousy, your assignment mundane, your church on the brink of closing, your kids hanging with the wrong people, and your body aching.

But God wants us to choose to rejoice in Him no matter what's happening, no matter what earthly ills have befallen us. He wants us to trust in Him, not our circumstances, and to find our joy complete in Himself. For in Him alone lies all our strength, hope, and joy.

I choose to rejoice in You, Lord. You are my all in all!

PRAYER JAR INSPIRATION:

Because I choose to trust in God and not my circumstances, I have joy!

Day 82

IN THE ROUGH SEASONS

For though we live in the world, we do not wage war as the world does. The weapons we fight with are not the weapons of the world. On the contrary, they have divine power to demolish strongholds. We demolish arguments and every pretension that sets itself up against the knowledge of God, and we take captive every thought to make it obedient to Christ.

2 Corinthians 10:3–5 niv

When the human body goes into shock, multiple things happen: You begin to shake uncontrollably, your ability to think clearly dissipates, and tears often come. Many times you can't think clearly to know what to do, so you must depend on others to guide you.

This isn't the time to beat yourself up for not being able to fix the situation. You have to give yourself grace throughout the crises that life throws your way.

Problems will come. But even in the thick of things, you can still feel the presence of God and recognize that He is with you. He will never leave you or forsake you—no matter how low things go.

And remember, even in the roughest of seasons, you've been given weapons to use for warfare. And those weapons have divine, God-breathed power to demolish strongholds!

You've given me powerful weapons, Lord. Now give me clarity of mind to know how and when to use them. Amen.

PRAYER JAR INSPIRATION:

God is with me in every crisis.

Day 83

A SERVANT'S HEART

As each has received a gift, use it to serve one another,
as good stewards of God's varied grace.

1 Peter 4:10 esv

"I don't want anything to do with your God."

Maybe you've heard those words from a family member, friend, or neighbor.

That hardheartedness has led many to lives of misery and isolation. But there are ways beyond those high fences they're building.

Take a pot of chicken soup to your friend when she is sick.

Let your neighbor know you're praying when her spouse leaves.

Offer to mow that elderly neighbor's lawn when she gripes that no one sees her or cares about her anymore.

Acts of service are an amazing way to show God's love.

So buy groceries for that single mom. And send a kind handwritten note to that grumpy man down the street, along with a plate of cookies. Watch those walls fall as you extend a hand of love to this hurting world.

Give me a servant's heart, Lord. Amen.

PRAYER JAR INSPIRATION:

When I don't know what else to do, I can always serve others.

Day 84

PROVING A PROVERB

The king's decree gave the Jews in every city authority to unite to defend their lives. . . . And the people of Susa celebrated the new decree. The Jews were filled with joy and gladness and were honored everywhere.

Esther 8:11, 15–16 NLT

A wicked man named Haman, who had wormed his way into the good graces of King Xerxes of Persia, had devised a scheme so that his enemy, Mordecai the Jew, would be killed, along with all the other Jews.

But, as if to prove Proverbs 10:28—that the hopes of the righteous would be happily realized and the hopes of the dastardly ones dashed—Haman ended up being hanged, Mordecai was given Haman's former position, and the Jewish people were not slaughtered but saved! And because the Jews were saved, they were filled with joy and gladness throughout the vast Persian kingdom!

Never doubt what God promises those who follow His way. Stick to the right path and have faith that you will see happiness bursting into your life once the storm has passed.

I believe in You and Your Word, Lord. My joy and hope of happiness rest in You alone!

PRAYER JAR INSPIRATION:

In His way and time, God grants happiness and joy to those He loves, proving His Word, love, and light to me over and over again.

Day 85

LET GO OF ANGUISH

Tell everyone who is discouraged, "Be strong and don't be afraid! God is coming to your rescue, coming to punish your enemies."

Isaiah 35:4 gnt

Trauma can be physical, psychological, or emotional. No doubt you've experienced various traumas through the years in all three areas. If you think about it, trauma is really a reaction (or a response) to what has happened. It seems to happen automatically.

The lingering effects of trauma can affect every area of your life. And we do all sorts of things to avoid future traumas because we know how devastating they can be.

That said, Jesus doesn't want you to live in fear. Part of the reason He heals you from trauma is so you can move forward into the future without being locked up in dread. If you're still holding tightly to anguish over an old trauma, today is a good day to let it go. Why? So it doesn't spill over into tomorrow.

I can only get past this with Your help, Jesus. Amen.

PRAYER JAR INSPIRATION:

I will ask God to provide the courage I need as I heal from my trauma.

Day 86

HEALED PEOPLE HEAL PEOPLE

LORD, I have heard of your fame; I stand in awe of your deeds, LORD. Repeat them in our day, in our time make them known; in wrath remember mercy.

HABAKKUK 3:2 NIV

Once you've survived a trauma and thrived on the other end of it, you have a story to tell. You also have lessons learned that could be beneficial to others. Healed people heal people.

Think about it this way: When you're going through an unexpected and unwanted divorce, who do you turn to for counsel? Probably someone who's walked that road ahead of you. Why? Because she (somehow) made it through, and you know she's going to share from her journey.

More than anything, she's going to give you hope that you'll be fine on the opposite side of this. And hope is a precious commodity when you're in the trenches.

One day that will be you. You'll be the one sharing and caring. Until then, hold tight to those who've already walked the road.

One day that will be me, Jesus. I'll be the one sharing my story. Heal me so that I can encourage others to heal, I pray. Amen.

PRAYER JAR INSPIRATION:

I will make it through this.

Day 87

GOOD NEWS

Sarah said, "God has made me laugh; all who hear [about our good news] will laugh with me." And she said, "Who would have said to Abraham that Sarah would nurse children? For I have given birth to a son by him in his old age."

Genesis 21:6–7 AMP

God had promised an aging Abraham a son through Sarah. Sarah, having overheard the news, laughed at the idea: "After I have become shriveled up and my lord is old, will I have delight?" (Genesis 18:12 HCSB).

Yet then God's promise and her hope came to fruition. "The LORD visited Sarah as he had said, and the LORD did to Sarah as he had promised" (Genesis 21:1 ESV). In their old age, Sarah and her husband did indeed have a child. And Sarah named him Isaac, which means "laughter."

God means what He says. You can trust and hope in His promises, for He cannot lie.

Lord of all creation, may I laugh and lift my voice in praise when Your promises, and my hopes, come to fruition!

PRAYER JAR INSPIRATION:

I rejoice that God follows through on His promises! And I revel in His good news!

Day 88

ON THE MOUNTAINTOPS AND IN THE VALLEYS

In all of this, Job did not sin by blaming God.

Job 1:22 NLT

Job was hard hit by disaster. He started out with an ideal life—great family, great home, great income, great friends, great health.

But he ended up losing nearly everything. Like dominoes, his nearly perfect life all came tumbling down. Job had the option of turning his back on God (of blaming Him, even) but he managed to hold tight to his faith.

When the dominoes are tumbling like that, it's natural to despair and to point fingers. After all, if God loved you, why would He allow all of this?

These challenges provide the perfect opportunity for God's intense love for you to shine through, even in the deepest valley. He doesn't plan to ever leave you or forsake you, so don't turn your back on Him either! You need Him in the valley. And on the mountaintop. And every place in between.

I won't point a finger at You, God. I'll keep trusting even when nothing is going my way. Amen.

PRAYER JAR INSPIRATION:

Even when the dominoes tumble, if I trust God, I won't fall.

Day 89

TRUST HIM TO STRAIGHTEN THE PATH

Trust in the Lord with all your heart and lean not on your own understanding; in all your ways submit to him, and he will make your paths straight.

Proverbs 3:5–6 NIV

When dreams seem to be irretrievably broken, you can feel completely alone. No one else had the passion for that dream like you did. No one else feels the disappointment you feel. In fact, many don't even seem to notice how deeply you're grieving this loss.

But you're feeling it to the core.

Those dreams, if God-breathed, will only come according to His calendar. And you simply don't know His timeline. It could be He's protecting you from pain by not letting it happen yet. Only time will tell.

But in the meantime, be reminded: You are never alone. Even when the path is brutally crooked, God is right there, holding you tight. If you're stuck, He's there. If you're moving forward, He's there.

He will never leave you or forsake you. You can still trust Him to make your path straight, no matter how crooked it has been.

I'm weary from the broken, crooked paths, Lord.
But I'm trusting You to straighten the road ahead. Amen.

PRAYER JAR INSPIRATION:

God can make my way straight.

Day 90

REJOICE!

Let the godly rejoice. Let them be glad in God's presence.
Let them be filled with joy. Sing praises to God and to his name!
Sing loud praises to him who rides the clouds. His name is the Lord—
rejoice in his presence! . . . Praise the Lord; praise God our savior!
For each day he carries us in his arms. Our God is a God who saves!

Psalm 68:3–4, 19–20 nlt

When you are working and resting, playing and reading, sunning and funning in the presence of God, you cannot help but be filled with joy.

Today, sing out your praises to the Lord. Look up to the clouds and imagine Him riding them, soaring across the sky, making things right in the lives of His people—all while remaining at your side, working within you, empowering you, helping you.

No matter what burden you may be carrying today, brush it aside. For there is one much greater, much more powerful than you. He is the supreme being who carries you in His arms. Every day. He will not let you go. He will save you.

Believe. Rejoice.

I can feel You carrying me in this moment, Lord. Hold me close!

PRAYER JAR INSPIRATION:
God carries me in His arms each day. Praise to God!

Day 91

DECISIONS, DECISIONS

"Why can't you decide for yourselves what is right?"

LUKE 12:57 NLT

How do you heal from a broken heart or wounded spirit? Slowly. Carefully. Methodically.

Some people tend to rush through the process. It's not unusual to see a newly divorced person immediately jump into the dating scene or even marry a near stranger. They think this will bring healing, but it usually just heaps more problems on top of an already traumatized heart.

Making quick decisions when you haven't taken the time to heal can land you in precarious positions—and that's not just with relational decisions. Financial decisions are harder when your mind and heart are still twisted up in the pain of what you've been through. (A lot of people drown their sorrows at the mall, spending money they don't need to be spending.)

Take time to heal before you make life-altering decisions. No rash ones or you might just have to pay a price.

Help me choose wisely, Lord. I don't want to make rash decisions I will later regret. Amen.

PRAYER JAR INSPIRATION:
Slow, careful, truth-filled decisions are always best.

Day 92

LIFE-GIVING POWER

All the people tried to touch him, for power was going out from him and healing them all.

Luke 6:19 GNT

Inanimate objects don't heal on their own. A broken platter doesn't miraculously come together over time like a broken bone would. A busted radiator won't fix itself. It takes a skilled worker with just the right instruments to bring those things back together again.

You're not an inanimate object but there really are times when you say, "I just can't. I don't have it in me." Aren't you glad in those times that the master craftsman is nearby, ready to put the pieces back together again?

Look at today's verse. People clustered around Jesus because He gained a reputation as a healer. They knew just where to go for their healing. And when they got close enough for a touch, power went out of Him!

That same life-giving power still flows from Jesus today. So look to Him for whatever you need.

Thank You, Lord, for healing Your children! Amen.

PRAYER JAR INSPIRATION:

When I can't, God can.

Day 93

UNFAILING LOVE

The Lord watches over those who fear him, those who rely on his unfailing love. . . . We put our hope in the Lord. He is our help and our shield. In him our hearts rejoice, for we trust in his holy name. Let your unfailing love surround us, Lord, for our hope is in you alone.

Psalm 33:18, 20–22 NLT

We've been told not to hope in anything or anyone but God. But sometimes that can be difficult. God is unseen, and it takes faith to believe the unseen will come to our aid. We may begin to rely on finances, other people, or other powers. But soon we come to realize that the Lord is the God of abundance, more powerful than people, things, or institutions.

So today, remember that God is watching over you. That His love will never fail you. That He alone can help and protect you.

Today, rejoice in the God of gods—the all-powerful, all-loving being who created you. The one who will always stand by you, never fail you. Put your hope in Him alone.

Remind me in this moment, Lord, that You are loving me, helping me, shielding me. That I can trust in You. May I feel Your presence, Lord, as my heart rejoices in You!

PRAYER JAR INSPIRATION:

My hope and joy rest in the God whose unfailing love surrounds me!

Day 94

UNEXPECTED

Behold, God is my helper; the Lord is the upholder of my life.

PSALM 54:4 ESV

When you're expecting a baby, you have nine months to prepare yourself for the baby's arrival. Nine months to buy baby furniture. Nine months to figure out your work situation. Nine months to choose the baby's name.

Not everything can be planned out like that. Sometimes things hit unexpectedly. A job loss. The death of a loved one. A stock market crash. And you've had zero time to prepare. So you go into it completely blind. There's been no sense of expectation, no clue this would hit. Yet here you are.

Isn't it comforting to realize that God knew this was coming and has already seen what's ahead for you? He loves you very much and will always take care of you, so you have nothing to fear. No matter what comes—expected or unexpected—He has already made provision for it.

I can trust You with the unexpected, Lord. Amen.

PRAYER JAR INSPIRATION:

God is my helper, even in the unexpected.

Day 95

FEELINGS

His anger lasts only a moment, his goodness for a lifetime.
Tears may flow in the night, but joy comes in the morning.

PSALM 30:5 GNT

If you've shut down after a trauma, the feelings will return. . . .

Sometimes feelings come in like a flood. A tsunami, even. Anger often leads the way. You don't really know why you're so angry, and you can't seem to control it, but there it is, rearing its ugly head.

Why? Because anger is one of the many stages of grief. (And let's face it, the stages of grief don't play nice!) Anger can lead to outbursts you might regret later.

When this tsunami hits, it's common to crash all over anyone who happens to be in your path. And while it might seem uncontrollable, you will begin to see patterns of reactionary behaviors that can be controlled, at least to some extent.

So watch out for the tsunamis. Don't let them sweep you out to sea. And remember: The Bible says that God gets angry too. But His anger lasts only for a moment. His goodness lasts a lifetime.

When angry moments come, help me keep them under control, Lord. Amen.

PRAYER JAR INSPIRATION:

I will not allow my emotions to rule me.

Day 96

GOD'S GIRL

"Fear not, for I have redeemed you; I have called you by name, you are mine. When you pass through the waters, I will be with you; and through the rivers, they shall not overwhelm you; when you walk through fire you shall not be burned, and the flame shall not consume you."

ISAIAH 43:1–2 ESV

You are not your own. You are God's. He created you, formed you, saved you. And He, the Master of the universe, wants you to live a life without fear because He needs you to live out the purpose He made you for.

You *can* live without fear by reminding yourself that when you pass through the waters, God will be in those waves with you. When you try to cross the flooded rivers, they won't overwhelm you because God is in the flood with you. And when you walk through fire, you'll not be burned nor consumed by the flames. Instead, you'll come out like Shadrach, Meshach, and Abednego—not only unsinged but lacking even the smell of smoke!

To live without fear, constantly remember who you are and where God is. You are His precious daughter, and He is the eternal power that nothing and no one can conquer!

Help me, Lord, to continually remember that I am Your girl— and that You will be with me through flood and fire!

PRAYER JAR INSPIRATION:

My hope and courage are found in who God is!

Day 97

SURVIVE. . .OR THRIVE?

"They will thrive like well-watered grass,
like willows by streams of running water."

Isaiah 44:4 gnt

Think of the people who've been through legitimate traumas: Holocaust survivors. Fire survivors. Abuse survivors.

All these people have one very important word in common: *survivor.* It's a powerful word to define them, but there's another word even more powerful: *thriver.*

God doesn't just want you to survive life's tragedies, He longs for you to thrive on the opposite side of them. It might seem impossible now, but you really can grow and become more like Christ from the hard road you've walked. When you do that, you can turn survival into a life of thriving.

You've been shaped and formed into His image as you've gone through the fire. Now you're ready to minister to others with a sensitivity and power you never had before. Nothing can hold you back now.

I want to thrive—like willows by streams of running water, Lord. Thank You for bringing me out on the other side so I can do that. Amen.

PRAYER JAR INSPIRATION:

Because of Jesus, I'm thriving like well-watered grass.

Day 98

BEAUTIFUL SCARS

"He went to him and bandaged his wounds, pouring on oil and wine. Then he put the man on his own donkey, brought him to an inn and took care of him."

Luke 10:34 NIV

Sometimes scars are visible. People notice them and are reminded to ask how you're doing post-trauma.

But sometimes scars are hidden, buried deep in your thought life or your heart. People don't see them and don't think to ask how you're doing. So you hunker down even more, convinced no one sees or knows what you're going through.

The truth is, we all have scars. And they are nothing to be ashamed of. They are a sign (to you and others) that healing is taking place. So don't hide those scars. They're a reminder that God is already at work.

Thank You for the healing that is already taking place in my heart and mind, Lord. I'm not ashamed of these scars. They're a sign that You are working in my life.

PRAYER JAR INSPIRATION:

My scars are beautiful.

Day 99

A CERTAIN KIND OF COURAGE

In your hearts set Christ apart [as holy—acknowledging Him, giving Him first place in your lives] as Lord. Always be ready to give a [logical] defense to anyone who asks you to account for the hope and confident assurance [elicited by faith] that is within you, yet [do it] with gentleness and respect.

1 Peter 3:15 AMP

The Bible tells us time and time again that we're to make God our priority (Psalm 70:4); we're to seek Him first above all other things (Matthew 6:33). For in doing so, we will not only eliminate needless worry in our lives but find the happiness, peace, and courage we long for.

Equipped with that joy, calm, and courage, we will find a way to speak confidently to others about God. We'll find the right words to tell them—with gentleness and respect—what Jesus has done and continues to do in our lives.

Today, lean into the confidence that walking closely with God provides.

Help me, Lord, to make You number one in my life!

PRAYER JAR INSPIRATION:

Making God a priority in my life is the first step toward spreading the good news!

Day 100

CHOOSE JOY

Always be joyful. Never stop praying. Be thankful in all circumstances, for this is God's will for you who belong to Christ Jesus.

1 Thessalonians 5:16–18 NLT

Can you imagine choosing not to heal? What if you looked at your broken arm and said, "Bones, I command you not to fuse back together!" That would be crazy, right?

It's equally strange that we go through seasons where we would rather wallow in our grief than pick up the pieces, get the healing we need, and move forward.

Maybe this is why the Bible says we are to "choose" joy. We choose joy even when we don't feel like it. (And let's face it: Some days we really, *really* don't feel like it.)

Why? Because it's hard to heal when you're down in the dumps. It's difficult to mend a broken leg if you keep removing the cast. Joy brings life to the bones and health to the body. And ultimately, that's God's way!

So choose joy today.

It's hard to imagine always being joyful, but I will do my best, Lord. Give me Your version of joy, the kind that rises above circumstances. Amen.

PRAYER JAR INSPIRATION:

Today I choose joy!

Day 101

FEAR OF REPEATS

Such love has no fear, because perfect love expels all fear. If we are afraid, it is for fear of punishment, and this shows that we have not fully experienced his perfect love.

1 John 4:18 NLT

When you've been hard-hit with a trauma, sometimes you slip into fear mode, convincing yourself that the trauma is going to hit again. If, for instance, a burglar breaks into your home and steals some of your belongings, you might live in constant fear that he's coming back, even though the police now have him in their custody.

This reaction is completely normal post-trauma, and you're certainly not alone. But God doesn't want you to live in fear.

The enemy would love nothing more than to keep you bound up, waiting for the next shoe to drop. But most of the things we worry about don't actually come to pass (thank goodness)! So don't give away hours of your life to fear of the unknown. Instead, acknowledge those fears. Be honest with God. Say, "I'm really scared this is going to happen again." Then allow Him to drive out that fear with His perfect love.

Thank You for the reminder that I don't have to live in fear, Lord. Amen.

PRAYER JAR INSPIRATION:

God's perfect love drives out fear.

Day 102

YOUR INNER FIRE

Fan into flame the gracious gift of God, [that inner fire—the special endowment] which is in you. . . . For God did not give us a spirit of timidity or cowardice or fear, but [He has given us a spirit] of power and of love and of sound judgment and personal discipline [abilities that result in a calm, well-balanced mind and self-control].

2 Timothy 1:6–7 AMP

When you first came to Christ, did you spend some time discovering your spiritual gift? Finding it most likely sparked your spiritual fire, so ready were you to serve God by using it to grow His kingdom. But, as the years went by, your initial spark may have died out.

It's time to fan back into a flame those embers of your gift so that you can serve God in a way no one else can. God equipped you with a unique talent. Use it, knowing that He has also given you the power, peace, love, and mind to do so.

Inspire me once more, Lord, to use the spiritual gift You've blessed me with. Help me see it with new eyes. Then give me the courage to use it in Your power!

PRAYER JAR INSPIRATION:

God of all gifts, thank You for giving me a spirit of power, love, and self-discipline!

Day 103

MILLION-DOLLAR WORDS

Like apples of gold in settings of silver is a ruling rightly given. Like an earring of gold or an ornament of fine gold is the rebuke of a wise judge to a listening ear.

PROVERBS 25:11–12 NIV

Do you have a friend or loved one who is struggling to find their way today? Speak words of life over them. Is someone grieving the loss of a job or a dream? Offer uplifting, hopeful words.

"Like apples of gold in settings of silver." What do you suppose that means? The ordinary becomes extraordinary with a few words of love poured on top. A child suddenly sees himself as special. A coworker's spirits are lifted as you share a pat on the back.

These might seem like small things, but they're not. If you could put a dollar value on encouraging words, the price would start at about a million dollars a word. That's how much they mean to the one on the receiving end.

So what's keeping you? Is a friend struggling? Drop some million-dollar words on her today!

I want to speak high-dollar words, Lord! Show me how to share positive, upbeat conversations with those who need them the most.

PRAYER JAR INSPIRATION:

Words matter.

Day 104

BETTER TOGETHER

Two people are better off than one, for they can help each other succeed. If one person falls, the other can reach out and help. But someone who falls alone is in real trouble. Likewise, two people lying close together can keep each other warm. But how can one be warm alone? A person standing alone can be attacked and defeated, but two can stand back-to-back and conquer. Three are even better, for a triple-braided cord is not easily broken.

ECCLESIASTES 4:9–12 NLT

Have you ever wondered why fish swim in schools? There are a host of reasons why they stick together; here are two. First, they are better protected against predators when they remain together. Second, they receive social benefits from being in a school.

It's the same with you. God designed you to live in community. This is especially critical when you're going through a crisis. It's almost impossible for the lone fish to survive the crisis. But when he's surrounded by his brothers and sisters, fully engulfed in that social circle of the protective school, his chances go way up.

One of the ways God wants you to heal from crises is by drawing close to those He's placed in your proverbial school. They're there, arms outstretched, waiting to walk you through this. Don't run from them. Instead, draw close.

Thank You for sending people I can share life with. Amen.

PRAYER JAR INSPIRATION:

We really are better together.

Day 105

STICK-TO-ITIVENESS

David continued to address Solomon: "Take charge! Take heart! Don't be anxious or get discouraged. God, my God, is with you in this; he won't walk off and leave you in the lurch. He's at your side until every last detail is completed for conducting the worship of God."

1 Chronicles 28:20 MSG

Young or old, we may at times lack the confidence and the courage to use the gifts God has given us. Perhaps we doubt whether we have the talent to do what we've been called to do. Or we imagine we'll run out of time to begin the project, much less complete it.

Yet, as Solomon was told and later discovered, whatever God has called us to do He will equip us to do—in both talent, resources, and time. So don't hesitate to begin the project God has tapped you for. And don't worry about having the time to complete it. Just continually seek God's direction, knowing He will be with you. He won't leave you in the lurch. He'll stick and stand with you till the end.

Help me focus on what You are doing in and through me, Lord, instead of what I may lack. Give me the courage and the faith to see a project through, from beginning to end.

PRAYER JAR INSPIRATION:

God is my comfort and stay!

Day 106

REALISTIC DREAMS

For when dreams increase and words grow many, there is vanity; but God is the one you must fear.

Ecclesiastes 5:7 esv

Today, look at some of your dreams that didn't come true—the ones you've grieved over—and give them a realistic look. Were they doable or some sort of get-rich-quick scheme? (Hey, there's nothing wrong with earning good money, but instant success is an illusion, not a reality.)

Perhaps it's time to reframe those dreams. Give them a longer timeline. Look at them from a different angle. Pray that God will reveal a better way to accomplish what He has put in your heart to do.

And don't give in to despair when those dreams don't come true. Hindsight, as they say, is 20/20. Later you'll be glad that all your dreams didn't come true. Some could have led you down a dark road, away from God and from His people. In other words, thank Him for the dreams that didn't work out. They might have been a saving grace!

When my dreams are unrealistic, Lord, show me! (I can take it!) Amen.

PRAYER JAR INSPIRATION:

Not all dreams will come true, and that's okay. God has something bigger—and better—in store for me.

Day 107

THE GOOD FIGHT

Fight the good fight of the faith. Take hold of the eternal life to which you were called and about which you made the good confession in the presence of many witnesses.

1 Timothy 6:12 esv

A fighter in the ring will get punched. He does his best to avoid it, ducking and turning, but he takes a lot of unexpected hits. Still, he has the knowledge in the back of his head that it's likely he will go down in the ring instead of coming out a victor.

Now think about your life. You're a lot like the fighter in the ring. But you forget that sometimes hard hits are to be expected. They catch you off guard. You don't have a strong defense. And then you find yourself on the floor of the ring, bloodied and wondering how you got there.

Life will knock you down from time to time. But a good fighter gets back up again. He lives to fight another day. Don't let the hard knocks keep you on the floor. That's what your opponent wants. Rise, get healed, and get back in the ring.

I want to keep on going, Lord, even after the hard hits. Heal me so that I can keep moving forward, I pray. Amen.

PRAYER JAR INSPIRATION:

After a hard hit, I will trust God for healing so I can get back in the ring.

Day 108

WHEREVER YOU GO

"Don't be afraid, for I am with you. Don't be discouraged, for I am your God. I will strengthen you and help you. I will hold you up with my victorious right hand. . . . For I hold you by your right hand—I, the Lord your God. And I say to you, 'Don't be afraid. I am here to help you.'"

Isaiah 41:10, 13 NLT

No matter what others tell you, you are not alone in this world. God is with you wherever you go. His presence will strengthen you and help you. He will lift you out of pits of despair, pull your foot out of snares, and haul you out of the deep waters into which you are plunged. He is there beside you, continually telling you not to be afraid. You can turn to Him for whatever help, strength, rescue, and empowerment you need, night or day.

It's this kind of knowledge that gave Joseph of Arimathea—"a respected member of the council, who was also himself looking for the kingdom of God" (Mark 15:43 ESV)—the courage, the boldness, to go to Pilate and ask for Jesus' body so he could prepare it for burial.

Daughter of God, sister of Christ, woman of the Holy Spirit, have courage. You never walk alone.

God, with You in my life, I will never fear.

PRAYER JAR INSPIRATION:

With God, I am never alone.

Day 109

AT THE CENTER

"But when he, the Spirit of truth, comes, he will guide you into all the truth. He will not speak on his own; he will speak only what he hears, and he will tell you what is yet to come."

JOHN 16:13 NIV

Is God at the center of your dreams? Maybe you have big ideas, big visions for the future. Great! But is He at the very center of them?

God dreams are most often bigger than yourself. They can seem impossible, even a little intimidating. But when God is in a thing, all things are possible!

Maybe you've had attainable dreams, things that should have come to pass but didn't. Perhaps God wasn't in them. You can walk away from those situations feeling defeated and hopeless. And let's face it, asking God to enter your dream isn't exactly a strategy for success.

It needs to be the other way around. If you are healing from a broken heart over crushed dreams, ask God to show you His plans, His dreams, His strategies. He wants you to succeed. And when you give Him His rightful place—the very center of it all—you will!

To keep You at the center, I have to invite Your Spirit to rule and reign. I choose to do that today, Lord. Amen.

PRAYER JAR INSPIRATION:

I will ask God to show me His dreams for my life.

Day 110

FIXING BROKEN THINGS

My son, be attentive to my words; incline your ear to my sayings.
Let them not escape from your sight; keep them within your heart.
For they are life to those who find them, and healing to all their flesh.

PROVERBS 4:20–22 ESV

There's your way, and then there's God's way. If you're like most, you just want to deal with things, put them behind you, and move on. God wants you to deal with the broken things on the sidewalk behind you. (Hey, if you leave the broken bicycle on the pathway, someone else is sure to trip. It's not helping anyone to leave broken things exposed.)

God wants to fix the bike, not just drag it off the sidewalk. And when that bike represents a broken friendship, He wants to repair it for several reasons: The longer you leave that broken relationship out in the open, the more it affects your loved ones. Other friends get caught up in the fray. Your family suffers when you're hyperfocused on the one who hurt you.

So, when you're able, take the time to fix those broken relationships. Not all are meant to be, but the ones that are could potentially last for a lifetime.

I'll admit, it's easier not to fix broken things, Lord. But I'll do it Your way! Amen.

PRAYER JAR INSPIRATION:

God's way is the healing way.

Day 111

CHAOS TO CALM

Why are you in despair, O my soul? And why are you restless and disturbed within me? Hope in God and wait expectantly for Him, for I shall again praise Him, the help of my [sad] countenance and my God.

Psalm 43:5 AMP

When ungodly people are unjustly attacking you, you might find yourself on the verge of losing your peace. So take a time-out to remind yourself who God is: your strength, a stronghold in whom you can take refuge (Psalm 43:2).

Ask God for direction, for help in staying calm. Ask Him to shine His light and truth on your path so that you can find your way back into His presence, a place where you can bend your knee in humility before Him, find a fountain of joy, and begin to praise instead of panic (Psalm 43:3–4). Lastly, speak to your soul, bringing it back to a place of hope, of expectation of God's shelter, love, and calm.

God, help me regain my peace. Remind me that You are my strength and my God of hope and joy! In Jesus' name, amen.

PRAYER JAR INSPIRATION:

God reigns within, guiding me out of the world's chaos and ushering me into His calm.

Day 112

PLENTY OF ROAD AHEAD

As you come to him, the living Stone—rejected by humans but chosen by God and precious to him—you also, like living stones, are being built into a spiritual house to be a holy priesthood, offering spiritual sacrifices acceptable to God through Jesus Christ.

1 Peter 2:4–5 NIV

Remember what it felt like as a teen to have a crush on a boy? Maybe you expressed your feelings, but then he rejected you.

The pain of rejection is a terrible thing to deal with, especially when you pinned all your hopes on that person. Now, as an adult, you've probably experienced the same pain in a variety of ways. Maybe you pinned all your hopes on a new job opportunity, and it didn't happen. Or maybe you felt certain you would have a child, only to have a pregnancy end in miscarriage. Broken dreams come in all forms.

It's never good to put all your hopes and dreams in one basket. But remember, God is there with you no matter what, traveling those broken roads. And He already sees into tomorrow and knows that great things are coming. So hang on! There's plenty of road ahead for you.

Thank You that broken dreams don't mean the end of the road, Jesus! Amen.

PRAYER JAR INSPIRATION:

It's not the end of the road for me!

Day 113

MUDDY WATERS

If the godly give in to the wicked, it's like polluting a fountain or muddying a spring.

PROVERBS 25:26 NLT

Have you ever been in a codependent relationship? Such relationships can be tricky to navigate, for sure. Things can get very complicated when the other person emotionally manipulates you or tries to make you feel guilty for things you're not really guilty of.

Sometimes the Lord allows these relationships to remain, but from a greater distance. Other times He calls you to break off the relationship—for your own sanity and for the good of the person who has become too dependent on you.

You weren't created to carry another person's load. That's not to say you don't care and don't pray. Of course you do both of those things.

If you're in a tricky relationship that needs healing, seek the Lord. Get His opinion. (It's the one that matters most, after all.) But do your best to stay out of muddy waters!

I won't muddy the waters by giving in to the nagging of someone who wants me to carry their load, Lord. Amen.

PRAYER JAR INSPIRATION:

I will seek the Lord in all my relationships—especially those that are tricky to navigate.

Day 114

CONSTANT PEACE

"You will keep in perfect and constant peace the one whose mind is steadfast [that is, committed and focused on You—in both inclination and character], because he trusts and takes refuge in You [with hope and confident expectation]."

ISAIAH 26:3 AMP

A million things could go wrong during a day: You could get a flat tire on the way home from the grocery store; the clothes dryer could break down, leaving you with sopping wet sheets; you could get a call from the school nurse to pick up your child in the middle of a workday; your husband could ask for a divorce; or you could get a diagnosis of cancer. From day to day, hour to hour, minute to minute, you don't know what may or may not happen. So many things are out of your control.

Yet you can still have peace by keeping your thoughts focused on God. By trusting in Him and taking shelter in Him. By confidently knowing that no matter what happens, He will bring out something good in the worst of circumstances.

Show me how to keep my mind on You, Lord, to run to You for refuge, trusting You to bring the best out of any situation. For I want, I need, I long for constant peace in You.

PRAYER JAR INSPIRATION:

Today I will trust and focus on God, my fortress, shield, and bringer of good.

Day 115

ONE DAY AT A TIME

"So do not worry about tomorrow; it will have enough worries of its own. There is no need to add to the troubles each day brings."

MATTHEW 6:34 GNT

If you're like most people, you've prayed for God to heal your emotions (say, a broken heart after a failed relationship), and He's done so. You walked in freedom for a while. Then it all started up again. And before you knew it, tears were rolling just like they used to.

There's a reason Jesus encouraged us to live one day at a time. Each day truly does have enough trouble of its own. And healing doesn't mean you'll never hurt again. It means you're not driven by the brokenness anymore.

Don't beat yourself up if you don't have it all together right away. These things take time, after all. Just rest easy in the fact that your heart is safe in the hands of the healer, who loves you more than life itself.

I know this is a process, Jesus. I will trust You,
even on the tear-filled days. Amen.

PRAYER JAR INSPIRATION:
I can trust God even on the hard days.

Day 116

OUT OF THE PIT

Bless the Lord, O my soul, and forget not all his benefits, who forgives all your iniquity, who heals all your diseases, who redeems your life from the pit, who crowns you with steadfast love and mercy.

Psalm 103:2–4 esv

Imagine you baked a loaf of bread a few days back and left it in plastic wrap on the counter. You're able to slice a piece of it, but you notice it has speckles of green mold on it.

The only way that moldy loaf of bread could actually hurt you would be if you ate it anyway. That's kind of what it's like when you return to the past to consume the guilt and sins of yesterday. The past is splattered in icky green mold, with nothing good to come of it.

When God redeems your life from the pit, His ultimate goal is to set you free from the past. No more pits. No more mold. He crowns you with steadfast love and mercy to remind you daily that pit life was a stinky life. And that's not the place for you anymore.

You're a child of the King, and He has great things planned for you. He didn't just save you *from* your old life, He saved you *for* something so much better!

Thank You for giving me new life, Jesus.
You've redeemed me and set me free! Amen.

PRAYER JAR INSPIRATION:
God saved me from *the pit* for *great things!*

Day 117

CARED FOR AND CARRIED

*"Listen to me. . . . I have cared for you since you were born.
Yes, I carried you before you were born. I will be your God throughout
your lifetime—until your hair is white with age. I made you,
and I will care for you. I will carry you along and save you."*

Isaiah 46:3–4 NLT

God has carried and cared for you not only since you were born. He's done so *before* you entered this worldly realm! And He will continue to carry and care for you even when your hair starts to turn gray then white with age.

Why? Because He loves you. He loves spending time with you. He made you to be in a relationship with Him. He loves to see you live out the purpose He created you for. Like any father, He is a proud Papa.

So don't worry about the past, present, or future. He'll be with you through it all, beaming His light, love, and protection on your path. Your job? Enjoy the ride!

I find great peace in knowing, Lord, that You have been and always will be caring for and carrying me! What a wonderful Savior!

PRAYER JAR INSPIRATION:

*God is my constant caretaker and carrier.
I rest easy in that knowledge!*

Day 118

WONDERFUL CREATOR

"You are worthy, our Lord and God, to receive glory and honor and power, for you created all things, and by your will they were created and have their being."

REVELATION 4:11 NIV

The same creative God who made blowfish, giraffes, and Siamese kittens made you. He doesn't suffer from a lack of creativity! Neither do you. You are created in His image, after all.

When you have your heart set on something—say, a big dream—and it doesn't come to fruition, it's tempting just to give up. But that's not what a child of God does. (God never gives up, after all.) You're creative enough, and tenacious enough, to begin again—even after a big disappointment.

Things might not look the way you expected. God might not even use the same people you expected. But your creative God is nudging you today to say, "Hey, don't stop now! We have work to do."

You do, you know. So stop fretting over what didn't happen and start looking ahead to what could happen.

Thank You, my creative Father, for making me in Your image! Help me to keep going even when I don't feel like it!

PRAYER JAR INSPIRATION:

I'm a child of the Most High God, and I won't give up!

Day 119

GET THE WORD IN

For the word of God is living and active, sharper than any two-edged sword, piercing to the division of soul and of spirit, of joints and of marrow, and discerning the thoughts and intentions of the heart.

HEBREWS 4:12 ESV

If you struggle with mind chatter, memorizing key Bible verses can be very helpful. When those reels begin to play in your memory, you can switch gears and begin to speak the Word over that situation.

If you're not able to memorize easily, here is a trick to help: Write down the Bible verses and pin or tape them in key places around your house.

Here's another fun way to get the Word inside you: Set the verses to music. Create a little melody to go along with the scripture verses you love.

You can even play the audio Bible as you have a quiet rest time midday. Refocus on the promises found in the Word of God and watch that mind chatter dissipate!

There are many ways to get the Word inside of you and keep it there. Use your imagination!

I will return to Your Word again and again to sustain me, Lord! Amen.

PRAYER JAR INSPIRATION:

I can—and will—memorize the Word of God.

Day 120

FINDING REST

"Come to Me, all who are weary and heavily burdened [by religious rituals that provide no peace], and I will give you rest [refreshing your souls with salvation]. Take My yoke upon you and learn from Me [following Me as My disciple], for I am gentle and humble in heart, and you will find rest (renewal, blessed quiet) for your souls."

MATTHEW 11:28–29 AMP

Jesus provides a simple pathway to realizing His peace. All you need to do is come to Him and lay down your burdens. He'll give you the rest you need if you're burned out on religion. He'll refresh you from the weariness you have suffered by wending your way through this world.

With Jesus you will be able to recover your true life, one that entails simply following Him. And in doing so, you'll not only find the peace you pine for but "learn the unforced rhythms of grace." As you endeavor to keep company with Him, "you'll learn to live freely and lightly" a life worth living (Matthew 11:29–30 MSG).

I come to You, Lord, ready to lay down my burdens and pick up Your peace and grace.

PRAYER JAR INSPIRATION:

In Jesus, I live and hope to "learn the unforced rhythms of grace" (Matthew 11:29 MSG).

Day 121

ULTIMATE MENDER

My sacrifice, O God, is a broken spirit; a broken and contrite heart you, God, will not despise.

PSALM 51:17 NIV

In Japanese tradition, a broken plate or piece of pottery is put back together with liquid gold (known as gold joinery or *kintsugi*). In this process, liquid gold fills the cracks of a broken vessel, forming a lovely finished product, even better than before.

No doubt you've been through some major breaks in your life. And you've done your best to mend and allow yourself to move forward. But you've still envisioned those cracks as something ugly—a negative testimony, as it were.

But they're not ugly at all!

Your master craftsman has used His own special version of gold, mending you and making you into a thing of beauty. So, as you look at where you've been—what you've been through—begin to see yourself as a beautiful work of art, pieced together by the master craftsman, with skillful artistry.

You have mended me into a thing of beauty, Lord, and I'm so grateful!

PRAYER JAR INSPIRATION:

Jesus is the ultimate mender!

Day 122

CAPTURED THOUGHTS

We demolish arguments and every pretension that sets itself up against the knowledge of God, and we take captive every thought to make it obedient to Christ.

2 Corinthians 10:5 niv

Imagine you're playing Ping-Pong with a friend. When it's your time to hit the ball, you accidentally knock it across the room. Off it goes, pinging off the floor, then the wall, then a table on the far side of the room. Just about the time you think it's slowing down, it rolls under a bench, out of sight. Now you'll never be able to capture it.

Thoughts can be like that ball sometimes. You give them too much attention and they start flying. Before you know it, they're completely out of control.

The Bible says you should take your thoughts captive before they start ping-ponging across the room and sweeping up all sorts of mischief. You need to squelch them when they're small, errant thoughts.

You really can capture them, friend. You can demolish every single stronghold that attempts to set itself up against the knowledge of God!

Help me capture my thoughts, Lord! Amen.

PRAYER JAR INSPIRATION:

I can demolish strongholds.

Day 123

BE STILL

"Be still and know (recognize, understand) that I am God. I will be exalted among the nations! I will be exalted in the earth." The Lord of hosts is with us; the God of Jacob is our stronghold [our refuge, our high tower].

Psalm 46:10–11 amp

When your world has been shaken up, when you see no way out of your troubles, when you feel friendless and fearful, be still. Take a few deep breaths. And settle your mind on God.

See the Lord as your refuge, strength, and helper. Remind yourself that you need not fear anything because He has you in the palm of His hand. So even if the earth quakes and the mountains topple into the sea, even though the waters may roar and foam, you have someone on your side: the Creator, sustainer, and maintainer of the universe.

God will never let you down, never allow you to falter. Jesus walks beside you, before you, behind you, and the Spirit resides within you.

Help me, Lord, to be still and know You are with me.

PRAYER JAR INSPIRATION:

I find God in the stillness of my soul, the calm of my heart, the peace of my spirit.

Day 124

BEST STORYTELLER

Better is the end of a thing than its beginning,
and the patient in spirit is better than the proud in spirit.

ECCLESIASTES 7:8 ESV

What if Cinderella didn't end up with the prince? What if Snow White didn't eat the poisoned apple? What if Rapunzel had short hair?

Not every real-life story ends the way you think it will. No doubt you've been somewhat conditioned by fairy tales to think there's a happily-ever-after, but reality often says otherwise. And the believer isn't exempt from pain and heartache. (Blame Adam and Eve! God created us to live in the bliss of Eden, and they blew it big time!)

You don't get to write the ending of your story, but you can most assuredly control the type of role you play in it. You can be a protagonist (working with God) or an antagonist (kicking and screaming, fighting Him all the way). When things don't go your way, bow your heart to the Creator of all and trust that no matter how tough the battle, He's planning to fight it for you.

I'm trusting You to write my story, Lord! Amen.

PRAYER JAR INSPIRATION:

God is the very best storyteller!

Day 125

GREEN PASTURES

"I will say to the prisoners, 'Come out in freedom,' and to those in darkness, 'Come into the light.' They will be my sheep, grazing in green pastures and on hills that were previously bare."

Isaiah 49:9 NLT

"I need a massage." "A day at the beach would do me a world of good." "I need a spa day." "A quiet evening by myself would be great for a change."

No doubt you've spoken some of these phrases over the years.

A massage can be great, but it doesn't always get to the root of the problem. A quiet evening alone might be good too, but perhaps what you really need is the shoulder of a friend.

God wants to lead you to green pastures to recline. In green pastures, you're replenished. You don't walk away the same way you came in.

Twenty-first-century solutions (like a spa day) are fun and probably do help. . .*some*. But remember, green pastures are the places where you're called to meet with the Lord—the one who will truly restore your soul.

Thank You for leading me to freedom, Lord! Amen.

PRAYER JAR INSPIRATION:

What does the phrase "green pastures" look like for me?

Day 126

RAY OF HOPE

Oh, how abundant is your goodness, which you have stored up for those who fear you and worked for those who take refuge in you!

Psalm 31:19 esv

When you can't take the world's woes anymore, when nothing seems to lift your lips into a smile, you can still uncover a significant ray of hope in God. But first you must turn away from the endless bad news and turn to God. Ask Him to help you focus on the good things that are coming your way, those He has stored up for you, the wonders that you cannot even begin to imagine.

Do what Jesus did—the one who has by example already shown you the way: Entrust your spirit into God's hands (Psalm 31:5). He will pull your foot out of the trap you are ensnared in (Psalm 31:4). He will rescue you from the negative thoughts pressing into your mind.

"I trust in you, O Lord. . . . My times are in your hand. . . . Blessed be the Lord, for he has wondrously shown his steadfast love to me" (Psalm 31:14–15, 21 esv).

PRAYER JAR INSPIRATION:

Shine Your rays of goodness on my path, Lord, so I may once more breathe hope.

Day 127

ALMOST

But the plans of the Lord stand firm forever,
the purposes of his heart through all generations.

Psalm 33:11 niv

Did you realize that Moses never actually made it to the Promised Land? Almost. . .but not quite.

Stephen, one of the early church leaders, wasn't able to meet his goal of reaching the world with the gospel message. He was stoned to death at a relatively young age.

Many times God places dreams and visions in the hearts of people who don't get to see them all the way to the end. But before you cry out, "That's not fair!" understand that He places those same dreams in the hearts of hundreds, if not thousands, of other believers too.

Moses wasn't meant to lead his people all the way into the Promised Land, but Joshua was. Stephen didn't live to spread the gospel, but a rogue-turned-believer named Paul did.

God always makes a way and always plants dreams in the hearts of men and women.

You always make a way, Lord. How grateful I am. Amen.

PRAYER JAR INSPIRATION:

God's purposes will stand.

Day 128

IN LOVE

Instead, by speaking the truth in a spirit of love,
we must grow up in every way to Christ, who is the head.

Ephesians 4:15 gnt

You're watching a friend go down the wrong path. You know she's on a course that's heading for a cliff. And you try to tell her, but she's not listening. Instead, defiant, she holds up her hand and says, "Let me live my own life."

So what do you do? Do you try once more to intervene, to bring healing to her heart and your relationship? Or do you walk away completely?

Though it might seem impossible, you might want to try one more time to speak the truth. You can do so in love, with her well-being at the forefront of the conversation. If she still won't receive it, then, for your own protection, it might be good to step away from the relationship—at least for now. You don't want her to drag you down with her.

It's not unkind to speak hard truth. In fact, it's unkinder not to. So, deep breath. Let's give this one more shot!

I don't know why I'm so nervous to speak the truth, Jesus.
Please give me courage and peace. Amen.

PRAYER JAR INSPIRATION:

Kindness and truthfulness go hand in hand.
I can be both kind and truthful.

Day 129

FINDING GOOD

He who pays attention to the word [of God] will find good, and blessed (happy, prosperous, to be admired) is he who trusts [confidently] in the Lord.

Proverbs 16:20 amp

God doesn't want you to be just a reader of His Word. He wants you to pay attention to it—to follow through on what it tells you to do and who it tells you to be. For when you really sink your heart, mind, body, soul, and spirit into what God through His Word is instructing you to do and be, you see yourself, the world, and your place in it with new eyes.

Make it a point each day not just to read a bit of the Bible and a short devotion but also to study His Word. Take one passage, one verse, one phrase and meditate on it. Chew on it. Then spend the day and night digesting it, asking God what He wants you to learn and then do with this information. Trust that He will bring scripture's meaning to life and into your life.

Help me, Lord, to be not just a woman of the Way but a woman of Your Word. Tell me what You would have me know. Then reveal to me the good, the blessings sparkling all around me.

PRAYER JAR INSPIRATION:

My hope is to see God's blessings to me through the lens of His good Word.

Day 130

TANGLED UP

"When you stand and pray, forgive anything you may have against anyone, so that your Father in heaven will forgive the wrongs you have done."

MARK 11:25 GNT

Have you ever tried to run a hairbrush through a little girl's tangled hair? There's only one way to untangle hair—gently. Slowly. Usually you work your way up from the bottom.

Some friendships are like that tangled hair. It's going to take time and patience to unravel the mess, and there may be a little crying along the way. (Hey, no one said healing was easy! It's a process.)

Think about the last time you reached for a string of Christmas lights from a storage box and found them all twisted up. It took a while to get them separated, but once you did, they shimmered as brightly as ever.

That's how relationships are too. Take the time to heal correctly, and in the end all tangles will be gone, all twists and kinks will be worked out, and the relationship will shine as never before.

I'm going to need Your patience as we unravel this mess together, Lord! Amen.

PRAYER JAR INSPIRATION:

Tangled messes don't have to be permanent. They can be untangled with patience and hard work.

Day 131

FIXATED

Fixing our eyes on Jesus, the pioneer and perfecter of faith.
For the joy set before him he endured the cross, scorning its shame,
and sat down at the right hand of the throne of God.

HEBREWS 12:2 NIV

Have you ever been fixated on something?

When we're fixated on something, it means our focus is so narrow we can't see past it. The house could be burning down around us, and we wouldn't notice when we're fixated.

The problem with twenty-first-century fixation is that we're usually not fixated on Jesus. More likely we're hyperfocused on stuff. Or our job. Or a relationship. Or a problem. We're staring so intently at it that we forget God is right next to us wishing He had our full attention.

Want to recover from the traumas that have plagued you? Take your eyes off whatever they're staring at and put them on Jesus, the author and finisher of your faith. He deserves every moment of your time and attention.

I will keep fixated on You, Jesus! Amen.

PRAYER JAR INSPIRATION:

Heavenly fixation is a good thing.

Day 132

LONGED-FOR GOOD

They cried to the Lord in their trouble, and he delivered them from their distress. He made the storm be still, and the waves of the sea were hushed. Then they were glad that the waters were quiet, and he brought them to their desired haven.

Psalm 107:28–30 esv

When we're in trouble, God will surely help us. But how can He do so if we do not ask?

It's not that God doesn't know what's happening in our lives. It's that He wants us to come to Him, to tell Him all that's on our minds, to ask for His help, to allow ourselves to conclude that *He* is God, not we. Our good comes from His hands, not our own.

Too often, we don't pray because we think we can get ourselves out of the jam we're in. But then, as we get more and more desperate, we finally pray—to our relief and God's pleasure—and find the good we've longed for come on the wings of heaven.

Today, consider what you've been holding back from God. Explain the situation and your feelings. Ask for His help. And before you know it, He'll calm the storm you've been riding through and bring you to where you desire to be.

Lord, I need Your help. . .

PRAYER JAR INSPIRATION:

God has good awaiting me. It's time to ask.

Day 133

THE BIBLICAL WAY

Therefore confess your sins to each other and pray for each other so that you may be healed. The prayer of a righteous person is powerful and effective.

James 5:16 NIV

It feels impossible. There's been a breach in your friendship. You haven't spoken in weeks. But there's a nudging in your heart that somehow things could mend. But you're clueless about what that should look like.

So you pray. You give the situation to God. Then He encourages you to reach out with a text. Just a few words: I MISS YOU.

And you wait. Time passes. And then a response comes: I MISS YOU TOO.

It's a start. You draw a deep breath and issue an apology for any role you might have played in the broken places. She responds in kind.

Broken relationships aren't always going to mend. Sometimes God separates you from people for your own protection. But there are still situations where you know in your heart that the friendship isn't truly over yet. So leave the door cracked if you feel that nudge from the Spirit. He'll show you what to do.

I trust You, Jesus. If the door is meant to swing wide, it will. Amen.

PRAYER JAR INSPIRATION:

I can't fix broken relationships, but Jesus can.

Day 134

DREAMER

Joseph had a dream, and when he told it to his brothers, they hated him all the more. He said to them, "Listen to this dream I had: We were binding sheaves of grain out in the field when suddenly my sheaf rose and stood upright, while your sheaves gathered around mine and bowed down to it."

GENESIS 37:5–7 NIV

If you've read the story of Joseph, found in Genesis 37, you know that he was a big dreamer. He had (literal) dreams that one day his brothers would bow down to him. They weren't amused. So they took that dreamer and tossed him into a pit, then sold him into slavery to the Egyptians.

Not everyone is going to like hearing about your dreams, especially if they're "big" dreams. You'll have naysayers. You'll have those who are angry when you succeed. And you'll have the "I told you so" crowd when your dreams don't come to pass the way you hoped (or expected) they would.

Joseph didn't let the negativity get to him. And, in the end, his dream actually came to pass.

Dreams will be broken. People will rub it in. But you can pick up the pieces and dare to dream again. Be a Joseph. Hang in there.

Thank You for the God-sized dreams You've placed inside of me, Lord! I won't give up when things don't go my way. Amen.

PRAYER JAR INSPIRATION:

I won't let the naysayers distract me from the dreams God has planted in my heart.

Day 135

DARE TO HOPE

It is because of the Lord's lovingkindnesses that we are not consumed, because His [tender] compassions never fail. They are new every morning; great and beyond measure is Your faithfulness. "The Lord is my portion and my inheritance," says my soul; "therefore I have hope in Him and wait expectantly for Him."

Lamentations 3:22–24 amp

When everything all around and within you seems to be coming apart—including your dreams, plans, and hopes—it's hard to focus on anything else. You may lament, " 'Everything I had hoped for from the Lord is lost!' The thought of my suffering and homelessness is bitter beyond words. I will never forget this awful time, as I grieve over my loss" (Lamentations 3:18–20 nlt).

Yet amid all your hardships, you must "still dare to hope" (Lamentations 3:21 nlt). You must remember that God's love is faithful. It will never end. And it's because of that love that you will not stay down and out.

Today and every day, remind yourself that God's faithfulness is beyond measure. His mercies come fresh to you every morning. He's yours. So live and breathe in hope!

Thank You, Lord, for Your continual love, Your abundant mercies that greet me anew each morning. Because You are in my life, I will continue to hope and pray—to expect Your good to come my way!

PRAYER JAR INSPIRATION:

Because God remains faithful to me, I will dare to hope!

Day 136

TIMELY WORD

The Lord God has given me the tongue of those who are taught, that I may know how to sustain with a word him who is weary. Morning by morning he awakens; he awakens my ear to hear as those who are taught.

Isaiah 50:4 esv

Think of a time when you were in intense physical pain. The pain gripped you in a way you couldn't properly deal with. All you wanted was relief—at any cost.

There are people out there who are in so much pain that they want release from it—at any cost. There are warning signs if you keep your eyes wide open. God wants you to be a light to those who have reached this point. You never know when a timely word will change everything in a person's situation.

So, instead of saying, "This really stinks!" say something like, "I'm looking forward to the day when this is behind you." Instead of saying, "This is so unfair," say something like, "How can I help?"

You can help, and often it requires simply being there with a person as they work their way through the valley. Be that kind word in due season. Offer hope.

Show me what to say to those who are truly struggling, Lord. Amen.

PRAYER JAR INSPIRATION:

I can speak a timely word and change someone's life forever.

Day 137

IN THE NAME OF THE LORD

David answered, "You are coming against me with sword, spear, and javelin, but I come against you in the name of the Lord *Almighty, the God of the Israelite armies, which you have defied."*

1 Samuel 17:45 GNT

David, the shepherd boy, was on his way to the battlefield to deliver food to the older, more capable warriors.

When he arrived, he saw that his people were squared off against a giant of a man—Goliath. Some say that Goliath was over nine feet tall!

Goliath stood at a distance, taunting and ridiculing the Jewish people, and David couldn't abide the vile words coming from the Philistine's mouth. So he flew into action. He didn't have dreams of being a giant-killer, but in the moment, God gave him the courage and tenacity to get the job done. With a slingshot and a stone, he took that giant down.

You might not dream of being a giant-killer either. But God has already placed inside of you the courage to do remarkable things when the situation calls for it. So don't worry about the giants in your path. The Lord is already making a way.

In Your name, I can take down my enemies, Lord! Amen.

PRAYER JAR INSPIRATION:
The name of Jesus is more powerful than anything I will ever face.

Day 138

SOMETHING NEW

This is what the Lord says—who makes a way in the sea, and a path through surging waters. . ."Do not remember the past events, pay no attention to things of old. Look, I am about to do something new; even now it is coming. Do you not see it? Indeed, I will make a way in the wilderness, rivers in the desert."

Isaiah 43:16, 18–19 HCSB

We are creatures of habit, and we often get stuck in a rut. We find it hard to imagine, to see, or to expect something new coming our way. Besides, there's comfort to be found in what's normal.

Yet God is always thinking up something new—something outside the box, unexpected, and wonderful. Remember, He's the one who made a path in the Red Sea so the Israelites could escape the thundering horses pulling the bloodthirsty Egyptians in their grand chariots.

Today, get your mind away from the old, the ordinary, the routine. Forget about what has gone before. Look for the new and good thing God is bringing your way. See how He is going to make a new path for you in the wilderness!

My eyes are off the old and looking for new good in You, Lord!

PRAYER JAR INSPIRATION:

Help me, Lord, to hope in something new from You!

Day 139

HERE AND NOW

Let your eyes look straight ahead; fix your gaze directly before you.

PROVERBS 4:25 NIV

Have you ever had a lingering cough or cold? At some point you may start thinking things like, *Am I going to have to live with this for the rest of my life?*

That's kind of how it is when you're struggling to let go of past hurts too. Some of the icky, nagging reminders keep showing up, whether you want them to or not. You do your best to press them down, but they pop up again—and often at the worst times. When your best friend announces her pregnancy. When a coworker celebrates a new romance. When your cousin gets a big job promotion.

Oops. There's that nagging cough again.

Perhaps this is why the writer of Proverbs so aptly said, "Fix your gaze directly before you." When you spend too much time looking over your shoulder, nothing good comes of it!

I'll keep my eyes fixed on the here and now, Lord!
Thank You for that reminder. Amen.

PRAYER JAR INSPIRATION:

I can "fix" my gaze and not fret over yesterday or tomorrow.

Day 140

RUN TO HIM

A woman in the crowd had suffered for twelve years with constant bleeding, and she could find no cure. Coming up behind Jesus, she touched the fringe of his robe. Immediately, the bleeding stopped.

Luke 8:43–44 NLT

Perhaps you feel alone in your heartache and brokenness.

No doubt the woman with the issue of blood felt the same. For years she had struggled. Years of bleeding. Years of humiliation, ostracized from society. Years of wishing for a different life, a different situation.

No doubt her emotional health was as poor as her physical health.

And then. . .Jesus. She saw Him from a distance and knew she had to make a move in His direction. Through the crowd she went, nudging her way toward the healer. And when she reached out to touch the hem of His garment, Jesus realized at once and said, "Who touched me?" The scripture says that He felt virtue going out of Him.

Maybe you feel like that woman. You're viewing Jesus from a distance. Through the crowd. Today, run to Him. Run with the assurance that He loves you and will pour Himself out on your behalf.

I know what it's like to press through the crowd to touch You, Jesus! I'm so grateful You welcome me every time. Amen.

PRAYER JAR INSPIRATION:

God is my healer.

Day 141

GOOD GIFTS

"You parents—if your children ask for a loaf of bread, do you give them a stone instead? Or if they ask for a fish, do you give them a snake? Of course not! So if you sinful people know how to give good gifts to your children, how much more will your heavenly Father give good gifts to those who ask him."

MATTHEW 7:9–11 NLT

Jesus tells us that God will give us what we ask for, what we seek. He will open the doors we come knocking on. Like any good parent, God will not give us a stone if we ask for bread. He won't give us a snake if we ask for a fish. If we, who have made mistakes, give good things to our children, how much more will our perfect God give good gifts to us!

Knowing this, we must make sure we go into our prayer closets with a strong expectation of receiving something good from God. We must look at Him as our compassionate and loving Father who wants to do all He can to give us joy, to equip us to serve Him.

I come to You in prayer today, Father, hoping—expecting—to receive nothing but good from You!

PRAYER JAR INSPIRATION:

Because I know my Father God is a giver of good gifts, my hope may be restored, my prayers more powerful!

Day 142

LETTING GO

Of course, my friends, I really do not think that I have already won it; the one thing I do, however, is to forget what is behind me and do my best to reach what is ahead. So I run straight toward the goal in order to win the prize, which is God's call through Christ Jesus to the life above.

PHILIPPIANS 3:13–14 GNT

Forgetting the past sounds easy enough in theory. But sometimes letting go of yesterday isn't as simple as one might think.

If anyone understood this, Job did. In his rearview mirror, he saw a man with the perfect life: a home, a family, crops, cattle, friends, money. All the things a person could ever wish for.

Through the windshield, however, things looked a lot different. All those things he once cherished had been stripped away. And now came the hard task: deciding where to set his gaze.

Maybe you can relate. Maybe your rearview mirror reflects better days gone by and almost lost from memory. Or perhaps your yesterdays were so painful you don't want to risk even a glance.

No matter what you've been through—good or bad—God can help you focus on today. Right here, right now, He can give you the courage and strength to heal from the pain of your yesterdays.

The only way I can truly forget what lies behind me is to keep my gaze fixed on You, Jesus. Amen.

PRAYER JAR INSPIRATION:

Yesterday is in the past. Today is a gift from God.

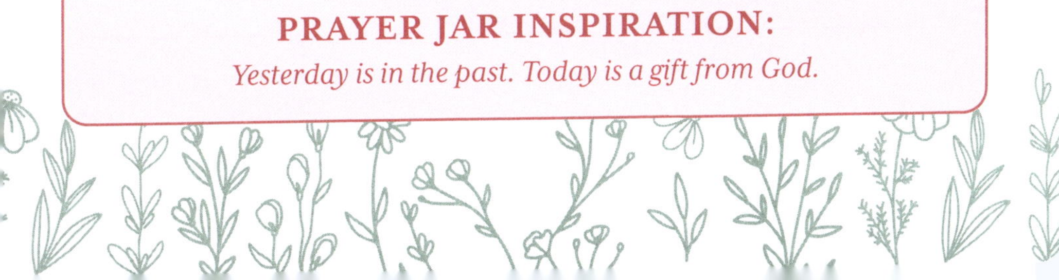

Day 143

GOD KNOWS

And it happened, before Isaiah had gone out into the middle court, that the word of the Lord *came to him, saying, "Return and tell Hezekiah the leader of My people, 'Thus says the* Lord*, the God of David your father: "I have heard your prayer, I have seen your tears; surely I will heal you. On the third day you shall go up to the house of the* Lord*."'"*

2 Kings 20:4–5 nkjv

Hezekiah lay on his deathbed, face to the wall. No doubt his spirits were low. Because, while others in Judah had turned their back on God and embraced pagan lifestyles, this man had not. And now here he was, mortally ill.

Hezekiah turned his face to the wall and prayed, reminding God of how he had lived a holy life. And God sent Isaiah the prophet to tell Hezekiah to dry his tears because God was going to extend his life by fifteen years.

Wow! An additional fifteen years!

No matter what you're going through, God knows the number of your days. He sees where you are. And He has a plan for your human body. So go right ahead. Pour out your heart to Him. He's listening. And He's going to guide you every step of the way.

I will trust You, even with my face to the wall, Jesus. Amen.

PRAYER JAR INSPIRATION:

Even when my face is to the wall,
God still sees and hears my every cry.

Day 144

NO LACK OF GOOD

Oh, taste and see that the Lord is good! Blessed is the man who takes refuge in him! Oh, fear the Lord, you his saints, for those who fear him have no lack! The young lions suffer want and hunger; but those who seek the Lord lack no good thing.

Psalm 34:8–10 ESV

Those who obey God, who revere Him as their Lord and Savior, Creator and sustainer, will find there is no one better than He. For no one and nothing in the world is *greater* than He.

So, at the first sign of trouble, don't count on yourself to work your way through it. Instead, run to the Lord. Take refuge in His protection, soak up the peace of His presence, breathe in His wisdom.

When you walk with God—minding His way, asking His advice, *and then taking it!*—you will surely lack nothing. After all, He is your all in all—your comfort, your calm, your faithful friend who is always looking to bless you with all good things.

Thank You, Lord, for always being there for me, providing refuge, making sure I lack no good thing–including hope in You. It is You alone I love with all my heart, soul, and mind.

PRAYER JAR INSPIRATION:

In and with God, I lack absolutely nothing.

Day 145

GOD'S HEART FOR FAMILIES

And the Word became flesh and dwelt among us, and we have seen his glory, glory as of the only Son from the Father, full of grace and truth.

John 1:14 ESV

It's important for people to heal, especially if they have children. After all, children are witnessing (and often mimicking) what they observe. But the kids aren't the only reason Mom and Dad need to get past the brokenness they're experiencing.

Let's face it: It's easy to say, "Get your act together for the sake of your children," but when we say that, we're overlooking the fact that Mom and Dad are as critical to God as those kids are.

God wants everyone to be healed, not just so the kids can grow up in a healthy environment but so that every single person in the household can experience the abundance of walking in healing and wholeness. *Every. Single. Person.*

Jesus didn't leave people out. When the woman with the issue of blood tugged on the hem of His garment, He didn't say, "I'm too busy to deal with you."

He's never too busy. He wants the whole family.

Today I offer myself and my whole family to You, Jesus!

PRAYER JAR INSPIRATION:

Healing—for Mom, Dad, and kids—
that's God's heart for the family.

Day 146

PEACEFUL SLEEP

I lie down and sleep; I wake again, because the Lord sustains me.

Psalm 3:5 niv

Sleep is a wonderful thing. But if you're like many twenty-first-century people, you don't get enough. Then you wonder why you're not healing (physically or psychologically) like you should.

God designed our bodies to heal while we're sleeping. How can that happen when you're staying up too late or falling asleep with a TV show blasting in the background?

Physical rest is critical, not just to your body but to your mind as well. Muddy, foggy thoughts come on the tail end of a poor night's sleep.

So plan for a better night's sleep. Take a warm bubble bath, put on your coziest jammies, climb between clean sheets in your warm bed and turn out the light.

And the TV. And the laptop. And your phone. And every other electronic device or distraction. Your body will thank you in the morning!

I confess, I don't always prioritize sleep, Lord.
Thank You for reminding me how important it is! Amen.

PRAYER JAR INSPIRATION:

Sleep is one of the best gifts I can give myself.

Day 147

MOST HIGH SHELTER

He who dwells in the shelter of the Most High will remain secure and rest in the shadow of the Almighty [whose power no enemy can withstand]. I will say of the Lord, "He is my refuge and my fortress, my God, in whom I trust [with great confidence, and on whom I rely]!"

Psalm 91:1–2 amp

Are you frightened? Stressed? Unprotected? Vulnerable? Then run to God. He'll save you from the fowler's snares. Like a mother eagle, He'll cover you with His wings. If any trouble does come your way, you'll be a spectator to it only. When you make God your refuge, no evil can befall you; He will command His angels to guard and defend you.

How can you get there from here? By loving God. By knowing who He is. By trusting in Him, knowing He will never abandon you. When you do these things, you can call on God, and He will answer you. He will be with you in trouble. He will rescue and honor you. He will cover you with His presence.

You, Lord, are my Refuge and Fortress, the God in whom I trust and hide!

PRAYER JAR INSPIRATION:

My hope and heart reside in the refuge of the Most High.

Day 148

START MOVING

Have mercy on me, Lord, for I am faint;
heal me, Lord, for my bones are in agony.

Psalm 6:2 NIV

If you're getting up there in years, the "bones are in agony" part of today's verse might hit a little too close to home. As we age, sometimes our bones seem to cry out in agony when we stand after sitting for a long period of time.

After a bit of stretching and flexing, we're finally able to make it from the sofa to the kitchen to start dinner. And once we get loosened up, we're good to go.

That's what it's like after you've been through an emotionally scarring time. Those scars can tighten things up. You're not as emotionally nimble as you once were. But you can learn to use those scars to your advantage. The key is to get up. Get going. Don't allow yourself to remain stagnant in one spot. True healing comes as you start moving.

I need Your help to start moving in faith, Lord!
Loosen up these emotional joints, and let's get going! Amen.

PRAYER JAR INSPIRATION:

With God's help, I can move even when I don't feel like it.

Day 149

HEALTHY CHANGES

"I know your works, your love and faith and service and patient endurance, and that your latter works exceed the first."

Revelation 2:19 esv

One of the problems with rushed living is that you don't have time to slow down long enough to make sure you're taking care of yourself. Oh, you've done the laundry for the kids. You've driven them to ball practice. Paid the bills. Fed the puppy. Cleaned up after the puppy.

But you're wiped out. And no one seems to notice. You barely have time to notice yourself. So you grab a quick snack to take the edge off the hunger from skipping lunch, and you put up with the ache in your belly.

Too many years of living like this will take a serious toll on your health, so maybe it's time to slow down long enough to analyze where you stand health-wise. It might be time for some significant changes so that you can live a long, healthy life.

I get it, Jesus. I'll pay more attention to my own health needs so I'm here for my loved ones even longer. Amen.

PRAYER JAR INSPIRATION:

My exhaustion is a sign that I need to take better care of myself.

Day 150

RELIANCE

We were crushed and overwhelmed beyond our ability to endure,
and we thought we would never live through it. In fact,
we expected to die. But as a result, we stopped relying on ourselves
and learned to rely only on God, who raises the dead.

2 Corinthians 1:8–9 NLT

This world can be a very difficult place. There may be days when you feel crushed and overwhelmed. You may begin to believe you'll never make it through to the dawn of the next day.

To rise above that depressed state, you must stop relying on yourself and learn to rely on God. As soon as you do, a calm will begin to sweep over you. When you give yourself into God's hands, you will find yourself in the most secure and loving place you can ever imagine on this side of heaven.

When you are crushed by trouble, look to God for all. Be secure in the knowledge that He who can raise the dead can and will save you.

Help me, Lord, even before the day of trouble
comes, to rely on You instead of myself.

PRAYER JAR INSPIRATION:
My hope of rescue lies in the God who can raise the dead.

Day 151

HEALING CAPABILITIES

This will bring health to your body and nourishment to your bones.

PROVERBS 3:8 NIV

We've all had those text messages from well-meaning friends trying to sell us their latest and greatest supplements or weight-loss plans. Those would-be salespeople are quite exuberant in their presentation—in part because they've seen results in their own bodies. (Hey, when you find something that works, you like to tell others so they can experience it too!)

The Word of God is like those supplements, only a thousand times better. The words you find inside the pages of the Bible really will bring life to your body and nourishment to your bones. They are a healing balm, better than anything you could ever swallow in pill form.

And no matter what you're walking through, there's a biblical remedy, easily found in the Word of God. Heartache? There are verses for you. Physical pain? You'll find verses for that too.

Talk about a miracle cure! The healing capabilities of the Word are endless!

I will turn to You and Your Word, Lord. I put my trust in You to heal the broken places in my heart.

PRAYER JAR INSPIRATION:

Thank You for the best supplement of all, Jesus—Your Word!

Day 152

OVER TIME

News about him spread all over Syria, and people brought to him all who were ill with various diseases, those suffering severe pain, the demon-possessed, those having seizures, and the paralyzed; and he healed them.

MATTHEW 4:24 NIV

Remember as a kid when you would scrape up your knee? Mom would put some medicine on it (maybe antibiotic cream) and then slap a bandage on it. "Now, don't mess with it!" she would say.

And you tried. You really did. But the temptation was too strong, especially after the bandage fell off and you saw that scab. So you picked at it. And then it started bleeding all over again.

That's how it is with emotional and psychological wounds too. When you allow the salve of the Holy Spirit to do its work, healing comes over time. But if you pull off God's protective layering and begin to pick at it, reliving it over and over again, it will never heal.

Leave that bandage on. Give God time. Resist the temptation to fix this yourself. Scabs serve a purpose. Leave them alone.

You are trying to heal me, Lord, and sometimes I make it worse instead of better. Give me the courage to leave this situation in Your hands. Amen.

PRAYER JAR INSPIRATION:

I will leave my healing in God's capable hands.

Day 153

WALL OF FIRE

"'For I,' declares the Lord, 'will be a wall of fire around her [protecting her from enemies], and I will be the glory in her midst.'" . . . "Sing for joy and rejoice, O Daughter of Zion; for behold, I am coming, and I will dwell in your midst," declares the Lord.

Zechariah 2:5, 10 amp

You are a woman of the Way, and you have a unique role to play in God's grand plan. For only a woman of your strength, history, and makeup can do what He asks of you. And because you are precious to Him, He will find a way to protect you while you are playing your part.

So, when you find yourself feeling insecure, defenseless, and vulnerable, remember that you are the daughter of an eternal King. He is your shield, your help—the wall of fire that surrounds you, protecting you from anything and anyone that might dare to cause you harm.

God dwells in your midst. So do not quiver in fear, but stand strong, fast, and firm. You do not walk alone but with the almighty God, whose power no foe can withstand.

Thank You, Lord, for being not only my life coach and planner but my great protector. With You in my midst, I can and will walk with confidence.

PRAYER JAR INSPIRATION:

God is my fire wall.

Day 154

REWRITTEN

By faith the prostitute Rahab, because she welcomed the spies, was not killed with those who were disobedient.

Hebrews 11:31 NIV

Have you ever read the story of Rahab? She's listed in the book of Joshua as a harlot, so (based solely on that description) you wouldn't think the Bible had much good to say about her. But Rahab's story changed dramatically when she allowed herself to be used by God to protect the Jewish people.

Rahab became the mother of Boaz. And if you know the remarkable story of Ruth, you know that she ended up married to Boaz, her kinsman-redeemer.

Rahab, who was known only to her neighbors and passersby as "the harlot," is one of the few women listed in the lineage of Jesus.

When your story changes, when you allow God to bring healing and wholeness, everything changes. A new plot is written. The old tale is no more.

Thank You for rewriting my story, Lord! I'm so glad You've given me a brand-new lineage! Amen.

PRAYER JAR INSPIRATION:

Plot twist! Jesus has changed my story!

Day 155

ON THE WALL

"For where two or three are gathered in my name, there am I among them."

MATTHEW 18:20 ESV

In biblical times, cities were fortified with high walls so that enemies couldn't come in and take them by force.

If you picture your body as a city, you can see some similarities. Sometimes the enemy (sickness, disease) tries to rush the walls and take over. When that happens, it can leave the city (you!) in disarray.

That's why it's so important to have watchmen on the wall. Having a team of prayer warriors can be a critical part of your journey as you work your way toward physical healing. They will do the hard work of fighting back the enemy while you take the time to heal.

There's power in numbers. And when you have a team of believers working together, praying together, believing together—watch out! Miracles can happen!

When I'm in need, I will gather my team of watchmen, Lord! Amen.

PRAYER JAR INSPIRATION:

Who are my watchmen on the wall?

Day 156

WINGS OF REFUGE

"Everything you have done for your mother-in-law. . .has been fully reported to me: how you left your father and mother and the land of your birth, and how you came to a people you didn't previously know. May the Lord reward you for what you have done, and may you receive a full reward from the Lord God of Israel, under whose wings you have come for refuge."

Ruth 2:11–12 HCSB

All those kindnesses you have done for others and all the ways you have stepped out of your comfort zone are things people—believers and non-believers alike—take notice of.

Your life may sometimes seem like an obstacle course as you meet challenge after challenge in your attempt to do the right thing: To help others selflessly. To walk with them when the road gets tough. But the end goal is finding your unique and secure place in the refuge of God.

Today, may the Lord reward you for what you have done and will do as you seek your place of refuge in Him.

Help me, Lord, to meet the challenges of this life as I steer my course to You.

PRAYER JAR INSPIRATION:

Under God's wings I find my eternal reward and refuge.

Day 157

RENEWABLE STRENGTH

Those who trust in the Lord will renew their strength; they will soar on wings like eagles; they will run and not grow weary; they will walk and not faint.

Isaiah 40:31 HCSB

The alarm goes off. Still heavy with sleep, you reluctantly pull your arm out from underneath the covers and hit the Snooze button. *Just one more minute,* you think to yourself, *and then I'll get up. Perhaps then I'll have the energy to face this day.*

Those kinds of thoughts speak to the spirit of women who aren't necessarily morning people. We wonder how and where we're going to get the strength to accomplish all the things we want or need to do today.

Yet God has another message He'd like you to engrave on your mind. And that's the hope that *He* will give you all the strength you need to get through your day. Only one ingredient is necessary: your trust in Him.

Lord, I hope in Your strength, knowing You will give me the energy to do what You would have me do today. Amen.

PRAYER JAR INSPIRATION:

God will renew my strength each day.

Day 158

WELL-BEING

For this is the love of God, that we keep his commandments. And his commandments are not burdensome.

1 John 5:3 ESV

When you're low on vitamin D, the doctor tells you to spend more time in the sunshine. When you're low on iron, he (or she) encourages you to eat more iron-rich foods like liver, beef, or eggs. Good foods can bring healing.

A lot of our medical woes in the twenty-first century come from wear and tear. Too much time on the computer causes eye strain, which leads to headaches and neck pain. Too many hours lounging on the sofa streaming movies leads to laziness or unwillingness to take that daily walk with your friend.

You get the idea. But the answers to most of these things come in the form of one simple word: *Obedience.*

Obedience gets up off the sofa.

Obedience pushes the chair away from the table.

Obedience steps out into the sunshine and breathes the fresh air.

Obedience leads to health.

Your commandments are for my well-being, Lord! Amen.

PRAYER JAR INSPIRATION:

God's commandments are never a burden.

Day 159

NEVER-ENDING STORY

Let us who live in the light be clearheaded, protected by the armor of faith and love, and wearing as our helmet the confidence of our salvation. For God chose to save us through our Lord Jesus Christ. . . . Christ died for us so that, whether we are dead or alive when he returns, we can live with him forever.

1 Thessalonians 5:8–10 NLT

Because we believe in Jesus, because we accepted Him as our Savior, we are children of the light (1 Thessalonians 5:5). And we do not live unprotected. We have surrounding us an impenetrable armor of faith and love. On our heads we wear a helmet of the hope of salvation. No matter where we are, regardless of whether we are alive or dead when Jesus returns, we can have the confidence that we will live with Him forever.

Yes, life on earth can be difficult at times. We will have our fair share of heartaches. But through good times and bad, we can live and die secure in the knowledge that our story with Jesus will never end.

Thank You, Jesus, for making me a child of Your light. For protecting me with Your love. For being my happily ever after.

PRAYER JAR INSPIRATION:

With Jesus in my life, I live a never-ending story.

Day 160

PERSONALLY AHEAD

"So be strong and courageous! Do not be afraid and do not panic before them. For the LORD your God will personally go ahead of you. He will neither fail you nor abandon you."

DEUTERONOMY 31:6 NLT

The world can be a very scary place. We never know what might be waiting for us around the next corner, the next bend in the road.

Moses had gotten God's people as far as the Jordan River. And just beyond that river was the Promised Land. From that moment on, Joshua would have to lead God's people. So, in his farewell address to the Israelites, Moses told them that they could be strong and brave. They need not panic nor be afraid—because God Himself was going ahead of them. He would always be there for them.

The same holds true for you. You are one of God's followers. So put all panic, fear, and weakness behind you. Instead, walk in the hope that God is going ahead of you personally. And always will.

Thank You, Lord, for giving me the strength and courage to go on, to go where You lead. Amen.

PRAYER JAR INSPIRATION:

God, lead the way in Your strength.

Day 161

EVERY NEED

And my God will supply every need of yours according to his riches in glory in Christ Jesus.

PHILIPPIANS 4:19 ESV

There's an interesting story in the Old Testament of a widow and her son. The prophet Elijah visited her during a lean season in her life. What did he ask for? Basically, a meal. He wanted water and a piece of bread.

The woman had just enough oil and flour to bake a loaf of bread for herself and her son. But she didn't hesitate. She was prepared to use the last of her ingredients to do as the prophet asked. But then something miraculous happened! God supernaturally supplied more oil and flour. The empty jar was suddenly full. And the jar of oil never ran out either.

This is what happens when you place your trust in God. He is your source, and He will provide in ways no one else possibly can. So turn your eyes upon Jesus. He's the one who will see you through.

You are my provider, Lord! I will keep my eyes on You, not others. Amen.

PRAYER JAR INSPIRATION:

God will supply all my needs.

Day 162

CONFIDENCE AND COURAGE

O God, my heart is steadfast [with confident faith]; I will sing, I will sing praises, even with my soul. . . . For Your lovingkindness is great and higher than the heavens; Your truth reaches to the skies. . . . Deliverance by man is in vain [a worthless hope]. With God we will do valiantly.

Psalm 108:1, 4, 12–13 amp

God has more love for you than you could ever imagine. And because of His love, you can live without worry or fear. Your heart can be warmed by your ever-present trust and firm faith in Him. No matter what's happening, no matter how many things skitter out of your control, no matter how many people desert you, no matter what comes against you. . .you have God, the supreme and holy being, in your corner—not just rooting for you, guiding you, and protecting you but fighting for you.

With God in your life, with Him walking by your side, you have all you need to be a confident and courageous woman, one who will live and do fearlessly.

I sing praises to You today, Lord. For with You, I have the courage and confidence to be what You would have me be and to do what You would have me do.

PRAYER JAR INSPIRATION:

God is my worthy hope, the author and supplier of my confidence and courage.

Day 163

FALSE HOPE

A king is not saved by a large army; a warrior will not be delivered by great strength. The horse is a false hope for safety; it provides no escape by its great power.

PSALM 33:16–17 HCSB

When you find yourself in trouble, you might look to friends and family for strength and power. You may even look to money or possessions to help you escape the evil that is coming your way.

Yet other people—no matter how much they love you or how much wisdom they possess—cannot deliver you. Neither can money or possessions. But God—the one before whom the entire earth trembles, the one who parted seas and made the earth open up—can save you.

If you are looking to be saved, to get yourself out of an impossible situation, turn to God. He is the one who has the strength to save you. He is the one who rules all peoples and all nature. He is the one who will remove the mountain of obstacles standing in your way and the evils barreling toward you. Put your hope in Him, the one who is never false.

Save me, Lord, by Your great strength.

PRAYER JAR INSPIRATION:

*God, the All-Powerful, is my only true hope.
To Him I entrust myself and all that I am.*

Day 164

A HOLY PLACE

Or do you not know that your body is a temple of the Holy Spirit within you, whom you have from God? You are not your own, for you were bought with a price. So glorify God in your body.

1 Corinthians 6:19–20 ESV

Why do you suppose God called the human body a temple? A temple is a holy place, a set-apart place. No one would dare desecrate a temple.

With those things in mind, it's getting easier to see why God called our bodies a temple. Each of us only has one, and we are to treat it with the reverence and respect we would treat the sanctuary of our church.

We wouldn't fill the sanctuary with trash or forget to vacuum the floors. We would make sure every light bulb was in place, the sound system was in working order, and the chairs or pews were in great shape to hold the incoming congregation.

These might seem like little details, but they're like taking care of your physical body. Exercise, vitamins, healthy foods, quiet time, adequate sleep—these are all things to keep your temple running smoothly!

Help me remember to care for this temple, Jesus. You've only given me one body, and I want to take excellent care of it. Amen.

PRAYER JAR INSPIRATION:

My temple is a holy place.

Day 165

THE FLOURISHING WOMAN

The godly will flourish like palm trees and grow strong like the cedars of Lebanon. For they are transplanted to the Lord's own house. They flourish in the courts of our God. Even in old age they will still produce fruit; they will remain vital and green.

Psalm 92:12–14 NLT

Our bodies are finite structures. As the years go by, our earth suits will eventually give out on us. Yet even then, if we stay close to the Lord, if we continue to obey, love, follow, and worship Him, we will remain a vital part of His body. We will be like the strong cedars of Lebanon, still green and able to produce fruit.

Today, make sure you are nourishing yourself in the Lord. Spend time in His Word. Stay steady in prayer, and afterward spend some time in God's presence. In doing so, you will not only be nourished but also find yourself flourishing in God's house for all your days.

I want to grow closer to You and in You, Lord, so that I can continue to be a viable and vital part of Your kingdom today and every day of my life.

PRAYER JAR INSPIRATION:

In God, I find my hope nourished and my heart flourishing.

Day 166

GOOD THINGS TO COME

"The grass withers and the flowers fade,
but the word of our God stands forever."

Isaiah 40:8 NLT

The things of this world are always changing. Every year, the grass turns brown and the flowers shrivel. The leaves fall and the trees stand bare. The butterflies and birds find other places to display their beauty. The snow comes, transforming the world into a white wonderland. Then just when you cannot take another day of ice and frigid winds, the crocuses begin to pop up, displaying their beauty once more. Upon seeing them, your hope of new things to come bursts through your winter doldrums, just as it did the year before.

Yes, much in this world is changeable. There's not much you can count on, as nothing remains the same. Except for God. And His Word. They never change. And because they never change, you can find your rock-solid strength in both.

Thank You, Lord, for the strength I find in Your
eternal presence and Word. Amen.

PRAYER JAR INSPIRATION:
In God's never-changing Word, I find my hope and strength.

Day 167

GOD-ESTEEM

For it is not the one who commends himself who is approved, but the one whom the Lord commends.

2 Corinthians 10:18 ESV

Pop psychologists and influencers talk a lot about self-esteem. According to their sage advice, self-esteem is critical. You must have it to thrive in this world. And so a lot of people look to themselves to heal. They follow the advice of the pros but don't find healing. Why?

The truth is, we can't heal ourselves. The answers were never inside of us. We must fix our eyes on Jesus. We need God-esteem if we're ever going to recover.

And when we realize God's deep love for us and His passion to see us healed and whole, we do become more confident from the inside out. Not because of anything we've done but because of what He did for us when He gave His life on the cross.

It's not a bad thing to love yourself. You were created in the image of God, after all. But to look at yourself as being all-knowing? That's just not wise.

I look to You, Jesus! I will have God-esteem! Amen.

PRAYER JAR INSPIRATION:

I can't find the answers inside myself.
I must look to the heavenly Father.

Day 168

WAIT AND HOPE

Are there any among the idols of the nations who can send rain? Or can the heavens [of their own will] give showers? Is it not You, O Lord our God? Therefore we will wait and hope [confidently] in You, for You are the one who has made all these things [the heavens and the rain].

Jeremiah 14:22 AMP

In this world, people seem willing to do anything to rise above others, to accumulate money, to obtain their fifteen minutes of fame. But none of those things, none of those "gods," can send rain. None can make the heavens pour down the water that we and our planet need. No one but God can save the bees, bats, and birds, the oceans, rivers, and lakes.

When you need something—when you are living in famine or drought, flood or fire—apply to God and Him alone. Acknowledge Him as Lord over all things seen and unseen. Then wait and hope with confidence in Him, that He who made the sky, clouds, earth, wind, and water will come through for you.

You, Lord, are my only God, my only security on this orb of earth. To You alone I pray. Upon You alone I wait. In You alone I hope.

PRAYER JAR INSPIRATION:

You only, Lord, are my God and my hope.

Day 169

ENCIRCLED WITH STRENGTH

The God who encircles me with strength and makes my way blameless? He makes my feet like hinds' feet [able to stand firmly and tread safely on paths of testing and trouble]; He sets me [securely] upon my high places.

Psalm 18:32–33 AMP

Society may consider you, as a female, to be a member of the weaker sex. But in God's eyes you are anything but weak. Why? Because it is God, the one who created and sustains the planet you're standing on, who encircles you with His strength. It is God who aims you in the right direction so that you won't run afoul of any evil.

And it is this same Lord of lords who helps you so that you can have a firm footing. You can walk safely on life's roadway of challenges and troubles. With God in your life, you can stand strong on the highest of heights!

Today, remember in whom all your hopes lie. Feel the Lord's power encircling your entire being—mind, body, spirit, and soul. Get it into your head that He not only shields you but gives you the energy and power to do all you need to do.

Encircle me with Your strength, Lord, and my feet will stay steady on Your path.

PRAYER JAR INSPIRATION:
God encircles my entire being with His strength!

Day 170

SAVED FROM YESTERDAYS

For all have sinned and fall short of the glory of God.

Romans 3:23 niv

So many believers come to faith in Jesus after living hard lives. They bring with them years of baggage and (oftentimes) guilt over the pain they've caused others and themselves.

This guilt can be debilitating if you don't let go of it. Jesus died for all of it, even the stuff you're incredibly ashamed of. So let your heart be mended. Let the guilt absolve.

Take another look at today's verse: We all sin. We all fall short. You didn't win some sort of award for being the worst-possible human before you gave your heart to Jesus. Everyone was just as messed up as you.

But God. . .

Those two words change everything—about your situation and your heart. God is the great healer of all broken things, and He sent His Son so that you could experience full spiritual healing.

So let it go. Yesterday is gone. Today is brand-new!

I've been ashamed of my past, Jesus, but You died to save me from my yesterdays! Amen.

PRAYER JAR INSPIRATION:

The blood of Jesus covers every sin, no matter how grievous.

Day 171

THE SATISFIER

The LORD always keeps his promises; he is gracious in all he does. The LORD helps the fallen and lifts those bent beneath their loads. The eyes of all look to you in hope; you give them their food as they need it. When you open your hand, you satisfy the hunger and thirst of every living thing.

PSALM 145:13–16 NLT

When you are afraid or under pressure, look to God's promises. Find one that fits your situation and sink your spirit into it. When it seems no one has any mercy or compassion for others, turn to the Bible stories where Jesus loves, heals, or lifts another; imagine yourself as the one He has helped. When you have fallen or can no longer get out from under that burden you've been bearing, ask God to help you up, to take on your load.

See God as the open hand that holds all you will ever hunger or thirst for on both sides of heaven. Tell Him what you need, and He will ensure you are satisfied and secure.

You, Lord, hold all I need, want, and wish for.
Thank You for looking after me in all ways, always.

PRAYER JAR INSPIRATION:

My eyes look to God in hope and love.

Day 172

TREASURED BY GOD

"How can someone like me, your servant, speak with someone like you, my lord? Now I have no strength, and there is no breath in me." . . . He said, "Don't be afraid, you who are treasured by God. Peace to you; be very strong!" As he spoke to me, I was strengthened.

Daniel 10:17, 19 HCSB

God reveals much to those who are humble, faithful, and praying followers of Him. For they are part of His plan. They have a role to play. And when those who are loved by the Lord feel weak, God sends a divine word to boost their strength and calm their hearts.

God has a plan for you. To work out that plan, you must realize who you are: a person loved and treasured by God. And if at any time you go weak in the knees when thinking about or playing your part, turn to God. Tell Him how you're feeling. Know that He will give you all the attention, love, peace, and strength you need to live out His word for you.

Thank You, Lord, for Your words of peace and strength.

PRAYER JAR INSPIRATION:

Treasured by God, I receive His peace and strength.

Day 173

FREE FROM WEEDS

Jesus told them another parable: "The kingdom of heaven is like a man who sowed good seed in his field. But while everyone was sleeping, his enemy came and sowed weeds among the wheat, and went away. When the wheat sprouted and formed heads, then the weeds also appeared."

Matthew 13:24–26 niv

Your spiritual life is like a garden filled with lovely flowers planted by the Lord. He has a lot in store for you, and it all starts with spiritual growth. The water of His Spirit. The fertilizer of His Word. Apply these things, and you'll do fine.

The problem is that gardens are often overrun with pesky things that don't belong there: weeds, pests, fungi. All these icky things can take over, ruining a perfectly good crop.

The same is true when you allow the enemy to enter your spiritual garden. He threatens to choke out the good with the bad. Before you realize it, poor theology has grown up: "God doesn't love me. God isn't fair. God must be mad at me." You name it, the enemy will try to get you to believe it.

These little beliefs become weeds in your spiritual garden, and they must go. Otherwise, healing will never come.

Weed the garden. Get rid of the stuff crowding out the truth.

I will do my best to keep the garden free of weeds, Lord. Amen.

PRAYER JAR INSPIRATION:

It's weeding day!

Day 174

FAITHFUL LOVE

"Oh, Lord God! You Yourself made the heavens and earth by Your great power and with Your outstretched arm. Nothing is too difficult for You! You show faithful love to thousands. . . , great and mighty God whose name is Yahweh of Hosts, the One great in counsel and mighty in deed."

JEREMIAH 32:17–19 HCSB

Do you know who God really is? He's the one who, by His great power and outstretched arm, made the heavens and the earth. He formed the very heavens above your head, that reach into galaxies and universes humankind has yet to uncover and discover! He created the very planet you are sitting, lying, standing on! He designed by hand the earth that rotates, the sun that shines on it, the moon that revolves around it. God made this orb that feeds and waters you, the one on which you first began your earthly life and will hold your body when you pass on to the other side.

This God for whom nothing is impossible loves you. When you feel insecure, remember who holds you every night and leads you every day. God's got you. With Him, anything is possible.

God of all creation and power, by You I stand and rest. Hold me close day and night. In Jesus' name and love, amen.

PRAYER JAR INSPIRATION:

God's faithful love and immense power rock me to sleep and awaken me to a new dawn.

Day 175

YOUR ARM

O Lord, be gracious to us; we have waited [expectantly] for You. Be the arm of Your servants every morning [that is, their strength and their defense], our salvation also in the time of trouble.

Isaiah 33:2 amp

You're sitting down to breakfast with eyes yearning to close. You reach for your coffee and take a sip, hoping it will give you the energy you need to shower and dress and then begin what you imagine will be a long, arduous day.

It's time to change that already-defeated mindset and attitude!

Remember who you are: a woman warrior. You are a follower of the all-powerful Creator God. Knowing He's on your side, allow Him to do what He is prepared to do: Be your arm, your strength, every morning. One who will not only fight for you but defend you. And in case there happens to be some trouble coming your way, He will be there to rescue you.

Lord, be my arm—my strength and defense!

PRAYER JAR INSPIRATION:

God's strength and protection await me each day!

Day 176

WORTH FIGHTING FOR

Dear friends, although I was very eager to write to you about the salvation we share, I felt compelled to write and urge you to contend for the faith that was once for all entrusted to God's holy people.

Jude 3 NIV

The world is full of people who have given up on God. Perhaps they have grown weary of waiting for an answer to prayer. Or maybe they're angry over the way they were treated at a church and have turned their anger toward the Lord.

There are all sorts of reasons why previously strong Christians turn their back on God, but here's the good news: He never turns His back on us, even when we're angry at Him or have completely given up on our faith.

Keep praying for those who've given up on the Lord. And if you're struggling in this area yourself, be reminded today that He still loves you, still wants you, still plans to move in your life. Open yourself back up to the possibilities if you can. Contend for your faith. Fight for it.

My faith is worth fighting for, Lord! You've entrusted it to me, and I will battle for it. Amen.

PRAYER JAR INSPIRATION:

The fight for faith is one battle worth fighting.

Day 177

YOUR SHELTER

I will sing praises to your name, O Most High.
My enemies retreated; they staggered and died when you appeared. . . . The LORD is a shelter for the oppressed, a refuge in times of trouble. Those who know your name trust in you.

PSALM 9:2–3, 9–10 NLT

God is amazing—and He is on your side!

When you're in trouble, when enemies seem to have surrounded you, just call on God. Ask for His help.

God can not only make forces that seem impenetrable stagger and fall but also repel them so that they begin to retreat, never to show their faces again! Meanwhile, for you He creates a place of safety. He shelters you; He hides you behind His hand until trouble passes by. When the dust has settled, when the spoils left behind by your enemies are ready to be plucked, only then will He open the shelter, allowing you to see what remains for you to glean.

Today, sing praises to your refuge, shelter, and provider.

You, Lord, are my amazing all in all!
Thank You for sheltering me in every storm.

PRAYER JAR INSPIRATION:

God, my sure shelter and everlasting song, it is You I praise!

Day 178

GOD SO LOVED

For God so loved the world that he gave his one and only Son, that whoever believes in him shall not perish but have eternal life.

John 3:16 niv

Let's take this verse apart and see what it may be telling us right now.

"God." The Master of all creation. The supernatural being with the ultimate plan. "So loved the world." God so loved *you*. *You* who are part of this world and the next. So great was His love for you that "he gave." He didn't hold back—never holds back—whatever you need. So He gave. "His one and only Son." Imagine having only one of something. So precious, so loved. Yet still, God gave this Son, *His* Son, His one and only Son. "That whoever." Any person. Anyone. *You*. "Believes." Hopes in, accepts, trusts. "In him." Not in just anyone, but in Him. "Shall not perish but have eternal life." Shall never die. Ever.

God so loved *you* that He gave His only Son so *you* who believe should live forever. Take these words to heart today and in all your tomorrows.

Lord, I put all of myself, all my hope in Your forever love!

PRAYER JAR INSPIRATION:
God's love for me is eternal.

Day 179

MESSAGE OF HOPE!

Because, if you confess with your mouth that Jesus is Lord and believe in your heart that God raised him from the dead, you will be saved.

Romans 10:9 ESV

Spiritual healing comes when you recognize your need for a Savior and place your life (and heart) into His capable hands. No matter where you've been, no matter what you've done, no matter how heinous your sins, that simple act of conforming to His image changes everything.

But it's a process to accept forgiveness. You'll probably still beat yourself up for the things you did wrong in the past. You might still have regrets. There might even be some things you still have to make right (people you need to apologize to).

But understanding that God now sees you not as a sinner but as a precious child purchased by the blood of His Son? Well, that's something to celebrate! And that news is so good that it's worth sharing with others so that they can come to know this amazing Savior too.

Accepting You was the best decision of my life, Jesus. Allowing You to break away the cobwebs surrounding my heart, letting You heal the broken places, accepting Your forgiveness—these decisions have changed me for all eternity, and I'm so grateful. Amen.

PRAYER JAR INSPIRATION:

I can proclaim salvation's message of hope!

Day 180

HELP AND RESCUE

I prayed to the LORD, and he answered me. He freed me from all my fears. . . . The angel of the LORD is a guard; he surrounds and defends all who fear him. . . . The LORD hears his people when they call to him for help. He rescues them from all their troubles.

PSALM 34:4, 7, 17 NLT

God wants you to know He is here for you. He is just waiting for you to call on Him, to acknowledge that you do indeed need Him. For when you allow Him into your life, He will free you from all the fears you have been harboring for so long.

God is the guide who goes before you and the guard who protects you from behind. He will surround you and defend you from whatever comes against you.

Today, consider all the things you have been trying to battle on your own. Then enter a time of prayer, asking God to take them all on His own massive shoulders. He will hear your calls for help and rescue you.

Lord, save me from those fears that tie me down. Rescue me from all that plagues me. I place myself completely in Your hands. Amen.

PRAYER JAR INSPIRATION:

God is my hope and help, my fear fighter!

Day 181

ALL THINGS

Love bears all things [regardless of what comes], believes all things [looking for the best in each one], hopes all things [remaining steadfast during difficult times], endures all things [without weakening].

1 Corinthians 13:7 AMP

It's difficult to love someone, to look for the best in every person, no matter what that person does. It can be hard to hope, especially when people are behaving as if they've never even heard of love—for God, themselves, or others! It seems arduous to endure every difficulty no matter how hard, to stay strong in love no matter what happens.

Yet if you really think about it, doing these things—bearing all, believing there is good in everyone, hoping for the best, and enduring whatever comes your way—is a wonderful plan! It's a great way to escape the grief and negativity the opposite attitude would hold.

Start today! Allow the love that God has poured into you to help you bear, believe, hope, and endure. Then take note of how your loving attitude and outlook changes your life—for the better, for the best, for God.

Lord, help my love to bear, believe, hope, and endure all things!

PRAYER JAR INSPIRATION:

With God's love in me and pouring out of me, I can bear, believe, hope, and endure anything!

Day 182

THE TRUST PROCESS

*Those who know your name trust in you, for you, Lord,
have never forsaken those who seek you.*

Psalm 9:10 niv

Part of the spiritual healing journey is simply learning to trust God again. If you've been disappointed and have pointed the finger at Him (say, after the death of a loved one or a tragic financial loss), it's easier just to go on distrusting. To place your hand in His again is tough.

But it's important. Because God isn't the one who let you down. We live in a fallen world where bad things happen to good people. And God still cares very deeply when you're hurting, so the last thing you need to do is pull away from Him.

Draw close. Even if it's hard. *Especially* if it's hard. He's right there, hand extended, ready to relight the flame that once burned bright between you.

It's going to be a process, Lord, but I want to learn to trust You again. I'll confess, there have been moments when my faith wavered, when my trust gave way to fear. But You have never abandoned me, and I know You never will. So I choose to trust You today. Amen.

PRAYER JAR INSPIRATION:
I can learn to trust again.

Day 183

THE SHEPHERD

The Lord God will come with might, and His arm will rule for Him. Most certainly His reward is with Him, and His restitution accompanies Him. He will protect His flock like a shepherd, He will gather the lambs in His arm, He will carry them in His bosom; He will gently and carefully lead those nursing their young.

Isaiah 40:10–11 AMP

There may be times in your life when you feel very vulnerable or weak. Weary from constant attack, you can barely raise up your hands in prayer. You no longer know what to do or where to go.

There is no need to worry, to panic, to sink further. Instead, rise up in the certainty that God can come in His strength and make all things right. That He will fend off your enemies. That He will protect you like a shepherd protects his sheep and will gather the young, the unsteady and carry them close to His heart. That He will gently lead the vulnerable, those spending their energy taking care of the needy.

Little lamb of God, follow your shepherd. He will lead you the right way.

My Lord the shepherd, come in Your strength. Protect me from all that has come against me. Gather me in Your arms and gently lead me home to You.

PRAYER JAR INSPIRATION:

Gentle Lord, renew me with Your presence. Lead me down Your pathway.

Day 184

THE GREATEST

And now there remain: faith [abiding trust in God and His promises], hope [confident expectation of eternal salvation], love [unselfish love for others growing out of God's love for me], these three [the choicest graces]; but the greatest of these is love.

1 Corinthians 13:13 amp

There are three things essential to a Christian. The first is faith. Only by believing in Jesus Christ can you get near to God, have your sins forgiven and forgotten, and find eternal life.

Then you need hope. Only by expecting that God will come through on all His promises to you will you keep going and get to the eventual finish line.

And lastly is love. Love is greater than both faith and hope. For there will come a day when your faith will actually become sight, and when all that you hoped for is finally realized because all God's promises have become a reality. Yet love will continue into eternity. Love is God, and God will abide forever.

Today, Lord, I choose to live in faith, hope, and love.

PRAYER JAR INSPIRATION:
Nothing is greater than love.

Day 185

SPIRITUAL HEALING

Dear friends, do not believe every spirit, but test the spirits to see whether they are from God, because many false prophets have gone out into the world.

1 John 4:1 NIV

If you look up the words *spiritual healing* online, you'll find all sorts of crazy suggestions. The majority of these come from New Age sources that don't believe in the Bible.

We know that we live in a fallen world and that the enemy will do everything he can to offer counterfeits. These fall into that category. The problem with all those things is that they don't offer real solutions.

Genuine spiritual brokenness requires healing from the one who created you. God pieced you together in your mother's womb. In fact, the Bible says He knew you even before the foundation of the world. Wouldn't it make more sense to trust your spirit to Him instead of some random crystals on the countertop? Best of all, God adores you. He has your best interest at heart. So turn away from worldly things and place your heart in His hands. You can trust Him to give you the very best.

Thank You for giving me discernment, Lord! Amen.

PRAYER JAR INSPIRATION:

Only the real deal for me—that's Jesus!

Day 186

STILL LISTENING

Be still before the Lord; wait patiently for Him and entrust yourself to Him; do not fret (whine, agonize) because of him who prospers in his way, because of the man who carries out wicked schemes. . . . Wait for and expect the Lord and keep His way.

Psalm 37:7, 34 AMP

When you pray, do you give God time to respond—or do you just pour out your heart and then walk away, not sitting still long enough to hear what He has to say? Or do you only pray for direction once, and then, in your desire to become as prosperous as the ungodly, determine your own strategy to obtain what you want, leaving God wordless, a silent figure standing on the sidelines?

If you don't allow God to speak after you've presented your requests to Him, you're not really praying.

Today, add listening to your prayer time. Determine to be still before the Lord, patiently waiting with open ears and heart, ready to hear what He may want to say.

Help me, Lord, to be a better listener, to be patient, to be still before You.

PRAYER JAR INSPIRATION:
In silence before God, I hope and wait.

Day 187

FLOODED WITH LOVE

Your left arm would be under my head, and your right arm would embrace me. . . . Love is as strong as death, its jealousy as enduring as the grave. Love flashes like fire, the brightest kind of flame. Many waters cannot quench love, nor can rivers drown it.

Song of Solomon 8:3, 6–7 NLT

There may be days when you doubt you are loved by anyone in heaven or on earth. Or perhaps you have grown so distant from God that you're ashamed to come back. Having fallen out of the fold, you're not sure how to get back in. Maybe you think or feel that God's love has flown not just from you but from the entire world. If so, think and feel again.

God, who is love personified, loves you like no one else can. He is not some distant God you cannot reach. He is with you, beside you, holding you in His arms!

And that love He feels for you is as strong as death. No amount of water can extinguish the flame of love God lavishes on you. No floods can drown it.

Today, hope in the strength and durability of God's abundant love. Allow it to pour into your heart and mind.

In the bounty of Your love, Lord, I hope and live.

PRAYER JAR INSPIRATION:

I'm flooded with God's unending love.

Day 188

BROKEN CHAINS

Truly I am your servant, LORD; I serve you just as my mother did; you have freed me from my chains.

PSALM 116:16 NIV

In biblical times, prisoners were bound with shackles around their ankles and wrists. The shackles ensured the prisoner wouldn't get very far if he tried to run.

The enemy of your soul has his own brand of shackles. He grips you with guilt and condemnation. Just about the time you think you've been set free (and you have) he convinces you that you're still shackled to those terrible feelings of shame and guilt.

But you're not! When Jesus died on the cross, He broke every chain. Every single one. Nothing holds you bound anymore. It's just an illusion. And let's face it: Satan is the master of illusions. He's great at bluffing!

There are no shackles on you. None. You can walk freely! The guilt from yesterday's sins is long gone now. You can walk in total freedom, shackle-free!

It feels so good to be relieved of the guilt and shame, Lord! I could never have freed myself. But Your sacrifice on the cross accomplished it all! How grateful I am. Amen.

PRAYER JAR INSPIRATION:

My chains are broken!

Day 189

A WOMAN'S WALK

The steps of a [good and righteous] man are directed and established by the Lord, and He delights in his way [and blesses his path]. When he falls, he will not be hurled down, because the Lord is the One who holds his hand and sustains him.

Psalm 37:23–24 AMP

God is working out a plan for your life, one that fits into His grand scheme. And because you are walking His Way, even when you stumble you won't be down for the count. God has a grip on your hand, and He's never going to let go.

How wonderful that God, the Lord of the universe, the Creator and master planner, has a plan. For you. Right now. In this moment. And all you have to do to tune in to that plan—to listen to His voice—is follow His Word, not letting the world bring you down or make you deviate from your path.

Thank You, Lord, for showing me how and where to walk, for having a firm grip on my hand, for making me a part of Your grand plan.

PRAYER JAR INSPIRATION:
With God, I can and will find firm footing.

Day 190

NO-FAULT LOVE

Always be humble and gentle. Be patient with each other, making allowance for each other's faults because of your love.

Ephesians 4:2 NLT

You belong to a God who Himself is the personification of love. And as such, He wants you to be humble, to put others before yourself. To be gentle, not abrasive or harsh. To be patient with others. To love them despite their faults—just as God loves you despite yours. Not sometimes, but *all the time.*

This kind of loving is going to take energy. You're going to have to dig deep to keep calm, cool, and collected when others provoke you. But with God in your heart and the knowledge that you too are not perfect, you can do what you are called to do. And all because you belong to the master of love who calls you to love others—no matter what.

God, help me cling to the hope that You and Your love can make me a humble, gentle, and patient woman.

PRAYER JAR INSPIRATION:
Lord, overwhelm me with love for others.

Day 191

BY HIS WOUNDS

"He himself bore our sins" in his body on the cross, so that we might die to sins and live for righteousness; "by his wounds you have been healed."

1 Peter 2:24 niv

Jesus was never content just to bring physical healing. He usually followed up with a spiritual message. For what would be the point of having blind eyes opened if not to also open spiritual eyes? And what would be the point of lame legs walking if not to walk in the newness of life?

Jesus cares about every aspect of your life, inside and out. He wants to see you healed in every single area, not one stone unturned. Why? So that you can live your fullest, healthiest life, complete and whole.

Today's verse shares a remarkable truth: It was Jesus' wounds that brought healing for our bodies, souls, and spirits. Because He went to the cross, because He bore the pain of the beatings and nails in His hands and feet, we have healing today. What a remarkable sacrifice on the part of our Savior!

I'll never be able to thank You for what You did for me, Jesus, but I'm so grateful for the wounds that brought my healing. Amen.

PRAYER JAR INSPIRATION:

By His wounds I am healed.

Day 192

SLOWING DOWN

The LORD is my shepherd; there is nothing I lack. He lets me lie down in green pastures; He leads me beside quiet waters. He renews my life; He leads me along the right paths for His name's sake. Even when I go through the darkest valley, I fear no danger, for You are with me.

PSALM 23:1–4 HCSB

It is so easy to get frazzled these days. Everyone seems to be in a hurry to get somewhere. Everyone's schedule seems to be full, *so* full that a woman can't help but feel like the proverbial chicken running around with her head chopped off! When we have lost sight of calm and are adrift in chaos, we need to slow down and recall the familiar words of Psalm 23.

God is your shepherd. With Him, you lack nothing. He'll get you to lie down in some soft green fields. He'll lead you beside those still waters where your soul and spirit can find refreshment and silence. He'll lead you where you are to go—on *His* schedule.

Even when things look dark, you don't need to fear anything. The Creator and sustainer of the universe walks with you. Today, slow down and go with God.

In You, good shepherd, I find the peace and rest I crave.

PRAYER JAR INSPIRATION:

My shepherd will lead me home to Him and His peace.

Day 193

CONSTANT LOVE

I will give You thanks with all my heart; I will sing Your praise before the heavenly beings. I will bow down toward Your holy temple and give thanks to Your name for Your constant love and truth.

Psalm 138:1–2 HCSB

Love is the greatest thing we have going. Love covers a multitude of sins, gives us joy, helps us heal, and blesses us beyond belief. For. . .God. . .is. . .love (1 John 4:16).

God loved us so much that He allowed His Son, His one and only Son, to die for us "while we were still sinners" (Romans 5:8 HCSB)! That means that when we were still selfish, mean, and nasty miscreants, God sent His precious Son to be whipped, stripped, beaten, mocked, and nailed to a cross. *That* is love.

So give your love back to God in the form of praise and thanksgiving. Thank Him that He keeps loving you, no matter how often you misstep or misspeak. In doing so, you will be reminding yourself of how wondrous, gracious, and mercy-filled God's love is.

I thank You, Lord, for Your constant love. In Jesus' name, amen.

PRAYER JAR INSPIRATION:

God's love for me will never die!

Day 194

IN HIS HANDS

He heals the brokenhearted and binds up their wounds.

Psalm 147:3 niv

If you sustained injuries on the battleground but had no one to bind them, what would happen? You would bleed out for sure. The medic, who appears from out of nowhere to bind your wounds, is ultimately the one who saves your life.

Jesus is the binder of wounds. Whenever you sustain an injury of any kind—emotional, mental, or spiritual, He's right there, ready to jump in and save you. You don't have to hope He shows up; He *always* shows up. And you don't have to give Him instructions. He knows just what to do.

He's the ultimate medic with supernatural vision and unlimited healing capabilities. You can trust Him with your body. You can trust Him with your thoughts. You can trust Him with your heart.

You can trust Him. Period. He's always there at just the right moment and knows just what to do.

You're the ultimate wound binder, Lord! My chances of survival went way up the moment I placed my life in Your hands. Amen.

PRAYER JAR INSPIRATION:

My medic, Jesus, is on the way!

Day 195

NO DEADLINES

"The vision is yet for the appointed [future] time. It hurries toward the goal [of fulfillment]; it will not fail. Even though it delays, wait [patiently] for it, because it will certainly come; it will not delay."

Habakkuk 2:3 AMP

God has planted a dream within your heart. He's making your vision, your part of His plan, a reality. That's His job.

Your job is to wait for your dream's fulfillment—to not become impatient but to trust God to bring things to fruition.

So stay on the track God has laid out for you. Disregard those voices that tell you to give up on your dream—unless the voice is God's (1 Chronicles 28:3).

Take heart, and even though delays come your way, wait. Relax. God has everything under control. You're on His timeline. All is well.

Lord, thank You for making me a part of Your plan. I find peace in knowing You never hurry. So I pray You would help me to slow down, to walk in Your rhythm, to patiently wait, knowing the fulfillment of my dream is on Your timeline, not mine.

PRAYER JAR INSPIRATION:

Because God is never in a hurry, I can relax in Him.

Day 196

LOST, THEN FOUND

"Son, you are always with me, and all that is mine is yours. It was fitting to celebrate and be glad, for this your brother was dead, and is alive; he was lost, and is found."

Luke 15:31–32 ESV

When the prodigal son returned, his father rejoiced over his return. He ordered his servants to dress him in a robe and to put a ring on his finger and sandals on his feet. Then he ordered a grand feast to be cooked and served to celebrate that his son who was once lost was now found.

But the dutiful older brother became miffed and refused to share in his younger brother's welcome-home dinner. So the father went out to plead with him. The older told his dad how good he had been, how well he had served his father and obeyed him. Yet he never got such a feast.

Some of us have been dutiful to God from the beginning. Others have not. Yet we all share in the joy the Father displays to the lost who are found and the found who stick around, praising the one whose love and hope for us never ceases.

Father God, help me not to begrudge or judge Your love and joy for the lost who become found.

PRAYER JAR INSPIRATION:

Make me a woman who rejoices when a lost follower rediscovers Your love and protection!

Day 197

THE GREAT HEALER

And now these three remain: faith, hope and love. But the greatest of these is love.

1 Corinthians 13:13 niv

Why do you suppose the Bible teaches us that love is the "greatest thing"? It's greater than faith. It's greater than hope. And both of those things are amazing all by themselves!

But love has the power to transform hearts, lives, and situations.

Love can heal relationships. Love can heal a broken heart. Love can heal a wounded spirit. Love can heal. . .pretty much anything.

Jesus shared the greatest example of love when He gave His life for us on Calvary. In that one act, He performed an act of love that surpasses all others. And as He did, He asked something of us: "Will you show (and share) My love with others?"

It's not a big task when you think about it. Sharing the good news is sharing a story of hope and healing. You really can change the lives of those around you simply by sharing the story of what Jesus did for them two thousand years ago on the cross at Calvary.

I am a good-news bearer when I share Your story with people around me, Lord! Thank You for Your sacrifice on the cross, not just for my sins but for the sins of all mankind. Amen.

PRAYER JAR INSPIRATION:

Through my story of hope and healing, I can bring hope and healing to others.

Day 198

OPEN EYES AND EARS

Your eyes shall see your Teacher. And your ears shall hear a word behind you, saying, "This is the way, walk in it," when you turn to the right or when you turn to the left.

Isaiah 30:20–21 esv

Often in life, we will find ourselves at a crossroads, looking for guidance as to which way we should go. Thankfully, we need not make that choice alone. We can ask God for help. Yet we need to have not only our eyes open but our ears as well.

Are you listening? Are your ears open? Or are you too busy making up a list of pros and cons for each route and trusting in your own judgment and wisdom over God's? Or perhaps you are so blind and deaf that you don't even know you are at a crossroads. You are not open to God's *"Pssssst! Daughter, there's an opportunity for you here!"*

Today, as you come before God in prayer, ask Him to open your eyes to His presence and your ears to His direction. Then walk where He wills.

Lord God, may my eyes be open to Your presence, my ears to Your voice. What would You have me see? What would You have me hear?

PRAYER JAR INSPIRATION:

The Lord is my guide.

Day 199

A BIG ASK

"I say to you who listen: Love your enemies, do what is good to those who hate you, bless those who curse you, pray for those who mistreat you. . . . Forgive, and you will be forgiven."

Luke 6:27–28, 37 HCSB

Jesus speaks to anyone who will listen, explaining the love He wants us to show each other, as well as the forgiveness He wants us to extend. For humankind, these things appear to be a big ask.

Yet Jesus urges us to bless the person who curses us. To the one who strikes us on one cheek, we're to offer the other. To the one who takes our coat, we're to offer our shirt. To the one who begs from us, we're to give what we have. To the one who takes a possession from us, we're not to demand its return. To the one who needs forgiveness, we're to forgive—then we too will be forgiven.

Although these ideas may on the surface seem difficult, in practice the result is delightful. Taking the high road leaves us with far more hope and joy than we find wallowing in the mud of the low road.

Show me who I can love and forgive today, Lord, while asking nothing in return!

PRAYER JAR INSPIRATION:

My hope for myself and humankind is found in loving the unlovable, forgiving the unforgivable.

Day 200

EVERY STRESS

"Do not let your hearts be troubled. You believe in God; believe also in me."

John 14:1 NIV

Whenever the disciples were stressed out, Jesus brought them back to center with this phrase: "Don't let your hearts be troubled. You believe in God; believe also in me." They had the God of the universe physically traveling side by side with them! And yet they still got stressed out at times.

Think about this: Before Jesus came, the Jews had a long-standing relationship with God, but they couldn't see Him with their eyes or hear Him with their ears. They trusted in the law and in all they had learned from their religious rituals.

But law and rituals will only take you so far. When you're hurting, when you're stressed, it helps to have the living, breathing God of the universe standing directly in front of you.

You might not see Jesus with your own eyes like the disciples did, but He's right there, hand tightly clasping yours. He's walking and talking with you!

You walk with me and talk with me, Lord! It's remarkable to imagine that the Creator of all cares about me too! I will put my trust in You! Amen.

PRAYER JAR INSPIRATION:

I can give all my stresses to the heavenly Father.

Day 201

SPRINGING INTO LOVE

"Feed the hungry, and help those in trouble. Then your light will shine out from the darkness, and the darkness around you will be as bright as noon. The Lord will guide you continually, giving you water when you are dry and restoring your strength. You will be like a well-watered garden, like an ever-flowing spring."

Isaiah 58:10–11 NLT

Feeling as if your life is a bit drab and dry? Are you finding yourself somewhat weak in your faith? Take God's advice and revive your life by stepping out of your comfort zone to help someone else. When you do, you'll start glowing with the light of God's love. People will notice. And so will God.

When you walk in the ways of love, you can be sure God will be guiding you every moment. He'll give you water when you feel dry. He'll renew your strength when you feel weak. And before you know it, you'll be flourishing in God's garden.

I've been feeling a bit blah, Lord. Show me who I can help, what I might do to ease someone else's burdens. Lead me in the ways of love and caring as I shine Your light into someone else's life and become revived myself along the way.

PRAYER JAR INSPIRATION:

Guide me, Lord, as I spring into love, sharing Your light with others.

Day 202

JESUS' PRAYER OF FORGIVENESS

When they came to a place called The Skull, they nailed him to the cross. And the criminals were also crucified—one on his right and one on his left. Jesus said, "Father, forgive them, for they don't know what they are doing." And the soldiers gambled for his clothes by throwing dice.

Luke 23:33–34 NLT

Imagine being one of Jesus' female followers, those who could only pray and watch from a distance as Jesus was deserted and denied by His own disciples, then arrested, tried, spit on, struck, scourged, stripped, mocked, and crucified by those who knew no better.

And in the middle of all this human heartlessness comes Jesus' amazing prayer to His Father: "Father, forgive them, for they don't know what they are doing."

Jesus never gave us any challenge that He Himself did not face. If He can forgive everything that was done against Him, surely we can forgive everything that is done against us.

Today, as you reflect on those who have injured you, look at what you endured in the light of what Jesus suffered. Then ask Him for the strength to forgive others, regardless of whether they knew what they were doing.

In Your name, Lord, I pray for the strength to forgive everything that has been done against me.

PRAYER JAR INSPIRATION:

Jesus, You are the Lord of the impossible. Help me forgive the seemingly unforgivable.

Day 203

KEEP CLIMBING

He will cover you with his pinions, and under his wings you will find refuge; his faithfulness is a shield and buckler. You will not fear the terror of the night, nor the arrow that flies by day, nor the pestilence that stalks in darkness, nor the destruction that wastes at noonday.

Psalm 91:4–6 esv

Have you ever visited the Statue of Liberty? It's a *l-o-n-g* climb to the top, and there's no other way to get up there. Once you commit to the process, you start climbing. And you keep on climbing until you either (1) reach the top or (2) turn around and head back down.

Recovering from a trauma is a bit like climbing those stairs to the top of the Statue of Liberty. Once you commit, you stay on the stairs until you arrive at the top. And from that lofty place, the view is a lot different than it was down below. From up there, you can see everything. Clearly.

Don't give up on the bottom stairs. Don't give up in the middle when you're out of breath. Stick with it to the very top, where the view will be spectacular. Up there, God will give you clarity and insight to bring everything into perspective.

I want to stop sometimes, Lord. But You nudge me on! Thank You for giving me the tenacity to keep climbing even when I don't feel like it. Amen.

PRAYER JAR INSPIRATION:

With God's nudging, I can keep going even when I don't feel like it.

Day 204

WORD WAITING

I wait for Your word. My eyes fail [with longing, watching] for [the fulfillment of] Your promise. . . . You are my hiding place and my shield; I wait for Your word. . . . I rise before dawn and cry [in prayer] for help; I wait for Your word. . . . The unfolding of Your [glorious] words give light; their unfolding gives understanding to the simple (childlike).

PSALM 119:81–82, 114, 147, 130 AMP

When you need direction, you'll find it in God's Word. His Word is a lamp to your feet; it shines a light on your path (Psalm 119:105). But you'll never find His direction unless you seek it. And in that seeking, you must have patience. For you may have to do some waiting.

In the meantime, rest in God. Hide in Him. Allow Him to cover you completely. For while you're in hiding, He'll restore, strengthen, and renew your mind, spirit, and soul, readying you for the task ahead. Know that in God's good time, His Word will give you the light and understanding you need to follow His path.

Lord, thank You for allowing me to rest, hide, and renew myself in You as I await Your good word—in Your time, not mine.

PRAYER JAR INSPIRATION:

I don't just hope but expect God's Word to shine a light on my path. His guidance will be worth the wait!

Day 205

ABUNDANT PARDON

Seek the Lord while He may be found; call on Him [for salvation] while He is near. Let the wicked leave (behind) his way and the unrighteous man his thoughts; and let him return to the Lord, and He will have compassion (mercy) on him, and to our God, for He will abundantly pardon.

Isaiah 55:6–7 AMP

Even when we mess up, we can seek out and call on God. We can leave behind our misdeeds, step off the wrong path we've embarked on, change our thoughts, return to God—and He will take us back in. As prodigal daughters, we can still run into the open arms of our loving God and be folded into His loving and forgiving embrace.

At the same time, we need to find a way to forgive ourselves—and perhaps ask others to forgive us for how we've wronged them. In asking God for forgiveness, forgiving ourselves, and apologizing to others, we will find the freedom to look forward to better days.

In what areas of life do you need to seek God and His forgiveness?

I call on You, Lord, seeking Your forgiveness.

PRAYER JAR INSPIRATION:

In seeking God, I find hope, mercy, and an abundance of forgiveness.

Day 206

WATCH FAITH GROW

Now faith is confidence in what we hope for and assurance about what we do not see. This is what the ancients were commended for.

Hebrews 11:1–2 niv

There's a misunderstanding, based in part on errant biblical teaching, that Christians will be immune to sickness and pain. Some believers feel that radical faith will keep them from walking through trauma.

Imagine their surprise when traumas come anyway. And when that faith, no matter how strong, is tested.

God never promised us a pain-free life. We live in a broken, fallen world, and troubles come in like a flood at times. Our faith is tested. Our belief system is shaken. But through it all, God remains the same. If you don't believe it, read Hebrews 11, where you will discover that great men and women of faith didn't always get what they prayed for.

Your faith will be challenged, but you can come out of life experiences stronger than ever before. The Lord hasn't promised to keep you *from* it, but He has promised to walk with you *through* it all.

When I place my trust in You, I can still have confidence, Jesus, even when things don't seem to be going my way. Amen.

PRAYER JAR INSPIRATION:

My faith can grow through life's challenges.

Day 207

FOREVER GUIDE

I will bless the LORD who has counseled me; indeed, my heart (mind) instructs me in the night. . . . Let me hear Your lovingkindness in the morning, for I trust in You. Teach me the way in which I should walk, for I lift up my soul to You. . . . This is God, our God forever and ever; He will be our guide even until death.

PSALM 16:7; 143:8; 48:14 AMP

Even while you're sleeping, God is guiding you through your dreams and visions; the divine touches your heart and mind. That's why some mornings you wake up with an amazing idea, a new direction you never imagined, a way you can please or serve Him.

Other times, your night might be filled with trouble and distress, leaving you to awake discouraged. That's when you must open the Good Book and read about the love and kindness God wants to pour over you again and again. Knowing He holds a forever love for you inspires you to trust Him not just to direct you but to teach you the way you should go.

Take courage! God's guidance is available to you morning, noon, and night. He will guide you, even until death.

Guide me, Lord, in Your love and wisdom, day and night.

PRAYER JAR INSPIRATION:

God is my forever guide on both sides of heaven.

Day 208

LETTING GO

From the depths of despair, O LORD, I call for your help. Hear my cry, O Lord. Pay attention to my prayer. LORD, if you kept a record of our sins, who, O Lord, could ever survive?

PSALM 130:1–3 NLT

Sometimes the things we have done can lead us to a state of despair. So burdened are we by our missteps that we can barely lift our heads. And we begin to wonder how many pages of our misdeeds God has on file. How many will He forgive?

Fortunately for us, we have a Lord who is "merciful and gracious, slow to anger and abounding in steadfast love" (Psalm 103:8 ESV). He's a God who doesn't "deal with us according to our sins, nor repay us according to our iniquities" (Psalm 103:10 ESV). Why? Because "as high as the heavens are above the earth, so great is his steadfast love toward those who fear him; as far as the east is from the west, so far does he remove our transgressions from us" (Psalm 103:11–12 ESV).

Lord, here's what happened. . .

PRAYER JAR INSPIRATION:

God's abundant love and mercy are mine!

Day 209

MUSTARD SEED

"Truly I tell you, if you have faith as small as a mustard seed, you can say to this mountain, 'Move from here to there,' and it will move. Nothing will be impossible for you."

MATTHEW 17:20 NIV

You might be in the middle of a terrible situation right now and your faith feels small. In fact, you wonder if there's even an ounce of it left after all you've been through.

This would be an excellent time to reread the verse above. The Bible says that faith is like a mustard seed. In case you've never seen one, a mustard seed isn't much bigger than a pen point. It's just a tiny dot of a thing. And yet here Jesus was, telling His disciples that all they needed was a pen point of faith to witness miracles.

Aren't you glad He didn't compare it to a watermelon? Or a cantaloupe, even?

But He said you don't need big faith. You just need a little. And whether you can see it or not, that tiny sliver of faith still residing in your heart is enough to get you through your rough patch.

Thank You for helping me through rough seasons, Jesus. I will place my faith in You. Amen.

PRAYER JAR INSPIRATION:

Mustard seed faith is all I need.

Day 210

PRESSING ON

I do not consider that I have made it my own yet; but one thing I do: forgetting what lies behind and reaching forward to what lies ahead, I press on toward the goal to win the [heavenly] prize of the upward call of God in Christ Jesus.

Philippians 3:13–14 amp

At times we become so mired in our past that we become trapped in our woulda, coulda, shouldas. We're left unable to find a way to walk freely in our present or hold any sort of hope for the future. This is not a pleasant or productive place to be. Fortunately, the apostle Paul gave us tips on how we can get unstuck.

Although we may have a long way to go in our walk of faith, there's one mindset we can adopt to move forward. We can forget what lies behind us and reach for what lies ahead. Doing so allows us to press on in the present. It allows us to keep our eyes on Jesus, the one who stands on the water waiting for us to walk into His arms.

Jesus, thank You for helping me forget what lies behind me and giving me the courage to reach forward.

PRAYER JAR INSPIRATION:

I'm reaching out for the hope that lies ahead of me!

Day 211

FORGIVENESS PRAYER

Do not remember the rebellious sins of my youth. Remember me in the light of your unfailing love, for you are merciful, O Lord. The Lord is good and does what is right; he shows the proper path to those who go astray. . . . O Lord, forgive my many, many sins.

Psalm 25:7–8, 11 NLT

We know that God is good and that His mercy and love are never ending. Yet it can be difficult to tell Him all the missteps we have made, because when we confess, we must admit them to ourselves.

Fortunately, we have the book of Psalms to help us. These verses from Psalm 25 are a prime example of how we can use what others have written to help us approach God in prayer.

The psalmist, David, asked God to see beyond his sins, to be viewed by God in the light of His love. He reminded God and himself that He is good and right and would show David how to get back on track. Most of all, he asked God to forgive his many sins.

Today, ask the Spirit to help you use the Psalms to address God in prayer as you seek His forgiveness. Take note of what happens when you do.

Lord, "do not remember the rebellious sins of my youth."

PRAYER JAR INSPIRATION:

Help me, Lord, to find the psalm prayer that fits me.

Day 212

RESURRECTED

For it is by grace you have been saved, through faith—and this is not from yourselves, it is the gift of God—not by works, so that no one can boast.

Ephesians 2:8–9 niv

Even the most faith-filled people sometimes fall into the pit of despair. Jesus' good friends Mary and Martha were personal witnesses to the miraculous things that happened at the hands of the Savior. But when they really needed Him (at the death of their brother, Lazarus), Jesus was busy tending to someone else's needs.

Martha gave Jesus a piece of her mind: "If You had been here, this wouldn't have happened."

Jesus already knew, of course, that He could (and would) raise Lazarus from the dead. And He's pretty good at raising your situations from the depths as well. Instead of arguing with Martha, He simply went to the tomb and cried out, "Lazarus, come forth!"

If you're in the middle of a faith crisis right now, picture Lazarus coming forth from that tomb, grave clothes falling away. If Jesus would do that for him, He can certainly resurrect you too!

Lord, I'm thankful that You're still in the business of peeling away grave clothes! Amen.

PRAYER JAR INSPIRATION:

I can trust Jesus with the resurrection of my faith.

Day 213

HANGING ON TO HOPE

"Look, God's home is now among his people! He will live with them, and they will be his people. God himself will be with them. He will wipe every tear from their eyes, and there will be no more death or sorrow or crying or pain. All these things are gone forever."

Revelation 21:3–4 NLT

The world can be a very harsh place. But those who trust in God, who believe in Jesus, and who walk with His Spirit know a better place lies ahead. And that place is heaven. There God will dwell among us. He Himself, His very presence, will be with us. In His compassion, our Father will gently wipe every tear from our eyes. No longer will we cry, suffer death or pain, or feel anguish.

This is the world we hope for and look forward to. A new place, a new home, a new life. The hope of that world is what will give us grace to live through this one. Hang on to that hope.

I look forward to living in that new world with You, Lord. To the hope of that world I cling.

PRAYER JAR INSPIRATION:

I live my life on earth with the hope of heaven in my heart.

Day 214

BELIEVE

"Do not let your heart be troubled (afraid, cowardly). Believe [confidently] in God and trust in Him, [have faith, hold on to it, rely on it, keep going and] believe also in Me."

John 14:1 AMP

This world continues its attempts to toss our hearts around and agitate our spirits. Outside forces vie for our attention, wanting us to put our hope and trust in the world's remedies, its cures for our seeming ills.

Fortunately, we have Jesus: The Word who never changes. The Lord of love and compassion who refuses to let us go, who urges us to turn to Him instead of getting swamped by worry, fear, frustration, and terror.

Believing in the goodness and compassion of Jesus and our Father God—remembering that they have given us the Spirit to help us cope—is all we need to find the happiness our hearts, souls, and spirits long for. Trust in them. And you will find the joy that will always be your strength.

It's You alone I hold on to, Lord. You are the secret of my happiness.

PRAYER JAR INSPIRATION:

Lord, "I do believe, but help me overcome my unbelief!" (Mark 9:24 NLT).

Day 215

FLIPPED

Do not be conformed to this world, but be transformed by the renewal of your mind, that by testing you may discern what is the will of God, what is good and acceptable and perfect.

ROMANS 12:2 ESV

Do you enjoy watching house-flipping shows on TV? It's remarkable, watching them take a filthy, run-down house and turn it into a thing of beauty.

We love transformational TV because, in an hour, we can watch something morph from ugly to beautiful.

God is still in the transformation business. And, while radical transformations don't always happen in rapid fashion like we see on TV, He can transform you from the inside out, no matter how rough your current situation might be.

Like some of those home builders, God might have to go to the bare bones and start from scratch with you. He will give you a new foundation in Him and build you into a person of strength and beauty. All you must do is submit to the process and allow Him to do the work.

There are areas of my life that need to be flipped, Lord.
And I give those areas to You today! Amen.

PRAYER JAR INSPIRATION:
God is still in the transformation business.

Day 216

THE SHEPHERD'S ROD AND STAFF

Even though I walk through the [sunless] valley of the shadow of death, I fear no evil, for You are with me; Your rod [to protect] and Your staff [to guide], they comfort and console me. . . . My cup overflows. Surely goodness and mercy and unfailing love shall follow me all the days of my life.

Psalm 23:4–6 amp

You need not live in fear or worry today or tomorrow. Because even though you may be walking in some hard places, the Lord is walking beside you. He's got His rod to fend off any evil that comes against you and His staff to make sure you keep on the right path.

Your life is filled with blessings—because you are the daughter of the Most High God. His goodness, mercy, and love will be with you, not just all the days of your life on earth but throughout eternity.

So shake off any doubts and fears. The one with you is so much greater than any other thing above you, below you, or on the earth. He has encompassed you within His protective arm, ensuring that nothing can get to you without His say-so.

Thank You, Lord, for staying close to me through good times and bad.

PRAYER JAR INSPIRATION:

God's goodness and mercy are following me!

Day 217

COMPLETE JOY

"Until now you have not asked [the Father] for anything in My name; but now ask and keep on asking and you will receive, so that your joy may be full and complete."

JOHN 16:24 AMP

Jesus told His disciples—and by extension, us—that our joy can be full and complete if we ask for things in His name. But what does it mean to pray in Jesus' name?

Praying in Jesus' name doesn't mean asking God for whatever you want and then just tacking on to the end of it "in Jesus' name I pray, amen." What it means is to pray to God in a way that is consistent with Jesus' character and His will.

Once again we are reminded to live our lives following in Jesus' footsteps—doing things, desiring things, asking and seeking things that He would have done, desired, asked, and sought. You can do that by thinking before you pray. Consider how Jesus would be speaking to His Father if *He* were in your shoes. Doing so will be your first step on the journey to complete joy.

Father, this is Your daughter here. Please, teach me how to pray to You like my friend and brother Jesus did. Lead me to complete joy. In Jesus' name I pray, amen.

PRAYER JAR INSPIRATION:

My hope is in finding joy as I live and pray Jesus' way.

Day 218

FREEDOM'S ROAD

Now the Lord is the Spirit, and where the Spirit of the Lord is, there is freedom.

2 Corinthians 3:17 esv

Freedom is a wonderful thing, and it's blissful to walk in it. No matter where you've been, no matter what has held you tightly in its grip, you can be set free. This is the message of the gospel—freedom from sin, freedom from the clutches of hell, and freedom to walk in newness of life.

That old life, the one that had you bound and frightened? It's gone now. When you say yes to Jesus, you become a new you, living in a new era, one filled with possibilities and opportunities.

Shackles have fallen, hope has risen, and there's a sparkle in your eyes now. That's what freedom in Jesus looks like. It doesn't mean you won't still face obstacles (you will), but you can tackle them one by one with your Savior's hand firmly clutched in yours.

So, what's keeping you? There are plenty of good roads ahead for you!

I'm so grateful to walk forward with my hand in Yours, Jesus. Amen.

PRAYER JAR INSPIRATION:

I will walk freedom's road with my head held high!

Day 219

FIXED FOCUS

Our present troubles are small and won't last very long. Yet they produce for us a glory that vastly outweighs them and will last forever! So we don't look at the troubles we can see now; rather, we fix our gaze on things that cannot be seen. For the things we see now will soon be gone, but the things we cannot see will last forever.

2 Corinthians 4:17–18 NLT

It's easy to get swallowed up by our trials and tribulations. But we need not go down that road at all. Even though our outer selves are continually wasting away, our inner selves are being renewed day by day. So these troubles we're passing through are miniscule, just little blips in the grand scheme of things. We can disregard them knowing good times are on their way and being prepared for us ahead of our arrival.

Today, look past your troubles. Fix your focus on the things that you cannot see. For they are what will be everlasting.

Lord, help me not to focus on all my troubles but to keep my eyes on the prize You have waiting for me at the end of this road.

PRAYER JAR INSPIRATION:

My focus is on God's goodness in the world to come!

Day 220

GREAT POWER

Are any of you suffering hardships? You should pray.
Are any of you happy? You should sing praises.

James 5:13 NLT

If you're wondering what to do when things are going right and you are delightfully happy, James tells you to sing your praises to God. On the other hand, when all has gone wrong and your bird of happiness seems to have flown, James advises you to pray. If you're not just unhappy but sick (or you've become sick because you are unhappy), James tells you to add to your prayer power by asking the elders of your church to pray for you and anoint you with oil in Jesus' name (see James 5:13–16).

If you offer a prayer in faith, you will regain your health. And if you have made any missteps, they will be forgiven. Why? Not just because your God loves you, but because "the earnest prayer of a righteous person has great power and produces wonderful results" (James 5:16 NLT).

Thank You, Lord, for blessing me with the power of prayer and praise!

PRAYER JAR INSPIRATION:

Knowing God stands with me in prayer and praise gives me hope for happiness!

Day 221

A COMPASSIONATE GOD

Then the Lord passed in front of him and proclaimed: Yahweh—Yahweh is a compassionate and gracious God, slow to anger and rich in faithful love and truth, maintaining faithful love to a thousand generations, forgiving wrongdoing, rebellion, and sin. But He will not leave the guilty unpunished.

Exodus 34:6–7 HCSB

God's love is lavish. Time and time again, we make mistakes, we revolt and rebel, we deviate from where He wants us to go and from what He wants us to be. Yet, our Lord still keeps loving His creation. Why? Because He is filled with compassion for us—even when we are cold-hearted.

Thankfully, God is slow to get angry. He is faithful with His love. He always speaks the truth. And He forgives whenever we stray.

How do we know that God has all these wonderful attitudes toward fault-ridden females such as us? Because He allowed His one and only Son to die to cover our sins so that we could be close to Him again.

Today, bask in the truth of who God was, is, and always will be: "a compassionate and gracious God, slow to anger and rich in faithful love and truth, maintaining faithful love to a thousand generations, forgiving wrongdoing, rebellion, and sin."

Thank You, Lord, for having compassion on me.

PRAYER JAR INSPIRATION:

Yahweh is my compassionate and gracious God!

Day 222

FOR GOOD

We know [with great confidence] that God [who is deeply concerned about us] causes all things to work together [as a plan] for good for those who love God, to those who are called according to His plan and purpose.

ROMANS 8:28 AMP

You are not just some woman adrift and alone, purposeless, forever meandering, shuffling around on planet Earth, putting in your time as best you can before you pass over to the other side. You are the daughter of the Most High God, a supernatural being who is seriously committed to helping you through this life and into the next.

Each daybreak, remember who you are: a woman of the Way chosen by God for a special purpose in His grand plan. He has all your todays and tomorrows charted out. So live your life with confidence and joy, knowing that good is coming your way—today and all your days to come.

Thank You, Lord, for loving me like You do, for making me a part of Your plan, for working all things out for my good.

PRAYER JAR INSPIRATION:

I have hope that I will see good today and in all my tomorrows.

Day 223

GOD'S PRESENCE

I know the Lord is always with me. I will not be shaken, for he is right beside me. No wonder my heart is glad, and I rejoice. My body rests in safety. . . . You will show me the way of life, granting me the joy of your presence and the pleasures of living with you forever.

Psalm 16:8–9, 11 NLT

Need a little more joy in your life? Take a tip from David. Remember that God is always with you. There is nowhere you can go that He cannot follow. There is no darkness so deep that He cannot find you, reach you, and rescue you.

God is always ready to help you. To teach you and guide you. To make sure you are on the right path, the one He designed for you from the beginning of time. He will show you how to do whatever needs to be done. If you allow Him, He will work right through you to accomplish things you never thought possible.

Open your eyes and your heart. Let God be an integral part of your life. And you will discover the joy of His presence today and every day to come.

Because You are with me, Lord, I can live in joy.

PRAYER JAR INSPIRATION:

Heart, open yourself up to God's presence and experience the joy it brings!

Day 224

READY TO FORGIVE

For You, O Lord, are good, and ready to forgive [our trespasses, sending them away, letting them go completely and forever]; and You are abundant in mercy and loving-kindness to all those who call upon You.

Psalm 86:5 AMPC

In Psalm 86, David begins by asking God to listen to him—to hear his words and answer his prayer. He describes himself as "poor and distressed, needy and desiring" (Psalm 86:1 AMPC) and reminds God he's faithful to Him (verse 2). David then appeals to God's mercy, explaining he has been crying to Him and calling on Him constantly (verse 3). David wants to rejoice as he lifts his soul up to the only one who can grant him the forgiveness he so desperately desires. He knows that God, out of the goodness of His heart and out of His abundant mercy and love, is ready, willing, and able to forgive.

You, like David, have the same assurance: When you come to God, He will be ready to forgive. You can be certain that when troubles come knocking, God will answer you (verse 7)!

O Lord, my God, I come with a heavy heart, knowing You are ready to forgive.

PRAYER JAR INSPIRATION:

My God is always ready to forgive.

Day 225

NO CHANGE

"I am the Lord, *I do not change [but remain faithful to My covenant with you]." . . . Jesus Christ is [eternally changeless, always] the same yesterday and today and forever.*

Malachi 3:6; Hebrews 13:8 amp

Three times a day, the exiled Daniel would get down on his knees, pray, and give thanks to God. He did so day after day after day—even after some men, jealous of his high position, convinced King Darius to pass an ordinance saying that anyone who prayed to anyone but the king would be thrown into the lions' den! Even then, Daniel did not stop worshipping, thanking, and praying to God (Daniel 6:10).

During our lives, we will go through many and varied transformations. But one thing should never change: our worship, thanks, and prayers to the God who never changes.

Nothing and no one, Lord, will ever keep me from being faithful to You. That is one part of my life that will never change.

PRAYER JAR INSPIRATION:

I pledge to remain faithful to the one who is faithful to me—today and all the days to come.

Day 226

AWESOME GOD

Father to the fatherless, defender of widows—this is God, whose dwelling is holy. God places the lonely in families; he sets the prisoners free and gives them joy. . . . God is awesome in his sanctuary. The God of Israel gives power and strength to his people. Praise be to God!

Psalm 68:5–6, 35 nlt

Someday you may lose your parents, your spouse, or your bestie. Yet even then, you need not despair. There is always one who remains with you. His name is the Lord.

He was with you before you were born, planning out your life, making things ready for your role in His plan. He is the one who timed your entrance on the earthly stage. He is and will remain with you 24–7. When you are alone, God places you in a family. When you are imprisoned, He sets you free. When you are weak, He gives you power and strength.

Why does God do all this? Because you are His beloved daughter. In this awesome God who cares for you like no other, may you not only rejoice but offer your eternal thanks!

I lift up my thanks to the God who is with me and cares for me eternally!

PRAYER JAR INSPIRATION:

Lord, I reach out today for Your gift of unending joy.

Day 227

FROM DARKNESS TO LIGHT

"I will rescue you from both your own people and the Gentiles. Yes, I am sending you to the Gentiles to open their eyes, so they may turn from darkness to light and from the power of Satan to God. Then they will receive forgiveness for their sins and be given a place among God's people, who are set apart by faith in me."

Acts 26:17–18 NLT

When it comes to forgiveness, God doesn't fool around. For proof, look no further than the life of Paul.

Before his conversion, Paul was called Saul. He actively persecuted Christians, and he even watched as Stephen was stoned (Acts 7:54–58). But then Jesus grabbed his attention. . .by striking him blind. He told Saul his new purpose: to open the eyes of others so that they could turn from darkness to light. These new believers would then receive forgiveness for their sins and join the company of God's people, set apart from nonbelievers.

If Jesus was that radical about forgiveness, all believers should stand up and take notice. We must strive to open the world's eyes to the light and blessing that comes from the one who holds the universe in His hands.

Lord, thank You for being radical, for rescuing me, for showing me the way to Your light.

PRAYER JAR INSPIRATION:

Keep me, Lord, in Your love and light!

Day 228

FEEDING THE SOUL

Eat honey, dear child—it's good for you—and delicacies that melt in your mouth. Likewise knowledge, and wisdom for your soul— get that and your future's secured, your hope is on solid rock.

PROVERBS 24:13–14 MSG

Just as good food nourishes your body and helps it to grow, knowledge and wisdom feed your soul. And the place to find that knowledge and wisdom is God's Word.

Seek to know more about God by reading your Bible. Perhaps begin with the Old Testament in the morning, dip your mind into the New Testament around midday, and then sink your soul into the Psalms just before you turn out the light. Doing so will not only help you keep your focus on God and off your problems all day but also plant a seed of hope in your spirit just before you drift off to sleep in God's everlasting arms.

Help me, Lord, to find a way to spend time with You three times a day. For then I know that my future will be secured and my hope will find its feet on solid ground.

PRAYER JAR INSPIRATION:

My hope rests on the solid rock of God's wisdom!

Day 229

LEARNING THE SECRET

Always be full of joy in the Lord. I say it again—rejoice! . . . I know how to live on almost nothing or with everything. I have learned the secret of living in every situation, whether it is with a full stomach or empty, with plenty or little.

PHILIPPIANS 4:4, 12 NLT

The Word tells us to rejoice in the Lord. Not just sometimes or some days. But all the time, every day!

Rejoicing always may take some focus, some intention from you. So, in those times when you are feeling as if your world is crumbling and tumbling down, do what others who have gone before you have done. Find a silver lining. Figure out how to rejoice in your situation no matter what you have lost or found. Teach yourself how to smile even when your heart is breaking.

This does not mean there will not be times when you need a good cry. It just means you are to make an effort to see the good in whatever circumstance you are facing. You are to rejoice in the Lord because He is with you wherever you are. And He will always be there to see you through.

Lord, teach me how to rejoice—always!

PRAYER JAR INSPIRATION:

I pray God will help me learn the secret of contentment—and rejoicing!

Day 230

SAFE AND SOUND

God so greatly loved and dearly prized the world that He [even] gave up His only begotten (unique) Son, so that whoever believes in (trusts in, clings to, relies on) Him shall not perish (come to destruction, be lost) but have eternal (everlasting) life. For God did not send the Son into the world in order to judge (to reject, to condemn, to pass sentence on) the world, but that the world might find salvation and be made safe and sound through Him.

John 3:16–17 AMPC

God loves you to the moon and beyond! He loves you, His daughter, so much that He gave up His only Son to save you. To cleanse you from your sins. To set you free.

Your part in being saved is to simply believe in Jesus. To trust in Him more than money, things, people, or other gods. You are to cling to Him when your feet can find no purchase. You are to rely on Him to meet all your needs.

When you believe, you're no longer subject to the penalty of sin; instead, you gain eternal life with the God who loves you more than anything in this world.

Lord, in You I believe and trust. To You I cling. Thank You, God, for sacrificing Your Son so that I, Your daughter, can live forever with You!

PRAYER JAR INSPIRATION:

Through Jesus, I am safe and sound.

Day 231

HE HEALS THE BROKEN

He heals the brokenhearted and binds up their wounds.

Psalm 147:3 niv

Picture Jesus, Savior of the world, bending down to heal a blind man. A beggar. An outcast. The Creator of all bent low to care for the needs of one whom others would walk by.

Isn't it just like Jesus to sweep in when least expected and bring healing to broken bodies, broken hearts, and broken lives?

No matter how long you've felt invisible, you are seen by the Savior of the world today. He bears witness to the brokenness, the heartache, and the confusion. In the middle of it all, He stops and looks you in the eye, with grace flooding the space between you.

And then, in that miraculous way of His, He bends low and touches you, driving out the brokenness. Your heart is mended and your thoughts transformed.

What a good, good Savior, who heals the broken!

Thank You, Jesus, for bending low and for touching me in my brokenness. Amen.

PRAYER JAR INSPIRATION:

From heaven to earth, Lord, You bring healing to all who call out to You!

Day 232

MEETING FACE-TO-FACE

Though I have many things to write to you, I don't want to do so with paper and ink. Instead, I hope to be with you and talk face to face so that our joy may be complete.

2 John 12 HCSB

There are so many ways we can connect with each other. We can send texts and emails or make phone calls. We can put a post on social media or engage in a video call. We can even write letters by hand and send them via snail mail. But none of these things can ever take the place of meeting face-to-face.

We are social creatures. We need those personal interactions. When we are face-to-face, we are more focused, communicate easier, and can pick up on nonverbal cues. We can, if appropriate, hug and kiss each other, feel each other's presence.

Today, for complete joy, plan a safe face-to-face meeting with a loved one. And remember to keep meeting as a church family to encourage each other (Hebrews 10:25) in the name of Christ.

Help me, Lord, to find a way to reach out to others, with Your love in my heart and Your message on my lips. In Jesus' name, amen.

PRAYER JAR INSPIRATION:

My hope is to complete my joy by spending time with others.

Day 233

FOR YOU

When they came to a place called The Skull, they nailed him to the cross. And the criminals were also crucified—one on his right and one on his left. Jesus said, "Father, forgive them, for they don't know what they are doing."

Luke 23:33–34 NLT

For you, Jesus was put on trial. For you, an innocent man was judged, interrogated, and falsely accused. For you, God's Son quietly bore insults, mocking, and degradation. For you, He was handed over to the crowd, forced to walk to His place of execution, and nailed to a cross, suspended between two criminals.

While hanging, Jesus prayed that God would forgive those who had abused Him. For you, He died.

When you begin to wonder if God loves you, when you feel unforgivable and all alone in this world, remember what God allowed to be sacrificed. He did it so that you would know that He loves you and wants to embrace you—that He would rather lose His Son than be separated from you.

God did it all for you.

May I ever praise You, Lord, who sacrificed so much for me!

PRAYER JAR INSPIRATION:

God's forgiveness for me is overwhelming!

Day 234

EVER CLOSE

The Lord is close to the brokenhearted and saves those who are crushed in spirit.

Psalm 34:18 niv

Have you ever walked through a valley so deep that you couldn't see beyond it? Oftentimes those gut-wrenching experiences cause us to withdraw from society, to pull away from family and friends, and to slip into isolation.

It's hard to stay connected when we're hurting, but it's vital. God created us to live in community. But here's a solid truth: Even when you're physically alone, you're never truly alone. God is always with you, even in the deepest valley. He's ever close to the brokenhearted and saves those who are crushed in spirit.

If you need healing for the emotional scars and psychological wounds you've endured, look up! Jesus is standing nearby with healing in His wings!

Thank You for sticking close, Jesus. Even when others leave me, You never will.

PRAYER JAR INSPIRATION:
The heavenly Father is as close as your next heartbeat.

Day 235

THE ROAD TAKEN

Barak said to her, "If you will go with me, I will go. But if you will not go with me, I will not go." "I will go with you," she said, "but you will receive no honor on the road you are about to take, because the Lord will sell Sisera into a woman's hand."

Judges 4:8–9 HCSB

Deborah was a woman, a prophet, a wife, and a judge of Israel. As she sat underneath a palm tree, the Israelites would come to her for judgment.

One day she called for Barak, a military commander of Israel. She told him that God wanted him to go to Mount Tabor with ten thousand men. There he would draw out Sisera, the general of the army of Jabin, a Canaanite king whose nine hundred chariots of iron were oppressing the people of Israel. And God would give Barak victory over Jabin's forces.

But Barak refused to go unless Deborah went with him.

Perhaps God is calling you to some face-off, but you hesitate because you are frightened, certain the other side will overwhelm you and your efforts.

Be like Deborah. Remember that your God is bigger than anything you're facing. And God will honor you on that road you take with Him.

Lord, give me the courage to step out in faith on the road You have placed before me.

PRAYER JAR INSPIRATION:

If I have faith and courage, God will deliver me!

Day 236

OVERWHELMING PRAISE

He has not dealt with us after our sins nor rewarded us according to our iniquities. For as the heavens are high above the earth, so great are His mercy and loving-kindness toward those who reverently and worshipfully fear Him.

Psalm 103:10–11 AMPC

When we see people committing despicable acts, our outrage brings us to our feet in protest. We may even cry or shout out when witnessing their evil. And then when those people receive their just deserts, we feel vindicated. Our hearts are less heavy, knowing the evildoers got what they deserve.

Yet our God must have the same feelings of outrage when we hurt His heart by sinning. But even then, He is so merciful that He doesn't give us our just deserts. Instead, His mercy and love, His kindness and grace—which are higher than the heavens are above the earth—come flowing out toward us. Why? Because He is more benevolent toward us than we deserve.

Today, reflect on God's mercy and love. Consider that because He does not treat you as you deserve but instead forgives all that you do, He deserves more than just your obedience and love. He deserves immeasurable praise.

Let me begin this day by lifting up a great amount of praise to You, Lord!

PRAYER JAR INSPIRATION:

God's mercy and love overwhelm me!

Day 237

RESTORED!

"'But I will restore you to health and heal your wounds,' declares the LORD, 'because you are called an outcast, Zion for whom no one cares.'"

JEREMIAH 30:17 NIV

Have you ever thought about how God created the human body to heal itself? Scrape your knee and a scab forms. Over time, healing comes to the area.

Sometimes mental, emotional, and spiritual healing take time too. God covers the wound, insulating it, much like a scab. Then, over time, you're able to begin to function properly again. The pain diminishes.

Don't get dismayed if your healing is taking time. Don't get angry at yourself if those old feelings crop up again. Just do your best to give them to God and trust the healing process.

He will restore you. That's a promise. He will heal those emotional and psychological wounds because He loves you and wants you to be set free. Trust the God of the process.

You're healing me even now, Lord! I'm grateful, no matter how long it takes.

PRAYER JAR INSPIRATION:

My healing will be worth the wait.

Day 238

PASSING POWER ON

"Have I not commanded you? Be strong and courageous. Do not be frightened, and do not be dismayed, for the LORD your God is with you wherever you go." And Joshua commanded the officers of the people, "Pass through the midst of the camp and command the people, 'Prepare your provisions, for within three days you are to pass over this Jordan to go in to take possession of the land that the LORD your God is giving you to possess.'"

JOSHUA 1:9–11 ESV

After Moses died, God *commanded* Joshua to be strong and courageous. To not be afraid or dismayed. Because He would be with Joshua wherever he went, whatever he attempted for God.

Filled with the assurance of God's presence and power, Joshua commanded the leaders in charge of each tribe to tell the people to get ready. They were soon going to head into the Promised Land God had prepared for them.

God gives you all the power you need to do what He would have you do. Today He *commands* you to be strong and courageous. To not live in fear or be waylaid by panic. *Because God is with you wherever you go.*

Lord, today I take up Your command to be strong and courageous, assured You are with me wherever I go. In Jesus' name, amen.

PRAYER JAR INSPIRATION:

I need not live in fear. For God is with me wherever I go!

Day 239

ETERNAL LOVE

You see, God takes all our crimes—our seemingly inexhaustible sins—and removes them. As far as east is from the west, He removes them from us. An earthly father expresses love for his children; it is no different with our heavenly Father; the Eternal shows His love for those who revere Him. For He knows what we are made of; He knows our frame is frail, and He remembers we came from dust.

Psalm 103:12–14 voice

God doesn't just forgive our countless misdeeds. He actually *removes* them from us! The sins that once stained our souls vanish. They are removed as far as the east is from the west.

That makes God the best Father in the universe. He is incomparable! He is wonderful! He is heavenly! His love can never be measured!

If you're wondering why God is so good to those who worship Him and respect His might and power, it's because He knows who we are. He knows that we are but dust. That our frame is frail, that our souls sometimes wander from His will. He knows that we sometimes have difficulty bearing up. And He cannot help but look upon us with compassion.

Thank You, Lord, for Your immense love and compassion. May I follow Your example in my own life.

PRAYER JAR INSPIRATION:

My God forgives and removes my sins with His eternal love and compassion!

Day 240

OFFERING PRAISE

Heal me, Lord, and I will be healed; save me and I will be saved, for you are the one I praise.

Jeremiah 17:14 niv

Part of the healing process is learning to praise even before your healing comes. It doesn't make sense in the natural world, but turning your eyes on Jesus—singing His praises and trusting in His promises—causes you to look away from your own problems and focus on Him.

Something amazing happens when you lift your eyes off your pain or your problem and place them squarely on Jesus. Suddenly you have a completely different perspective. Trust increases. Hope increases. Faith rises.

So praise Jesus today! He's worthy of your praise whether you've seen complete healing yet or not. Praise Him, not just as a distraction from any pain you might be facing, but as a simple act of love and obedience to a Savior who gave His very life for you. That's how much He loves you!

Today I offer praise to You, my Savior, even before full healing comes. You are worthy, no matter what I'm walking through.

PRAYER JAR INSPIRATION:

Even when I'm in the valley, my God is still worthy of praise.

Day 241

NOT KNOWING

By faith Abraham, when he was called, obeyed and went out to a place he was going to receive as an inheritance. He went out, not knowing where he was going.

HEBREWS 11:8 HCSB

God had told Abram to leave his home and his father's family and head to a land that God would show him. There, God promised, He would make Abram a great nation. He would bless him. He would make his name great and make him a blessing.

Abram left what he knew to go to a place he knew not. . .all because God told him to do so. When was the last time you went to a place without first checking a map or planning your route through an app on your phone?

Blindly going where God would have you go, especially when that place and the route to get there is unknown to you, takes a lot of faith and courage. But if you ask, God will willingly give you an abundance of both.

I am ready, Lord, to go where You would have me go. Please provide the faith and courage to get there from here.

PRAYER JAR INSPIRATION:

God is with me and will equip me with the courage I need to travel into the unknown.

Day 242

GOD'S PROGRAM OF FORGIVENESS

Jonah was furious. He lost his temper. He yelled at God, "God! I knew it—when I was back home, I knew this was going to happen! That's why I ran off to Tarshish! I knew you were sheer grace and mercy, not easily angered, rich in love, and ready at the drop of a hat to turn your plans of punishment into a program of forgiveness!"

Jonah 4:1–2 msg

Poor Jonah. Now that God had relented from destroying Nineveh, Jonah complained to Him about what He'd done! He had the gall to yell at His Creator and sustainer, to gripe at the fact that He is so rich in love that He's always eager to turn His punishment into forgiveness!

God's response to Jonah's irrational tirade? "What do you have to be angry about?" (Jonah 4:4 msg). But that didn't keep Jonah from stomping out of the city and sulking in the shade. That's when God caused a gourd to spring up and shelter Jonah to cool him off. But then God sent a worm that bored into the gourd and killed it. When Jonah prayed for death, God "mercifully reprove[d] him who would pity himself and this gourd, and yet would keep God from showing his compassion to so many thousand people" (Geneva Study Bible).

May I, Lord, thank You for Your amazing compassion no matter whom You bestow it upon!

PRAYER JAR INSPIRATION:

My God has a program of forgiveness for all!

Day 243

HE KNOWS

The sacrifices of God are a broken spirit; a broken and a contrite heart, God, You will not despise.

Psalm 51:17 NASB

Aren't you glad God doesn't frown down on you when you have the blues? It would be awful to think that your sadness was somehow upsetting Him. Of course He wants you to put your trust in Him, but if anyone understands a broken heart, God does! He gave His only Son, after all.

Yes, your heavenly Father certainly understands your broken and contrite heart. He knows what to heal, when to heal, and how to heal. And you can trust Him with every single step of that process, even when it feels like the pain will never end.

Today, give God your broken heart. Picture it in His capable hands, being gently wooed back to hope and joy. Only the God of the universe is capable of such a miracle. But He loves you enough to perform it on your behalf.

Lord, I place my heart in Your capable hands! I know I can trust You! Amen.

PRAYER JAR INSPIRATION:

My God isn't frowning down on me—not today, not ever.

Day 244

"ALL IS WELL"

She called to her husband and said, "Send me one of the servants and one of the donkeys, that I may quickly go to the man of God and come back again." And he said, "Why will you go to him today? It is neither new moon nor Sabbath." She said, "All is well."

2 Kings 4:22–23 esv

A prominent Shunammite woman talked her husband into making a room in their home for the prophet Elisha. In return, Elisha told her she would hold a son in her arms by the next year.

And it happened just as Elisha said.

Years later, the Shunammite's son fell ill and died in his mother's arms. So she took her child up to Elisha's room, gently laid him on the prophet's bed, then told her husband she was going to see the man of God. When he asked why, she simply responded with "All is well."

She said the same thing to Elisha's servant. And when she reached Elisha himself, she explained all. Later, he brought the child back to life and placed him in his mother's arms once again.

When you trust God, you can have peace knowing that no matter what's happening in your life, all is truly well.

Lord, in You I trust. With You, I know all is and will be well.

PRAYER JAR INSPIRATION:

I live in the hope that no matter what's happening in my life, all is truly well.

Day 245

THE SLATE WIPED CLEAN

When you were stuck in your old sin-dead life, you were incapable of responding to God. God brought you alive—right along with Christ! Think of it! All sins forgiven, the slate wiped clean, that old arrest warrant canceled and nailed to Christ's cross.

Colossians 2:13–14 msg

Because of Jesus, you've been transformed. Instead of being dead in your sins and alienated from God, you are a new woman with a new life! Every sin and mistake you've ever committed has been forgiven. All those black marks against you have been erased from you and added to Christ's cross. You've been reborn!

That's one major do-over! The question now is: Where will you go from here? In what ways are you going to thank God for this miraculous erasure? How are you going to repay a debt that could never be repaid?

As you live your new life with a clean slate, one thing you can do is to show as much mercy and love to others as God has shown to you.

Help me, Lord, find a way to show love and mercy to everyone I meet!

PRAYER JAR INSPIRATION:

Because of Jesus' love and God's mercy, I am alive and forgiven! I am a woman reborn!

Day 246

CELEBRATE NOW

A joyful heart is good medicine, but a broken spirit dries up the bones.

Proverbs 17:22 nasb

What a wonder joy is! It transforms everything. When you add joy to the recipe, the outcome is always good. And best of all, it's a gift that comes along with salvation.

Joy energizes. Joy lifts. Joy engages you with the Giver. Joy casts your vision off yourself and onto Him. Is it any wonder we sing "Joy to the World!" at Christmastime? That is our ultimate wish for every heart, every nation, to experience the fullness of joy that Christ brings, the blissful message of hope!

Whatever you're walking through today, apply the joy of your salvation, and then watch your circumstances change. Healing comes on the wings of a celebration, the kind that begins to praise even before answers come. (What are you waiting for? Start praising!)

I'll start celebrating now, Lord, because my joyful heart will give me hope! Amen.

PRAYER JAR INSPIRATION:

I can be transformed by joy.

Day 247

PURSUING PEACE

What man is there who desires life and loves many days, that he may see good? Keep your tongue from evil and your lips from speaking deceit. Turn away from evil and do good; seek peace and pursue it. The eyes of the LORD are toward the righteous and his ears toward their cry.

PSALM 34:12–15 ESV

It's good to promote peace. But God wants you to go beyond that. God wants you to *pursue* peace! To go after it any way and any day you can! Why? Because that's one way to shed His light in this world.

One approach to pursuing peace is to make sure that what you say helps, not hinders, the hearer. Say things that are encouraging, that build others up. Another approach is to turn away from evil. Instead, do good.

Throughout His Word, God makes it clear that He has His eyes focused on those who are doing the right thing—reverencing Him, obeying His commandment to love Him and others. It's the prayers of those who are following Him that He hears and responds to.

Woman of God, what can—what will—you do to pursue peace today?

Show me, Lord, how I can promote and pursue peace today.

PRAYER JAR INSPIRATION:

What the world needs now is love and peace.
Help me, Lord, to be a promoter and pursuer of both.

Day 248

SET FREE IN FORGIVENESS

Visualize this: His blood freely flowing down the cross, setting us free! We are forgiven for our sinful ways by the richness of His grace, which He has poured all over us. With all wisdom and insight, He has enlightened us to the great mystery at the center of His will. With immense pleasure, He laid out His intentions through Jesus, a plan that will climax when the time is right as He returns to create order and unity—both in heaven and on earth—when all things are brought together under the Anointed's royal rule.

EPHESIANS 1:7–10 VOICE

Close your eyes. Imagine your body, spirit, soul, and mind being immersed in God's grace and soaked in His forgiveness. Streams of mercy flow freely within and without. God has poured His grace all over you. What an amazing picture!

Think of how precious you are to God. He has bequeathed wisdom and insight to you. You're now clued into His plan and the mystery of His will.

Because you are one with the Word (Jesus), you can rest assured not only that you are forgiven but that He will one day return and make *all* things right!

You amaze me, Lord! Thank You for making me a part of Your grand plan!

PRAYER JAR INSPIRATION:

Forgiveness and grace flow freely from my God!

Day 249

END DATE

The human spirit can endure in sickness, but a crushed spirit who can bear?

Proverbs 18:14 NIV

Having a cold is nothing to sneeze at. But even in the worst of it, you hang on to one important fact: You will get better. You might need medicine. You need rest. But the common cold passes in time. And knowing your negative situation has an end date helps so much psychologically.

Now think about those who are heartsick. They can't see an end date. They're in the thick of it, thinking the pain will go on forever. That's why it's so critical to give hope to the hopeless—so they can see a way out.

No matter how difficult the situation, no matter how bruised your heart, there is an end date to your pain. Focus on Jesus, the author and finisher of your faith. And remind yourself, "This too shall pass." It will, you know. But you must give it to Him first.

Today I make a visible demonstration of giving You my pain, Jesus. I'm ready to see the end date and to walk in hope once again!

PRAYER JAR INSPIRATION:

This intense pain has an end date. When I give a difficult situation to Jesus, I can live in hope, knowing it will pass in time.

Day 250

DO WHAT YOU CAN

Jesus said, "Leave her alone. Why are you bothering her? She has done a noble thing for Me. . . . She has done what she could; she has anointed My body in advance for burial. I assure you: Wherever the gospel is proclaimed in the whole world, what this woman has done will also be told in memory of her."

MARK 14:6, 8–9 HCSB

While Jesus was dining at the table of Simon the leper, a woman came in with a jar of expensive perfume. She broke the jar then poured the ointment over His head.

Some who were present admonished her, wondering why she'd been allowed to waste such expensive perfume when the money from selling it would have been better spent on the poor. But Jesus scolded them, telling them to leave her alone, for His followers would always have the poor with them. They could help them however they wanted when He was gone. But this woman had done what she could to prepare Him for His upcoming burial.

Let's do what is in our heart, power, ability, and budget to do for God. And He will commend us for it.

Remind me each day, Lord, to do what good I can—and to leave the rest of the world's problems and burdens in Your capable hands.

PRAYER JAR INSPIRATION:

I need not be a superwoman. All I need to do is focus on being a godly woman.

Day 251

FORGIVEN AND FORGOTTEN

So let's get this clear: it's for My own sake that I save you. I am He who wipes the slate clean and erases your wrongdoing. I will not call to mind your sins anymore.

Isaiah 43:25 voice

God is so great, loving, wonderful, and full of mercy that He wipes the slate clean of your sin. Whatever charges are against you—whatever ways you've erred, disobeyed, or taken the wrong path—He pardons. Then, He goes a step further by never again even thinking about the errors you've made!

Why would a holy God forgive and forget your wrongs?

It's not because *you* can pardon sin. No, that's His role alone. And neither is it because you have any power to coerce Him into doing so. Instead, the reason God forgives and forgets is because He wants to show the world how much love and compassion He feels toward you—how *He alone* can wipe away your wrongs.

Today, meditate on the fact that God has made you innocent. Realize that He alone can wipe your slate clean. Then praise Him for the love and compassion that prompts Him to fully forgive and forget.

I praise Your name, Lord, for Your love and compassion that erase my record of wrongs!

PRAYER JAR INSPIRATION:

My God both forgives and forgets!

Day 252

BEAUTIFUL SCARS

Make me hear joy and gladness, that the bones You have broken may rejoice.

PSALM 51:8 NKJV

Some scars are visible on the outside. They're difficult to mask. When you meet a person who has been burned in a fire, for instance, they share their scars as a testimony to what they've survived.

Other scars are buried deep, not visible to the outside world. Oh, you know they're there. But sometimes you wonder if they're getting in the way.

Here's the truth: Scars are the body's way of healing. They're an outward sign that internal healing has taken place. And when the heart is involved, internal scars form. But those scars are tough! They're working like glue to bind things together. And they're a clear sign of what has been, not of what is or what is coming.

So embrace those scars. Wear them proudly as a sign of victory. God has done an amazing work in your life!

I'm grateful for the scars, Lord. They're a reminder of all You've brought me through.

PRAYER JAR INSPIRATION:

My scars are beautiful because they announce, "Healing has come!"

Day 253

REMAIN CALM

"Do not be afraid! Take your stand [be firm and confident and undismayed] and see the salvation of the Lord which He will accomplish for you today; for those Egyptians whom you have seen today, you will never see again. The Lord will fight for you while you [only need to] keep silent and remain calm."

Exodus 14:13–14 AMP

When you're between a rock and a hard place, it's hard to stand still, to be calm, to keep your peace. But it is possible—just ask the Israelites.

The Egyptians with their chariots had come after the Israelites. The Israelites were trapped between an infuriated army and the Red Sea. Panicked, they cried out to God. Then they complained to Moses, asking why he'd brought them out here into the wilderness to be killed when they could've just stayed in Egypt and died there.

So Moses reassured them, telling them not to be afraid but to stand firm. They would soon witness the Lord saving them from their peril. He assured them that the enemy they saw today they'd never see again. All they had to do was remain calm and watch.

God is telling you the same thing today. Don't panic. He's got this battle.

Lord of my salvation, help me remain calm, cool, and collected in You.

PRAYER JAR INSPIRATION:

Because God is in control, I aim to stay calm.

Day 254

ONE SACRIFICE FOR ALL

"This is the new covenant I will make with my people on that day, says the LORD: I will put my laws in their hearts, and I will write them on their minds." Then he says, "I will never again remember their sins and lawless deeds." And when sins have been forgiven, there is no need to offer any more sacrifices.

HEBREWS 10:16–18 NLT

Under the old agreement with God, a priest had to make daily sacrifices so that the people would be cleansed of sin. But this method never solved the sin problem. Then, Jesus came along. He sacrificed His own body once and for all, and *voila*! This single sacrifice took away sins for all time. Jesus Christ's death "was a perfect sacrifice by a perfect person to perfect some very imperfect people" (Hebrews 10:14 MSG). His work alone "completely cleansed and perfected those who are consecrated and made holy" (Hebrews 10:14 AMPC).

The Holy Spirit backed this up by prompting the prophet Jeremiah to pronounce this new covenant, one that would not be written on stones (as the Ten Commandments were) but on peoples' hearts and minds (Jeremiah 31:33). Now, God forgives and forgets His peoples' wrongdoing—no additional sacrifice required.

Oh, what a God! Oh, what a Savior!

Spirit of God, thank You for reminding us that Jesus Christ's work has, in one fell swoop, saved and sanctified all—including me!

PRAYER JAR INSPIRATION:

Thank You, Jesus, for Your single great sacrifice for me!

Day 255

FICKLE EMOTIONS

So I say, walk by the Spirit, and you will not gratify the desires of the flesh. For the flesh desires what is contrary to the Spirit, and the Spirit what is contrary to the flesh. They are in conflict with each other, so that you are not to do whatever you want.

GALATIANS 5:16–17 NIV

Emotions are fickle things. They change with the wind. Maybe you've been there—up one minute, down the next. Excited about life, then plummeting to the depths of despair.

Emotions often show up after the real issue hits you. Tears come when you're grieving. A broken heart brings you to your knees after your spouse leaves you. Joy rises in your soul after you get great news.

Emotions come after. But you know what comes before, during, *and* after? The God of creation. He's there before the crisis. He's there in the center of it. And He's there to bring healing and comfort after the fact.

I'm so glad you see past my emotions, Lord!
You created me and know me best of all.

PRAYER JAR INSPIRATION:
I won't let my emotions rule me.

Day 256

EVERLASTING ARMS

There is none like the God of Jeshurun, who rides the heavens to your aid, the clouds in His majesty. The God of old is your dwelling place, and underneath are the everlasting arms. He drives out the enemy before you. . . . He is the shield that protects you, the sword you boast in.

DEUTERONOMY 33:26–27, 29 HCSB

Other people may have power, wealth, and false gods, but you have the God of Jeshurun. And there is no one and nothing like Him. He is the one who actually rides the heavens to reach you, to help you. He is your rock, your refuge, your dwelling place. And underneath are His almighty arms that are ready to catch you, protect you, lift you, comfort you.

This God unlike any other will drive your enemy away from you. He is the shield of protection that encases you and the sword that fights for you.

Knowing that you have this God in your life should and can fill you with an overwhelming sense of calm. All you need to do is look upward, look inward. He is there for you—and always will be.

Lord, there is none like You! Help me keep myself in You, my rock, my refuge, my protection.

PRAYER JAR INSPIRATION:

I live within reach of God—the one with everlasting arms!

Day 257

GOOD AND CLEAN

Learn to do good; commit yourselves to seeking justice. Make right for the world's most vulnerable—the oppressed, the orphaned, the widow. Come on now, let's walk and talk; let's work this out. Your wrongdoings are bloodred, but they can turn as white as snow. Your sins are red like crimson, but they can be made clean again like new wool.

Isaiah 1:17–18 voice

God continually tries to get His people to stop doing evil. He wants them to turn to good, to seek justice, to make things right for the afflicted, homeless, parentless, and widowed. Why? Because God wants His people to be like Him. To show mercy, love, and compassion. To remember that He made us for good and that good things come to those who do good!

There's no stain tougher to remove than blood. But God is the doer of the impossible. There's no challenge He can't meet, no problem He can't solve, no sin He can't cleanse, no wrong He can't right.

So, while Jesus has saved you once and for all from your sins, the Word still urges you to be like Him: good, loving, forgiving, and merciful, seeking justice for all.

Look around your corner of the world. How can you lift someone who's down today?

Lord, please show me where and how I can bring more good into this world!

PRAYER JAR INSPIRATION:

With God's help, I am good and clean!

Day 258

WITH A WHISPER

My sacrifice, O God, is a broken spirit; a broken and contrite heart you, God, will not despise.

Psalm 51:17 niv

When you're in an emotionally challenging season, you might feel like it's never ending. When a loved one dies. When a spouse leaves. When your best friend betrays you. When you lose your job. These kinds of things are a kick to the gut. And the pain is real. It's deep. It's relentless.

Picture that broken heart, the one with all the cracks, being picked up by your heavenly Father. He takes it into His very capable hands and, with just a whisper, every crack is filled. Love glues it all back together. Somehow that fragile heart is now capable of holding more than pain.

Joy returns. Hope returns. Peace returns. And all because you were willing to give your heart to Him. So, what's holding you back? Place it in His capable hands today.

Take my brokenness and make me whole, Jesus!
In Your hands, my heart can be mended. Amen.

PRAYER JAR INSPIRATION:

Jesus mends every crack in my broken heart.

Day 259

RETURNING TO GOD

The Lord God, the Holy One of Israel has said this, "In returning [to Me] and rest you shall be saved, in quietness and confident trust is your strength."

Isaiah 30:15 amp

In Isaiah 30, God warned the people of Judah not to make an alliance with Egypt. He said they'd be sorry if they carried out a plan that was not His. . .if they made an alliance, but not one of His Spirit. . .if they went down to Egypt without talking to Him about it first. . .if they took refuge in Pharaoh's stronghold, not in Him.

God wants His people to stop turning to others for help. He is longing to be gracious to them, to have compassion on them, to bless them.

When your peace has flown from your mind, your heart, your situation, your circumstances, take stock of where you are. Then do whatever you need to do to return to God. For there you will find not just Him but rest and rescuing.

My peace has flown, Lord. Grant me peace as I return to You for rest and rescue. Help me regain my strength in quietness and confident trust in You.

PRAYER JAR INSPIRATION:

My hope of shelter, guidance, rest, salvation, and peace lies in my returning to God!

Day 260

THE LOVE OF GOD

Love is patient; love is kind. Love isn't envious, doesn't boast, brag, or strut about. There's no arrogance in love; it's never rude, crude, or indecent—it's not self-absorbed. Love isn't easily upset. Love doesn't tally wrongs or celebrate injustice; but truth—yes, truth—is love's delight! Love puts up with anything and everything that comes along; it trusts, hopes, and endures no matter what.

1 Corinthians 13:4–7 voice

First John 4:16 (voice) teaches that "God is love. Anyone who lives faithfully in love also lives faithfully in God, and God lives in him." And since God is love, it only stands to reason that God is also all the things listed in 1 Corinthians 13! Love (a.k.a. God) is patient and kind. It is not self-absorbed but selfless. Nor is it easily angered. It doesn't keep a record of wrongs, and it delights in truth!

First Corinthians 13 is a wonder-filled description of who God is. Hearing that love puts up with everything rings true, especially when we remember all our past missteps. . .and all the times God has forgiven and forgotten those misdeeds.

Today, reflect on how much God loves you. Then, think of some ways you can reflect His love to others.

Lord, I am overwhelmed with gratitude for Your extravagant love for me!

PRAYER JAR INSPIRATION:

May I live as a reflection of God's love!

Day 261

CONTROL

A time to weep and a time to laugh, a time to mourn and a time to dance.

Ecclesiastes 3:4 NIV

There are so many things in life you simply can't control. Many of the circumstances that swirl around you are unchangeable. You can't fix them.

That's why it's important to control the things you can. Behaviors. Attitudes. Forgiveness. Discipline. Taking charge of the areas of your life that are controllable honors God.

No matter what's swirling outside your door, pause and do business with the Lord over the things you have control over. Give Him your heart. Your thoughts. Your attitude. Your past. Your present. Your future.

You do your part. He does His part. Together you're an amazing team.

Thank You for guiding me through this tough season, Jesus! Amen.

PRAYER JAR INSPIRATION:

Jesus is on my team!

Day 262

LORD OF LOVE

"Do not let your hands fall limp. The Lord your God is in your midst, a Warrior who saves. He will rejoice over you with joy; He will be quiet in His love [making no mention of your past sins], He will rejoice over you with shouts of joy."

Zephaniah 3:16–17 amp

Peace can be difficult to obtain when your mind ruminates on all the things you have done wrong in the past—all the misdeeds you cannot undo, the words you cannot take back. When your mind is fixated on such things, it's hard to move forward, to turn to God, to live the life He created you to live.

Take heart, woman of God. For He is with you, in your midst. He is a mighty warrior who is ready to save you. All He wants to do is love you and do so without bringing up all that you have done wrong. He will not harp on all the ways you have messed up. Instead, He will rejoice over you with songs and shouts of joy.

Thank You, Lord, for substituting my shame with Your peace.

PRAYER JAR INSPIRATION:

My hope of peace lies in my vision of a loving Lord!

Day 263

LAVISH WITH FORGIVENESS

Seek God while he's here to be found, pray to him while he's close at hand. Let the wicked abandon their way of life and the evil their way of thinking. Let them come back to God, who is merciful, come back to our God, who is lavish with forgiveness.

Isaiah 55:6–7 msg

Every morning, God's Word reaches out to you, wanting to bring you closer to Him. While He is near, pray to Him. Spend time in His presence. Ask Him to tell you what He wants you to do, say, be, and desire. . .and what He wants you to give up or turn over to Him.

To get your head on straight—your heart and will aligned with God's—ask Him to change your thinking, to fill your mind with love, kindness, humility, gentleness, and generosity. Ask Him to make you more like Him, transforming you into the woman He originally designed you to be. Run into His arms, confessing whatever is burdening your heart, whatever the Spirit is prompting you to put right. All the while, remember your God is lavish with forgiveness.

Sensing Your nearness in this moment, Lord of my life, I come to You with all my thoughts, dreams, and actions. Change within me whatever is not of You. Bless me with Your lavish forgiveness.

PRAYER JAR INSPIRATION:

I need not fear fessing up to my God for He is lavish with forgiveness.

Day 264

WHAT YOU CAN'T SEE

That is what the Scriptures mean when they say,
"No eye has seen, no ear has heard, and no mind has imagined
what God has prepared for those who love him."

1 Corinthians 2:9 nlt

Emotions aren't visible or audible (unless there's sobbing or laughter involved). They're illusive, invisible things. And yet they're very real.

So how do you go about fixing what you cannot see?

You put your trust in God. He sees. He hears. He knows. To Him, your emotions are completely visible. And He already has a plan to take you beyond where you are to a land of plenty, a place where broken things will all be mended.

While you're waiting and while you're trying to figure out why the pain is still so fresh, do your best to place your trust in God and to imagine a time (it's coming!) when things will be better.

They will, you know.

I put my trust in You, Lord. You see all things. You know all things.
And You love me even more than I love myself! Amen.

PRAYER JAR INSPIRATION:

I can't see, but Jesus can.

Day 265

JESUS' PEACE

"Peace I leave with you; My [perfect] peace I give to you; not as the world gives do I give to you. Do not let your heart be troubled, nor let it be afraid. [Let My perfect peace calm you in every circumstance and give you courage and strength for every challenge.]"

JOHN 14:27 AMP

When an angel appeared to announce Jesus' birth to simple shepherds, his first words to them were "Don't be afraid" (Luke 2:10 HCSB). Good news that would bring great joy had entered the worldly realm. Immediately after the angel's announcement, the heavenly host joined him, proclaiming glory to God and peace on earth.

When Jesus told His followers He would be leaving soon, He began with "Your heart must not be troubled" and "Peace I leave with you" (John 14:1, 27 HCSB). Then, having risen from the dead, Jesus greeted His followers with the words "Peace to you!" (John 20:19 HCSB).

Daughter of God, Jesus has left you His peace for the asking, taking, and sharing. The peace He offers you, the peace within your reach, is one that will enable you to be calm in every situation; it will give you strength for every challenge.

Bless me, Lord, with Your peace.

PRAYER JAR INSPIRATION:

My hope lies in the peace Jesus brought and spread, from His beginning to His never ending.

Day 266

RESCUED FROM DARKNESS

Thank You, Father, as You have made us eligible to receive our portion of the inheritance given to all those set apart by the light. You have rescued us from dark powers and brought us safely into the kingdom of Your Son, whom You love and in whom we are redeemed and forgiven of our sins [through His blood].

Colossians 1:12–14 voice

What a wonderful thank-you prayer the apostle Paul sent to the church in Colossae. He made a point in telling his readers what God has done for those who believe in Him—a point we should take to heart today.

If you're looking to be rescued by a white knight, it's already happened! Because Jesus—God's one and only Son—took our sins upon Him, we've been saved, redeemed, and forgiven! We've been freed from the darkness and delivered into the light of Jesus' kingdom.

Know that no matter what happens in your life, you are no longer in the clutches of evil but in the arms of a Savior who loves you more than you can imagine!

Lord of light, thank You for pursuing me, for rescuing me from the darkness so that I can live in the light of Your forgiveness and love!

PRAYER JAR INSPIRATION:

God is my true knight in shining armor who has brought me into the light of forgiveness!

Day 267

EVERY AREA OF YOUR HEART

Keep your heart with all vigilance, for from it flow the springs of life.

PROVERBS 4:23 ESV

If you do a deep dive into emotions, you'll learn that there are (categorically) six of them: happiness, sadness, fear, disgust, anger, and surprise. Some of the things we deal with (like frustration, for instance) might fall under the category of disgust or anger.

Now think about emotional healing. If you experience brokenness in any one of these six categories, imagine how it would affect the others. If sadness consumes you, it wipes away happiness. If you're overwhelmed by disgust at something a spouse has done, it triggers anger. They all play together (or squabble together) in the same play yard.

Now you see why it's so important to allow God to fully heal every area of your heart. One area usually overlaps another. So allow Him to do a deep dive into all six areas so that total healing can come.

I give all my emotions to You, Jesus, not just a few!

PRAYER JAR INSPIRATION:

Jesus sees every emotion and knows how to bring healing.

Day 268

INNER CALM

Let the peace of Christ [the inner calm of one who walks daily with Him] be the controlling factor in your hearts [deciding and settling questions that arise]. To this peace indeed you were called as members in one body [of believers].

Colossians 3:15 amp

Colossians 3:15 says we're to let the peace of Christ—the inner calm of the woman who walks with Him every day—rule in our hearts. But to understand that peace, we must understand the man who embodied it.

No matter how large the crowds, how stubborn the unbelievers, how dense the disciples, how unkind the religious leaders, how needy the people, or how little the time, Jesus kept His peace by tapping into the power of His Father.

To grasp that peace of Christ—to know it, to understand it, to claim it—we must spend some time each day in the New Testament accounts of Jesus. We must tap into the calm we uncover there. We must allow it to rule our hearts and settle any questions that have arisen. We must permit it to direct our lives.

Help me, Lord, to understand and tap into the calm of Christ.

PRAYER JAR INSPIRATION:

My hope of peace lies in grasping and making mine the inner calm of Christ.

Day 269

MERCY IS GOD'S SPECIALTY

Where is the god who can compare with you—wiping the slate clean of guilt, turning a blind eye, a deaf ear, to the past sins of your purged and precious people? You don't nurse your anger and don't stay angry long, for mercy is your specialty. That's what you love most. And compassion is on its way to us. You'll stamp out our wrongdoing. You'll sink our sins to the bottom of the ocean.

MICAH 7:18–19 MSG

When it comes to mercy, love, and forgiveness, your God is incomparable. You can't gain such things from idols, possessions, or power. Only God can pardon all of your wrongdoing. Only He can purge you of sin's stain. But that's not all!

Your God will not hold a grudge against you. He won't give you the silent treatment nor abuse you for your past missteps. Instead, He'll shower you with His love, affection, and devotion. He'll look upon you with mercy and compassion. He'll correct the wrongs you've committed—and cast them all into the bottom of the ocean! So, whenever guilt and the fear of God's anger begins creeping into your heart, remember that mercy is His specialty.

There is no one like You, Lord! Thank You for Your mercy!

PRAYER JAR INSPIRATION:

God absolves me with His abundant mercy and compassion!

Day 270

LET HEALING BEGIN!

Dear friend, I pray that you may enjoy good health and that all may go well with you, even as your soul is getting along well.

3 John 2 NIV

Imagine you had an open wound in a hidden place where no one could see it. You did your best to treat it, but without proper antibiotics, the infection continued to spread.

A hidden wound affects everything. And if left untended, it can become septic. At that point, there's no hiding the problem anymore. Your very life is in danger.

This might seem like an extreme example, but when you refuse to acknowledge the problems going on in your broken heart, they will eventually catch up with you. There will be no hiding the problem once you reach the septic point.

So don't wait. Run to Jesus today. Allow the spiritual antibiotic of His love, His peace, His joy to wash over the wound so that true healing can come.

I've waited long enough, Lord. Today is my day for healing to begin!

PRAYER JAR INSPIRATION:

Why wait for healing when God can begin the work today?

Day 271

FIXED THOUGHTS

Fix your thoughts on what is true, and honorable, and right, and pure, and lovely, and admirable. Think about things that are excellent and worthy of praise. Keep putting into practice all you learned and received from me—everything you heard from me and saw me doing. Then the God of peace will be with you.

PHILIPPIANS 4:8–9 NLT

When our minds are fixed on bad news, it's easy to get depressed, feel hopeless, and lose our peace. That's why God's Word encourages us to fix our thoughts on things that are true, noble, authentic, pure, and lovely.

Fixing our thoughts on good things may mean turning away from social media or news outlets that are looking more for a high number of readers than truth. It may mean not streaming a program that's filled with violence and instead watching one that raises our spirits or fills us with awe.

Today, start making a conscious effort to feed yourself only those things that meet the requirements of Philippians 4:8–9. Try doing so for a week or two, taking note of whatever changes occur. See how fixing your thoughts on what's good brings you closer to the peace of God.

Lord, remind me to keep my thoughts fixed on the good. Lead me to Your peace.

PRAYER JAR INSPIRATION:

Today my mind is looking for good!

Day 272

AN IMPORTANT CAVEAT

If you forgive people their trespasses [their reckless and willful sins, leaving them, letting them go, and giving up resentment], your heavenly Father will also forgive you. But if you do not forgive others their trespasses [their reckless and willful sins, leaving them, letting them go, and giving up resentment], neither will your Father forgive you your trespasses.

MATTHEW 6:14–15 AMPC

God is abundantly forgiving. But there is one caveat: to be forgiven by Father God, you must forgive those who have sinned against you.

This caveat is so important that Jesus included it in the Lord's Prayer! In Luke 11:4 (AMPC), the line reads: "And forgive us our sins, for we ourselves also forgive everyone who is indebted to us [who has offended us or done us wrong]." Matthew 6:12 (AMPC) puts it like this: "And forgive us our debts, as we also have forgiven (left, remitted, and let go of the debts, and have given up resentment against) our debtors." But both mean the same thing: If you want God to lovingly forgive you when you wrong Him, you must do the same to whoever wrongs you.

Are you ready?

Lord, help me find the compassion to forgive others as You have forgiven me.

PRAYER JAR INSPIRATION:

My God forgives me to the extent I forgive others!

Day 273

PAST HURTS

The human spirit can endure in sickness, but a crushed spirit who can bear?

Proverbs 18:14 niv

Have you ever met someone who lived in the past? Maybe she buried herself in the memories of yesteryear. Or, perhaps (as many do) she camped out in the valley of past hurts.

Some people just can't seem to get past yesterday's wounds. They lick them. They baby them. They talk about them. They peel the scab off—on purpose. They draw attention to them.

But why? Why would someone live like that? Why adopt a "woe is me" mentality when it does nothing but drag you down? In part because some people have made those past hurts their identity. They choose to identify as a wounded warrior, one with a crushed spirit.

God doesn't want you to place your identity in your battle wounds. He wants you to heal from them and move forward. So don't nurture those wounds. Don't rehearse them. Don't continue to publicize them. Instead, allow the King of kings to heal you from them once and for all.

Today I choose to allow healing of my past hurts, Jesus. Completely. Totally. Heal me, I pray. Amen.

PRAYER JAR INSPIRATION:

I won't lick old wounds.

Day 274

ENDLESS GOOD

Don't be afraid, O land. Be glad now and rejoice, for the Lord has done great things. Don't be afraid, you animals of the field, for the wilderness pastures will soon be green. The trees will again be filled with fruit; fig trees and grapevines will be loaded down once more. Rejoice, you people of Jerusalem! Rejoice in the Lord your God! For the rain he sends demonstrates his faithfulness. Once more the autumn rains will come, as well as the rains of spring.

Joel 2:21–23 NLT

There will be days when hope seems to have deserted us and we cannot remember the ways God has done so much good. That's our cue to go outside, revel in nature, bathe ourselves in the forests, look up into the starry night, and remind ourselves how God continues to bring good things into our lives, sometimes without us even asking for them.

Today, look for and take joy in the good things God is bringing your way!

May all nature rejoice with me, Lord, as I revel in You and Your goodness to me!

PRAYER JAR INSPIRATION:
My hope is revived by God's endless good!

Day 275

RICH IN MERCY

God, who is rich in mercy, because of His great love that He had for us, made us alive with the Messiah even though we were dead in trespasses. You are saved by grace! Together with Christ Jesus He also raised us up and seated us in the heavens, so that in the coming ages He might display the immeasurable riches of His grace through His kindness to us in Christ Jesus.

EPHESIANS 2:4–7 HCSB

Time after time, the Word tells us how rich God is in His mercy, how immeasurable His kindness is to us fallible female followers. And it's all due to His unfathomable and never-ending love for us!

When you begin to doubt the extent of God's forgiveness for you, read today's verses. Remember that you are not just forgiven but made alive with Christ! That God's grace has saved you from the darkness and brought you into the light! That you have been raised up and seated in the heavens with Jesus.

What blessings upon blessings!

When I doubt the extent of Your forgiveness to me, Lord, lead me to Your Word so that I can comprehend the blessings upon blessings You shower on me!

PRAYER JAR INSPIRATION:

All praise to God who is rich in mercy and has saved me by His grace!

Day 276

TO THE FULL!

"The thief comes only to steal and kill and destroy; I have come that they may have life, and have it to the full."

John 10:10 niv

Sometimes we seek healing for the hurts in our past but hold on to behaviors that prevent us from living life to the full. Perhaps we go through a painful romantic breakup and manage to forgive the one who left, but we leave walls up. The next time someone comes along, we inadvertently push them away. These things happen.

It's important to pray for healing from hurts but also healing from behaviors that might bring us further harm. God wants the whole you healed—every part. So don't let anything remain behind. (Scrub those spots clean, and then move forward with confidence, guarded behaviors behind you.) The same is true of your healing: Get every single spot cleaned out so you can move forward in peace.

I truly want to leave the past in the past, Lord. If there's anything left in me to be dealt with, I give it to You wholly and freely.

PRAYER JAR INSPIRATION:

God will sweep away every cobweb if I let Him.

Day 277

SOWING GOOD

Don't be deceived: God is not mocked. For whatever a man sows he will also reap. . . . So we must not get tired of doing good, for we will reap at the proper time if we don't give up.

Galatians 6:7, 9 hcsb

Every moment of your life, you have the choice to sow either good or bad. And whatever it is that you sow, that is what you will also reap.

So how do you sow good? You follow the promptings of the Spirit. When the Spirit hints that you should donate to a shelter or work at a food pantry, you follow that hint. When the Spirit prompts you to take a tin of cookies to an elderly neighbor, you start gathering the ingredients. When the Spirit urges you to do a pledge walk, you begin finding some sponsors and checking out the tread on your sneakers.

And no matter how well or not so well your work at the pantry or your cookie baking or your walk goes, take it in stride and just keep doing good. For in doing that, you will someday reap an amazing harvest for God!

Spirit, show me what good works I can do!

PRAYER JAR INSPIRATION:

May I not only spread good but increase others' hope!

Day 278

HE WILL FORGIVE

If My people, who are called by My name, shall humble themselves, pray, seek, crave, and require of necessity My face and turn from their wicked ways, then will I hear from heaven, forgive their sin, and heal their land.

2 Chronicles 7:14 AMPC

Having built a temple for God's presence, King Solomon then prayed to the Lord (2 Chronicles 6). He began by praising His name, proclaiming that He was like no other God in the heavens or earth. Why? Because this God keeps His promises and shows love and mercy to those who walk before Him with all their hearts. King Solomon then asked God to hear the prayers of His people and forgive them.

After Solomon's prayer, the Lord's glory filled the entire temple. Later that night, He appeared to Solomon, telling him that if His people humble themselves, pray, seek after and crave His face, and "abandon any actions or thoughts that might lead to further sinning" (2 Chronicles 7:14 VOICE), then God would forgive them.

To this day, God keeps His promises. If you follow the prayer outline in today's verses, He will hear. . .and He will forgive.

I humble myself before You, Lord. Hear my prayer.

PRAYER JAR INSPIRATION:

God hears—me! God heals—me! God forgives—me!

Day 279

TODAY

God again set a certain day, calling it "Today." This he did when a long time later he spoke through David, as in the passage already quoted: "Today, if you hear his voice, do not harden your hearts."

Hebrews 4:7 niv

When you read the word *yesterday*, what comes to mind? Did you realize the word only refers (specifically) to the day that came before today?

When we say, "God wiped away the pain of all my yesterdays," we're talking about a lot of days, not just one. That's a lot of work on God's part! He took yesterday and did a work. He also took yesterday's yesterday and cleaned it up too. And so on.

He wants you to look beyond your yesterdays to the todays. Yesterday will give you a crick in your neck if you stare at it too long. Today is right in front of you, an empty page ready to be written on.

Just don't give God too much to have to deal with tomorrow, okay?

But even if you do, tomorrow's yesterday (today) is currently fresh and ready for amazing things to happen!

All my days are held in Your hands, Jesus. I trust You with them all! Amen.

PRAYER JAR INSPIRATION:

I will redirect my attention—from yesterday to today!

Day 280

GOD IS SO GOOD

"I am Joseph your brother, whom you sold into Egypt. Now do not be distressed or angry with yourselves because you sold me here, for God sent me ahead of you to save life and preserve our family."

GENESIS 45:4–5 AMP

Joseph experienced many hardships beginning on the day his jealous older brothers threw him into a pit and then sold him to traveling traders, who in turn sold him to an Egyptian officer to serve as a slave in his home. That same officer's wife later accused Joseph of attempted rape, after which an innocent Joseph was thrown into a dungeon. There he successfully interpreted the dreams of the king's baker and cupbearer, but upon his release, the latter soon forgot about Joseph—until the king himself needed dreams interpreted. . .

No matter what happened, Joseph never complained to God. Instead, the Lord was with him and so would bless him, making Joseph a successful man (Genesis 39:2–3, 5, 21, 23).

When others intend evil against God's children, we can be assured He will turn that evil into something good. When we stick with God, He sticks with us, blessing us even in times of trial.

Regardless of what comes my way, Lord, I'm sticking with You, the God of good!

PRAYER JAR INSPIRATION:

God will turn all evil against me into good!

Day 281

NO FOOLING

If we claim that we're free of sin, we're only fooling ourselves. A claim like that is errant nonsense. On the other hand, if we admit our sins—simply come clean about them—he won't let us down; he'll be true to himself. He'll forgive our sins and purge us of all wrongdoing. If we claim that we've never sinned, we out-and-out contradict God—make a liar out of him. A claim like that only shows off our ignorance of God.

1 John 1:8–10 msg

None of us is perfect. At some point, we're going to trip, stumble, or downright fall from the path God has outlined for us in His Word. The apostle John makes it clear in today's passage that if we don't admit this, we're only fooling ourselves.

On the other hand, if we admit that we have done wrong and confess our mistakes to God, He will do what He does best: He'll forgive us and rinse us off! And He'll do so over and over again for as many times as it takes to get us back on the right track.

Thank You, Lord, for reminding me that no one is perfect. . .but that You will forgive all!

PRAYER JAR INSPIRATION:

Praise the God who forgives faulty females!

Day 282

P.A.S.T.

See! The winter is past; the rains are over and gone.

Song of Solomon 2:11 NIV

What if you took the word *past* and broke it down into an acronym that looked like this:

P: Put
A: All
S: Situations
T: There (at the feet of Jesus)

What if you took all those situations from the past—the ones you couldn't control and even the ones you could (but messed up)—and laid them at the feet of Jesus? How different would today look if you could stop fretting over yesterday?

When you lay something down, you remove your hands from it. It's not yours to fix anymore. And that's what the Bible encourages us to do with the things from the past anyway. There's no longer anything you can do with the stuff from days gone by. Even if you choose to pick it up, you can't change it. So put it there—at Jesus' feet.

I don't know why I tend to pick things up after I've already laid them down, Jesus, but I want to stop. I'm going to need Your help. Amen.

PRAYER JAR INSPIRATION:

Today is tomorrow's yesterday.

Day 283

GOOD BREEDS KINDNESS

"You planned evil against me; God planned it for good to bring about the present result—the survival of many people. Therefore don't be afraid. I will take care of you and your little ones." And he comforted them and spoke kindly to them.

GENESIS 50:20–21 HCSB

Joseph understood that because he'd not lost faith in God—but grew even closer to Him amid his ordeals—God turned the evil that had been done to him into good for himself and for others! Because of this knowledge, Joseph had no desire to seek revenge for what his brothers had done to him—even though his brothers' actions meant Joseph had to go without the love and affection of his earthly father for many years. Even then, Joseph determined not only to forgive his brothers and their families but also to be kind to them after his father's death.

Today, consider those who have wronged you. Consider how God already has or sometime will turn that evil into something good. Then resolve not only to forgive the wrongdoers but also to show them kindness, just as God has done for you.

God, turn all evil done against me into good. Then help me forgive and treat gently those who have done me wrong.

PRAYER JAR INSPIRATION:

Only God can turn evil into good, cruelty into kindness.

Day 284

HOLY TRUTHS

Ananias, have you allowed Satan to influence your lies to the Holy Spirit and hold back some of the money? Look, it was your property before you sold it, and the money was all yours after you sold it. Why have you concocted this scheme in your heart? You weren't just lying to us; you were lying to God.

ACTS 5:3–4 VOICE

The community of Christian believers in Jerusalem were deeply united in heart and soul, sharing their possessions with each other. Many even sold their land and houses and brought the money to the church leaders to distribute among all! As a result, no one lived in need.

Then one day, a man named Ananias and his wife, Sapphira, sold some property but kept back some of the proceeds. Yet Ananias "pretended to make a full donation to the Lord's emissaries" (Acts 5:2 VOICE). He could've been honest and said it was a partial donation. But instead, Ananias decided to deceive. In doing so, he was lying not only to his fellow believers but to God. The result: struck dead where he stood!

Even a half-truth can trip you up. To live a full life (instead of a *fool's* life), you must be totally honest with yourself and with God.

Help me, Lord, to be a woman of holy truths not half-truths!

PRAYER JAR INSPIRATION:

May I be a woman of truth, belonging to a God of truth!

Day 285

DEFINING HURT

And after you have suffered a little while, the God of all grace, who has called you to his eternal glory in Christ, will himself restore, confirm, strengthen, and establish you.

1 Peter 5:10 esv

If you look up the definition of the word *hurt*, you'll see a lot of words like *distress*, *physical damage or pain*, *injury*, *mental or emotional suffering*, *hinder*, *impair*, *discomfort*, and *damage*.

There's not a positive word in the bunch.

When you're hurt, things can get complicated. There are varying layers to the pain you've suffered. And they must be peeled back like an onion, one layer after another. This takes time. And effort.

As the onion is being peeled, go easy on yourself. Grace is necessary, and you can be the one both offering and receiving it at the same time.

Healing rarely happens all at once. But God will strengthen you. You can count on it.

Thank You for the promise of Your Word, Lord, that You will restore and establish me. Amen.

PRAYER JAR INSPIRATION:

When nothing seems positive, God's Word always is!

Day 286

WOMAN AT WORK

By grace you have been saved through faith. And this is not your own doing; it is the gift of God, not a result of works, so that no one may boast. For we are his workmanship, created in Christ Jesus for good works, which God prepared beforehand, that we should walk in them.

Ephesians 2:8–10 ESV

God has showered His grace on you. Not because of anything you've done, but because He loves you and has a plan for your life.

You, God's masterpiece in Christ, have been designed to do good works—ones that He prepared long ago, way ahead of time, so that you would walk in them, perform them.

Today and every day, live with that intention. Keep your eyes on where God is working around you. Seek what He would have you get involved in.

And don't worry that you may not be ready or have the time to do what you've been called to do. Instead, remember that God will prepare you for whatever needs your doing. . .in His time.

Thank You, Lord, for designing me and equipping me for the work You have in mind for me. My sleeves are rolled up. I'm ready to go. Now, Lord, reveal what You would have me do—for You!

PRAYER JAR INSPIRATION:

Lord, make me a woman at work for Your good!

Day 287

WORD WATCHERS

For the mouth simply shapes the heart's impulses into words. And so the good man (who is filled with goodness) speaks good words, while the evil man (who is filled with evil) speaks evil words. I tell you this: on the day of judgment, people will be called to account for every careless word they have ever said.

Matthew 12:34–36 voice

Your mouth can get you into a whole lot of trouble—not just in this life but in the one to come! On Judgment Day, "the righteous will be acquitted by their own words, and. . .evildoers will be condemned by [their] own words" (Matthew 12:37 voice).

Jesus makes it clear that what comes out of your mouth can come back to haunt you. Like actions, words can never be taken back. Once they've left your mouth, they stay out there, ricocheting and perhaps finding homes in your hearers' minds.

The point? Watch your words. Don't let your tongue form anything that can wound. Keep your head and heart in God's Word and your mouth on alert. Become a good woman who, filled with goodness, speaks only good words!

Help me, Lord, to keep my mind and heart on You. . .and a careful eye on my mouth!

PRAYER JAR INSPIRATION:

Fill my heart with good, Lord, so that my words please You!

Day 288

DON'T RUSH GOD

"Nevertheless, the righteous will hold to their ways, and those with clean hands will grow stronger."

Job 17:9 NIV

If you're traveling out of a season of past hurts, no doubt you're anxious to hit the road and put that old town or city behind you. You're asking God, "Are we there yet?" and He's asking you to look around you and appreciate the journey that takes you out of that old place.

So take a moment to do just that. Instead of trying to rush God, offer up a prayer of thanks that the place you're in today doesn't look like the place you were in yesterday. Your minivan is pointed in a more hopeful direction now. You're growing stronger.

And even though the journey might be taking longer than you expected, you are well on your way, with a brand-new spiritual GPS that's guaranteed to get you to your destination on God's perfect timeline.

The road might be long, Lord, but I'm in a better place than I was. Thank You for that! Amen.

PRAYER JAR INSPIRATION:
With God's help, I am growing stronger.

Day 289

CONQUERING EVIL

Never return evil for evil or insult for insult [avoid scolding, berating, and any kind of abuse], but on the contrary, give a blessing [pray for one another's well-being, contentment, and protection]; for you have been called for this very purpose, that you might inherit a blessing [from God that brings well-being, happiness, and protection].

1 Peter 3:9 AMP

Wondering why you've not had a lot of good, an abundance of blessings, come your way? Perhaps it's because you're giving back what you get.

Many people find it easy to slap back when they're slapped, to insult when they're insulted, to pay back evil for evil. But God wants us to do the complete opposite—God wants us to pay back evil with good (Romans 12:21). Why? Because that's what Jesus did.

After so much evilness had come upon Him—after He'd been harassed, threatened, deserted, beaten, denuded, and crucified—Jesus did an amazing thing: *He died for us! Even before we knew Him!* Jesus was good to us when we were evil, and God wants you to go and do the same.

Lord, to be like Jesus, I too must find a way to conquer evil with good. So the next time I'm yelled at, reviled, insulted, and abused, give me the strength to return that evil with a blessing. In Jesus' name, amen.

PRAYER JAR INSPIRATION:

Lord, help me join You in conquering evil.

Day 290

FAULTS AND FORGIVENESS

Your servant will find, hidden in Your commandments, both a strong warning and a great reward for keeping them. Who could possibly know all that he has done wrong? Forgive my hidden and unknown faults. As I am Your servant, protect me from my bent toward pride, and keep sin from ruling my life.

Psalm 19:11–13 voice

Let's face it: We all have our faults. We are fallible females. That's not an excuse—just a fact.

Because not one of us is perfect, we sometimes err and don't realize it. So while our life aim is to keep God's commands so that we can find our way in the darkness, we still want to go deeper. We want God to shine His light within us and cleanse us from our unconscious faults.

The fact that God has the power to bring these hidden faults to light and forgive them is an absolute blessing. For He can save us from any pride and sin that may be working their way to the surface. Ask God today to take those faults away.

Lord, You know me inside and out. Please forgive my hidden faults!

PRAYER JAR INSPIRATION:

Shine Your light within me, Lord! Forgive what lies hidden.

Day 291

LET HOPE BLOSSOM

"Forget the former things; do not dwell on the past. See, I am doing a new thing! Now it springs up; do you not perceive it?"

Isaiah 43:18–19 NIV

One good thing about yesterday is that it's, well. . .*yesterday*. It's not today. *Yester* means "last past," after all.

Today means "this present day." It's pretty specific, isn't it?

Really, "today" is a mentality. That mentality includes phrases like "fresh start," "new beginnings," and "new outlook." But guess what happens when you drag yesterday into today? You forget those phrases. You're not feeling that fresh start, which means hope has no place to reside.

Give hope a chance to blossom by living in today. Yester is no more. So forget the former things. Don't dwell on the past. God is doing a brand-new thing!

I'm so grateful that "yester" is behind me, Lord! Thank You for today. Amen.

PRAYER JAR INSPIRATION:

I won't dwell in the past.

Day 292

HOPE THROUGH PRAYERS

At the same time also prepare a guest room for me [in expectation of a visit], for I hope that through your prayers I will be [granted the gracious privilege of] coming to you [at Colossae].

PHILEMON 1:22 AMP

Nothing in your life seems to be going the way you thought it would. Your expectations of things getting better are falling by the wayside. And then a fellow sister in Christ tells you she's been praying for you; she's been asking God to bring an abundance of good your way, to more than fulfill your many needs, small and great.

When you hear her words, you cannot help but feel her and God's precious love. Your hope is revived. Because of the abundance of good she began rolling your way through her prayers, you cannot help but feel joy, knowing it was God who prompted her to fold her hands in prayer for you.

Prayer reaches over houses, communities, states, and time zones, bringing much-needed good to those who are praying and those who are prayed for.

Lord, who would You prompt me to pray for today?

PRAYER JAR INSPIRATION:

When prayer is in my hands, the hope of good will be restored in others.

Day 293

THE HOLY HELPER

Here's my instruction: walk in the Spirit, and let the Spirit bring order to your life. If you do, you will never give in to your selfish and sinful cravings. For everything the flesh desires goes against the Spirit, and everything the Spirit desires goes against the flesh. There is a constant battle raging between them that prevents you from doing the good you want to do. But when you are led by the Spirit, you are no longer subject to the law.

GALATIANS 5:16–18 VOICE

God continues to hold the power of forgiveness in His hands. And He wants us to run to Him at the first sign of a misstep, to tell Him all and ask His forgiveness. However, He also gives us a helper, one who can keep us from stumbling in the first place. That holy helper is the Spirit.

To keep you from wandering off God's way and stepping into sin, the apostle Paul provides instructions: Walk in the Spirit and allow Him to rule over your life. When you let the Spirit overrule the flesh, all your selfish and sinful cravings will dissipate!

Teach me, Lord, how to walk in the Spirit!

PRAYER JAR INSPIRATION:

Thank You, Lord, for Your gift of the Spirit!

Day 294

LIVE LIKE IT!

For I will forgive their wickedness and will remember their sins no more.

Hebrews 8:12 niv

Moving forward from shame or regret can be difficult. One reason so many of us feel shame is because the actions of yesterday don't line up with our morality (or Spirit-infused beliefs) today.

Those things might be shameful, but Jesus was clear that we're not to carry guilt and shame. One of the most amazing things about His grace is that it completely covers our shame. It's a free ocean of forgiveness and mercy, wide enough to wash away those feelings associated with shame and regret.

Everyone makes mistakes. But what bliss to move into the freedom of healing in Christ. No matter what you did back then, you don't have to live in the past anymore. You are a new creation in Christ Jesus. Live like it!

You remember my sins no more, Jesus, so I will do my best to let go of the shame associated with them. Amen.

PRAYER JAR INSPIRATION:
I am a new creation. Old things have passed away.

Day 295

GOOD IN ABUNDANCE

He took the five loaves and the two fish, and looking up to heaven, He blessed and broke them. He kept giving them to the disciples to set before the crowd. Everyone ate and was filled. Then they picked up 12 baskets of leftover pieces.

LUKE 9:16–17 HCSB

Jesus had gone into the wilderness and a crowd had followed Him. So He taught the people and healed those who were sick. As evening approached, the disciples asked Jesus to send the people away. They had nothing to feed such a huge crowd—only five loaves of bread and two fish. That certainly wasn't enough to feed five thousand men along with all the women and children with them.

But Jesus told the disciples to have the people sit down. He then blessed the meager meal, broke it up, and kept giving the pieces to the disciples to distribute to the crowd. In the end, everyone had eaten their fill—and there were twelve baskets filled with leftovers!

Give what you have to God. He will not only bless it but increase it beyond what you could ever hope or imagine!

I offer to You what I have, Lord. Bless it and me!

PRAYER JAR INSPIRATION:

God increases my offerings more than I could ever hope or imagine!

Day 296

SPIRIT WALKER

Walk and live [habitually] in the [Holy] Spirit [responsive to and controlled and guided by the Spirit]; then you will certainly not gratify the cravings and desires of the flesh (of human nature without God).

Galatians 5:16 AMPC

It's great that we have access to the Holy Spirit, one who is ready, willing, and able to help us stick to God's way and not veer off in a sinful direction. But how do we walk in the Spirit?

To get yourself on the Spirit's wavelength, you must pray—and commit to doing so all day, every day. You also need to trust that God knows best. That means when the Spirit prompts you, you should follow His lead, regardless of whatever else seems the "better" path.

To build up your prayer muscle and your trust in God, tell Him at the end of every day what you're grateful for. And mean it!

Last, but certainly not least, keep your eyes and thoughts on Jesus. Make His Word the first thing you read in the morning and the last thing you read at night!

Lord, make me a Spirit walker, following His lead, not mine!

PRAYER JAR INSPIRATION:

Lead me, Lord, down the Spirit led pathway to You!

Day 297

A PROCESS

And I am sure of this, that he who began a good work in you will bring it to completion at the day of Jesus Christ.

Philippians 1:6 esv

Consider the word *process*. It can be used as either a verb or a noun. When you *process* something, you think long and hard about it. You examine it carefully from every angle. But when you use *process* as a noun (e.g., "It's a process"), the word takes on a whole new meaning.

Whether you use the word as a verb or a noun, there's an implication of time. "Process" doesn't happen instantly. It requires effort and patience as things progress. (Funny how similar process and progress are.)

In other words, no matter what you're processing today, it's going to be a process. But here's a promise in the middle of the process: The same God who started a good work in you is going to be faithful to complete it. He is not giving up, and neither should you.

You started a good work in me, Jesus, and I know You're going to see it through. Thank You! Amen.

PRAYER JAR INSPIRATION:

I can trust God with the process.

Day 298

REALIZING GOD'S GOOD

Jacob awoke from his sleep and he said, "Without any doubt the Lord is in this place, and I did not realize it."

Genesis 28:16 amp

Sometimes we get so caught up in our own lives that we forget to look around us. We forget to add God to the equation or to open our eyes to what He might be doing in or near us.

Jacob tricked his older brother out of his blessing and his inheritance. Then, literally running for his life, Jacob headed to his uncle's home to find a wife. On the way, he stopped and lay down to sleep, using a stone for a pillow.

That night Jacob dreamed of a stairway to heaven that had angels climbing up and down between heaven and earth. God told Jacob He'd always be with him, that He'd watch over and provide for him wherever he went. When Jacob woke, he realized what he hadn't before—that God was in that place.

Today, open your eyes. Look for God, His work, His face. Listen for His voice. He is where you are, waiting to bless and keep you, to do you good.

God, open my eyes to Your good.

PRAYER JAR INSPIRATION:

May I walk in a hope-filled way, continually open to God's blessings.

Day 299

WOMAN BLESSED FOUR WAYS

Blessed (happy, fortunate, to be envied) is he who has forgiveness of his transgression continually exercised upon him, whose sin is covered. Blessed (happy, fortunate, to be envied) is the man to whom the Lord imputes no iniquity and in whose spirit there is no deceit.

Psalm 32:1–2 AMPC

When you're counting your blessings at night, thanking God for all He does, don't forget to mention how happy you are for His continual forgiveness. Each time you confess your missteps, God is there to listen and to grant you His forgiveness (blessing number one). He then wipes your slate clean, removing your sins far out of sight (blessing number two).

God's next blessing (number three) is that He doesn't bear a grudge! Once you've been forgiven, He holds nothing against you—so neither should you! And finally, blessing number four stems from how clean and honest your spirit becomes when you are upfront with God about your wrongdoings. Whew! Doesn't that feel great?

Examine yourself today. If you've been hiding something from God, run into His arms. Tell Him all, holding nothing back. Those four blessings await!

Lord, help me examine myself and bring all my missteps before You.

PRAYER JAR INSPIRATION:

God's forgiveness is a four-fold blessing! What joy!

Day 300

DON'T CAMP THERE

And he who was seated on the throne said, "Behold, I am making all things new." Also he said, "Write this down, for these words are trustworthy and true."

Revelation 21:5 ESV

Some people make their tragic past their full identity. They rehearse the story over and over. It's one thing to share your testimony; it's another thing altogether to constantly bring up how badly you were hurt by someone because you're looking for ongoing empathy.

The past hurt you. That part is obvious to all who know you and know your story. But if you camp out there, if you identify as that hurt person, then your current friends will always tiptoe around you. They won't relax and be themselves.

It's great to share your testimony, but if it has become altogether different than a praise report, and you find yourself sharing it often, you might need to reanalyze it. Just something to ponder as you heal from the traumas of yesterday.

I won't rehearse it, Jesus! I've rehashed that story enough already! With Your help, I can put it behind me. Amen.

PRAYER JAR INSPIRATION:

Rehearsal is over! I'm putting the past in the past where it belongs!

Day 301

CLINGING TO HOPE AND FAITH

Throwing off his cloak, he sprang up and came to Jesus. And Jesus said to him, "What do you want me to do for you?" And the blind man said to him, "Rabbi, let me recover my sight." And Jesus said to him, "Go your way; your faith has made you well."

Mark 10:50–52 ESV

As Jesus, His disciples, and the crowd following them made their way out of Jericho, they passed Bartimaeus, a blind beggar who happened to be sitting on the side of the road. When he heard it was Jesus walking by him, he cried out for His mercy. And when people told him to be quiet, Bartimaeus cried out even more!

So Jesus had them call the blind man to Him. In his eagerness to get to Jesus, Bartimaeus threw off his coat and ran to Him. Jesus asked him what he wanted. Bartimaeus said, "Rabbi, I want to see."

Jesus replied, "Go; your faith [and confident trust in My power] has made you well" (Mark 10:52 AMP).

Consider what you may need to shrug off so that you can receive the good that God wants to give you. Cling to the hope and faith that Jesus can and will give you exactly what you need.

Lord, I cling to my hope and faith in Your goodness.

PRAYER JAR INSPIRATION:

Today I will shrug off __________ to receive __________ from Jesus.

Day 302

IN PRAISE OF PROMISES CONTINUALLY KEPT

O Eternal One, Israel's God, there is no other God who compares to You in heaven or on earth. You have guarded Your covenant and revealed Your loyal love to those who serve You with all their being. You have kept Your word to Your servant, my father, David. You have promised with Your mouth and fulfilled Your promise with Your actions as it is today.

1 Kings 8:23–24 voice

When King Solomon finished building the Lord's temple, He prayed a prayer of dedication which covered a myriad of topics. . .and which gives us an excellent example of how we too should pray.

The first thing Solomon did in his prayer was to praise God, declaring that there is no God that compares to Him. For this God not only keeps His agreements intact but proves His loyalty by lovingly providing for those who follow Him with all their hearts. Each day, we experience the fulfillment of His promises.

Before praying to God for forgiveness, spend some time in praise. Think back to the promises He has kept. Know that He will continue to pardon and provide.

You are a God like no other, Lord. . .

PRAYER JAR INSPIRATION:

My God keeps His promises!

Day 303

THE PROMISED LAND

Live as free people, but do not use your freedom as a cover-up for evil; live as God's slaves.

1 PETER 2:16 NIV

Sometimes life is so crazy busy that we get overwhelmed and overlook basic things. (What else would explain that time you showed up at work wearing mismatched shoes?)

If ordinary daily tasks are so easy to forget, why do you suppose we have such a hard time forgetting the past? Even if we're able to heal from it, forgetting is another thing altogether!

The Bible says that God forgets our sins once we repent. As far as the east is from the west—that's how far our sins are removed from us.

If God can forgive and forget the past, maybe we need to work harder at letting it go. Clearly He doesn't want us to dwell there! (Why go on living in the desert when you've been offered the Promised Land?)

Step into the Promised Land, friend. Forget yesterday. Live for today!

The Promised Land sounds mighty good to me, Lord! I can't wait to cross the Jordan! Amen.

PRAYER JAR INSPIRATION:

I choose freedom!

Day 304

GOOD INTENTS

A woman who had suffered from a hemorrhage for twelve years came up behind Him and touched the [tassel] fringe of His outer robe; for she had been saying to herself, "If I only touch His outer robe, I will be healed."

MATTHEW 9:20–21 AMP

Self-talk can be a good thing. That is, *if* what you're telling yourself is aligned with God's promises, who Jesus is, and what truth the Spirit would have you understand. Such was the case with the woman who had an issue of blood.

This poor woman had been hemorrhaging for twelve years. She'd seen many doctors who took her money but left her no better off. So when she heard that Jesus was coming her way, she made an effort to reach out to Him, telling herself, "If I only touch His outer robe, I will be healed."

Because of the good she hoped for, expected, prayed for, believed in, and acted on, Jesus' power went out from Him to heal her. Seeing her, He said, "Take courage, daughter; your [personal trust and confident] faith [in Me] has made you well" (Matthew 9:22 AMP).

Help me, Lord, to hope for, expect, pray for, believe in, and act on the fact that You intend good for me. Amen.

PRAYER JAR INSPIRATION:

May my faith in God's good intentions make me hopeful and whole.

Day 305

THE BEST PATH

When the heavens are dried up and no rain is given to the earth because Your people sinned against You, if they turn and pray in the direction of this place and praise Your name and turn away from their sins after You afflict them, then hear them in heaven and forgive the sins of those who serve You and of Your people Israel. Show them the best path, the good path, upon which to walk.

1 Kings 8:35–36 voice

Sometimes, God teaches us by our troubles. This portion of Solomon's prayer reminds us that everything we receive is a blessing from God. And when something is held back from us, it's time to take stock of where we've been, where we are, and where we're headed.

With each misstep, consider where, how, and *why* you stumbled. Your thoughts may be so scattered that you need God to tell you where you went wrong. Then you need to ask God to not only forgive you but show you a better way.

Lord, where did I go wrong? Lead me down a better path.

PRAYER JAR INSPIRATION:

My God forgives and then guides me to the best path, the good path.

Day 306

NO PAST REPEATS

Now the Lord is the Spirit, and where the Spirit of the Lord is, there is freedom.

2 Corinthians 3:17 niv

The reason so many of us get stuck in the past is because we're terrified of a repeat in the present. We put walls up and walk around guarded because we're so afraid to trust again. Or to love again. Or to walk in close relationship with a friend again.

If you've been hurt by a friend or loved one in the past, it can be hard to trust again. But part of the journey out of that pain is the recognition that not all people are alike. Not all men are alike. Not all friends are alike. Not all preachers are alike. Not all churches are alike.

We must stop lumping people into groups and making assumptions, and that can happen only when we become vulnerable once again.

And remember, there's freedom in Christ. That's not just a saying. There's literal, actual freedom!

You are my answer, Jesus! In You, I can find freedom. There will be no repeats from the past. It's all behind me now, and I have You to thank for that. Amen.

PRAYER JAR INSPIRATION:

No repeats from the past for me, Lord!

Day 307

PRAY AND PRAISE REGARDLESS!

Paul and Silas were praying and singing hymns of praise to God, and the prisoners were listening to them; suddenly there was a great earthquake, so [powerful] that the very foundations of the prison were shaken and at once all the doors were opened and everyone's chains were unfastened.

Acts 16:25–26 AMP

While Paul and Silas were on their way to pray, they met a slave girl whose fortune-telling talents had made a great amount of money for her masters. After Paul exorcised her of this spirit, her owners dragged Paul and Silas to the magistrates in the marketplace and made charges against them. Then a mob stripped the duo of their clothes and beat them with rods, and the men were thrown into prison with their feet clamped in stocks.

Even though all these hardships had come upon them, Paul and Silas prayed and sang praises to God. In return, God sent an earthquake to shake up the jail, open its doors, and unfasten all the prisoners' chains.

This story teaches us that when we pray and sing praises to God regardless of our circumstances, He will bring us a wealth of good—and then some!

I am a woman of Your Way, Lord, ready to pray and praise every day!

PRAYER JAR INSPIRATION:

No matter what my circumstances, my hope for God's good reigns!

Day 308

HEARTFELT PRAYERS

Hear in heaven, Your dwelling place, and forgive and act and give to every man according to his ways, whose heart You know, for You and You only know the hearts of all the children of men, that they may fear and revere You all the days that they live in the land.

1 Kings 8:39–40 AMPC

When you come to God and confess your missteps, He knows if you're being sincere. He knows if you are truly sorry for what you've said or done. For God alone knows your heart.

So when you open yourself up to God, you must be honest. After praising Him, perhaps you could ask God to search your heart and to point out any wrong intentions that may lurk therein. Ask Him to correct any fault He finds. Perhaps you're misjudging someone. Perhaps you're going down the wrong path. Perhaps what your heart intends is not what God intends for you.

The point is to remember to whom you're talking: someone who knows you better than you know yourself. So go to Him with your heart on your sleeve, questions on your lips, praises and petitions on your tongue. Let your prayer be heartfelt.

Lord, You know me better than I do myself. Make me "heart smart."

PRAYER JAR INSPIRATION:

God knows my heart best.

Day 309

FOR HIS GLORY

Blessed is the man who remains steadfast under trial, for when he has stood the test he will receive the crown of life, which God has promised to those who love him.

James 1:12 ESV

Letting go of a relationship, especially one you enjoyed for years, can be devastating. And heartbreaking. It takes a supernatural move of God to bring comfort to your broken heart after losing a good friend.

No matter what has happened, God will bring comfort, hope, and peace once again. He will. That heart of yours will heal over time. And no doubt you'll learn some lessons—however hard—about the next friendship that comes your way. In some ways you're sadder, but you're wiser.

God will use this situation for your benefit and for His glory. He always does. So go ahead and grieve, but anticipate healing. It's just around the corner. And remember, Jesus is a friend who sticks closer than a brother. That's one friendship that will never end.

I anticipate healing, Jesus. Amen.

PRAYER JAR INSPIRATION:

No matter what, God will use my situation for His glory.

Day 310

EYES ON HIS GOODNESS

Therefore if you have been raised with Christ [to a new life, sharing in His resurrection from the dead], keep seeking the things that are above, where Christ is, seated at the right hand of God. Set your mind and keep focused habitually on the things above [the heavenly things], not on things that are on the earth [which have only temporal value].

Colossians 3:1–2 AMP

You've had a pretty good week. The next morning you awaken with great expectations for the day ahead. That's when the dishwasher breaks—and its warranty expired last week. Or one of the kids missed the bus. In your rush to drive your child to school before you head to work, you spill coffee on the report you spent weeks on. Or you head down to the basement to let the puppy out of its kennel, only to discover it had escaped on its own the night before and begun eating your drywall.

All the things that can and sometimes do go wrong in one day are enough to drive a woman to the brink of tears. But God would rather you lift your eyes off these earthy things and focus on heavenly ones. The good things. The things that really matter. When you do, He'll give you the strength to deal with the rest.

Help me keep my eyes on Your heavenly good, Lord.

PRAYER JAR INSPIRATION:

Today my eyes are on You, Lord! Things are looking up!

Day 311

SPIRITUAL EARS AND EYES

Then Job said to the Lord, I know that You can do all things, and that no thought or purpose of Yours can be restrained or thwarted. . . . [I now see] I have [rashly] uttered what I did not understand, things too wonderful for me, which I did not know. . . . I had heard of You [only] by the hearing of the ear, but now my [spiritual] eye sees You. Therefore I loathe [my words] and abhor myself and repent in dust and ashes.

Job 42:1–3, 5–6 AMPC

After an intense conversation with the Lord, Job finally gets his head straight. He realizes that God's purpose stands above all things. That no matter what happens in our lives, His will cannot be restrained. That there will always be so many things we neither understand nor know about God's methods.

Like Job, we sometimes don't exactly get the gist of what God is saying. Sometimes, we don't understand what He's doing. During these times, we must hear and see with our spiritual ears and eyes. We need to trust that God has only good in store for us. And we must apologize to Him when we get things wrong.

Thank You, Lord, for loving me even when I get things wrong!

PRAYER JAR INSPIRATION:

Lord, help me hear and see with spiritual ears and eyes!

Day 312

SOMETHING'S GOTTA GIVE

The vexation of a fool is known at once, but the prudent ignores an insult.

Proverbs 12:16 ESV

Relationships are hard, but codependent relationships are over-the-top difficult. When you're in a precarious friendship where the other person has an unhealthy attachment to you, situations can get tricky.

You want to be a good friend. You've tried. But she's consuming you. Draining you. Accusing you of not being caring enough, no matter how much you give. . .

You weren't meant to fix everything. If you sweep in and play the role that only God should play, your friend will never learn anything. You have to take steps backward from the friendship until she gets the message that you're not her be-all, end-all.

It's not going to be easy, but when relationships reach the codependent stage, something has to give. So take this as a sign. Back away from the fire—for your safety and your loved one's as well.

Show me what to do with the tough ones, Jesus! Amen.

PRAYER JAR INSPIRATION:

I'm not the fixer of all things. But my God is.

Day 313

EXPECTATIONS

The lame man looked at them eagerly, expecting some money. But Peter said, "I don't have any silver or gold for you. But I'll give you what I have. In the name of Jesus Christ the Nazarene, get up and walk!"

Acts 3:5–6 NLT

Apostles Peter and John were heading to the temple for prayer. As they approached, they saw a man lying beside the Beautiful Gate. Lame since birth, he was carried to the gate every day so that he could beg for money from temple-goers.

When the man saw Peter and John approaching, he looked at them with hope in his eyes, expecting them to give him some money. But Peter said that instead of money he would give what he had: healing in Jesus' name. Peter then grabbed the man's arm and raised him up. All at once the man's feet and ankles were filled with strength, allowing the man to leap, stand, and walk, praising God.

Your best security, help, and answer to prayer lie in looking to God, not to money. Today, take your problem, your expectations, your hopes and dreams to Jesus, knowing that in His power, you will receive exactly what you need.

I look to You, Lord, for all that I need.

PRAYER JAR INSPIRATION:

My eager expectations lie in Jesus.

Day 314

OFFERING UP

Unto You, O Lord, do I bring my life. O my God, I trust, lean on, rely on, and am confident in You. . . . Remember, O Lord, Your tender mercy and loving-kindness; for they have been ever from of old.

Psalm 25:1–2, 6 AMPC

When we're looking to God and seeking His forgiveness, we often have trouble finding the words to say. That's when we can look to the psalms for help.

Psalm 25 has the perfect opening: "Unto You, O Lord, do I bring my life." These words tell God that you're bringing your entire self into His presence. You're offering Him not just your mind, heart, soul, spirit, and body but your past, present, and future.

The next sentence is a reminder of what God means to you—how much you can lean on Him and trust His promises. Lastly, the passage says you can find assurance by remembering His unchanging mercy, gentleness, and loving kindness.

Allow these words to linger in your mind. Then, in your petition for God's forgiveness, offer up your whole life to God, knowing He is—and always will be—the Lord of forgiveness.

"Unto You, O Lord, do I bring my life."

PRAYER JAR INSPIRATION:

I trust and rest in God's mercy.

Day 315

A PEACEMAKER

If it is possible, as far as it depends on you, live at peace with everyone.

Romans 12:18 niv

Have you ever watched a litter of puppies at play? They're having so much fun, tossing and turning, yipping at one another. Until one of them decides to bare his teeth. Then all bets are off!

Sometimes that's how friend groups are. You all get along great. You play together. You eat together. You even worship together. Then someone decides to stir up trouble. Before you know it, the whole friend group is going at it.

It's hard to reconcile with one person, let alone a whole friend group! That's why it's important to be a peacemaker when you can.

Look at today's verse. Home in on the words "*as far as it depends on you.*"

God knew it wouldn't be easy. But you really can be a peacemaker, even when the rest of your friends are squabbling!

You see to the very heart of my friend groups, Jesus. Help me to be the best friend I can be and to be a peacemaker to the best of my ability. Amen.

PRAYER JAR INSPIRATION:

Just because everyone else is squabbling doesn't mean I have to.

Day 316

WELL-PLACED CONFIDENCE

And he did rescue us from mortal danger, and he will rescue us again. We have placed our confidence in him, and he will continue to rescue us. And you are helping us by praying for us.

2 Corinthians 1:10–11 NLT

When you had no hope of surviving a mortal danger, when all you saw was certain death on your horizon, you learned to rely on God instead of yourself. And He saved you.

We humans have short memories. When life calms down a bit, we may once more begin relying on ourselves instead of God. After all, we can handle anything, really. . . Can't we?

No. We can't. Every breath is a gift from God, and so we must continually work to put and keep our confidence in Him, our good shepherd, knowing He is our constant Rescuer, even from hazards we may never see!

Prayers from others will help us continue to rely on God alone. So today, choose someone that you would willingly pray for daily. And ask that person to pray for you. In doing so, you'll be helping each other remember to be securely confident in God.

Who, Lord, would You have me pray for in my effort to help them keep their confidence in You?

PRAYER JAR INSPIRATION:

My continual hope and confidence rest in God and prayer!

Day 317

YOUTHFUL INDISCRETIONS

Remember not the sins (the lapses and frailties) of my youth or my transgressions; according to Your mercy and steadfast love remember me, for Your goodness' sake, O Lord. Good and upright is the Lord; therefore will He instruct sinners in [His] way. He leads the humble in what is right, and the humble He teaches His way.

Psalm 25:7–9 AMPC

We all have a history. Some things you might look back on with humble pride; others you might shudder to think about or admit to God. But everything you've done has made you the woman you are today—a woman seeking God's love, guidance, and forgiveness.

Once again, the psalms come to your aid in helping you find the right words—this time for a prayer of repentance over a not-so-upright past. To help your past become the past, you must own up to the missteps you made in your youth. With today's verses, you can ask God to *forget* about your past misdeeds. . .while at the same time asking Him to deal with you in the light of His love and mercy and instruct you in the way you should go.

Lord, remember not the missteps I made when young.

PRAYER JAR INSPIRATION:

God, forgive and forget my prior missteps. Teach me to walk rightly.

Day 318

GRACE AND MERCY

If we confess our sins, he is faithful and just to forgive us our sins and to cleanse us from all unrighteousness.

1 John 1:9 ESV

Grace and mercy—two things you hope others will extend to you when you mess up.

Here's the thing: God doesn't just want you to receive grace and mercy. He wants you to extend it to others, even the ones who've hurt you. He's not asking you to be a doormat, but there are situations where you should probably just forgive the person who hurt you and let it go, especially if she has asked for your forgiveness and tried to make things right.

Why is it so important to forgive and offer grace? Because God forgives. . .as you forgive. If you don't let it go, then He doesn't have to let your sins go either.

That's pretty heavy stuff, but it's what the Bible says. So choose grace. Choose a merciful response to the ones who've wounded you. Then watch as God pours mercy and grace out on you too!

It's not easy, but today I will choose to extend grace to the ones who've hurt me, Jesus. Amen.

PRAYER JAR INSPIRATION:

Grace and mercy are gifts I can offer to others.

Day 319

DEATH-DEFYING REFUGE

The wicked is overthrown through his wrongdoing, but the righteous has hope and confidence and a refuge [with God] even in death.

Proverbs 14:32 amp

Cruel and wicked people are driven away from God's favor and His presence. They do not keep company with those who are right with God. They will forever remain separate from any hope of happiness—in this life and the next.

Things are, of course, different for those who are in good standing with God. She who is righteous can fly to God amid the calamities and catastrophes in life. She can pour her heart out to Him in prayer, talk to Him when her heart is crushed. She knows she will find a safe place in, receive comfort from, and garner a listening ear with God because all her confidence is in Him. Even when she faces death, she has hope that she will be delivered to a life everlasting.

Today, remember where your hope and confidence lie: in the everlasting, death-defying refuge of God.

To You, Lord, I fly for safety, knowing You are and will be my sure refuge, even in death.

PRAYER JAR INSPIRATION:

My hope and safety lie in God, my refuge, in life and death.

Day 320

LIVE IN GOODNESS

O LORD, the Eternal, bring glory to Your name, and forgive my sins because they are beyond number. MAY anyone who fears the Eternal be shown the path he should choose. His soul will NOT only live in goodness, but his children will inherit the land.

Psalm 25:11–13 voice

Preceding these verses, the psalmist asks God to teach him His ways and feed him His Word. Why? "Because You are the True God who has saved me," he writes. "I wait all day long, hoping, trusting in You" (verse 5 voice). It's clear this petitioner is very familiar with God. Yet along with His devotion to the Lord, he feels the overwhelming sense of sin in his life. He knows He needs God's pardon for the countless wrongs he has done.

Have you ever tried to list all the ways you've stumbled in your life? Perhaps yours would also be numerous. But thankfully, you belong to a God who is more than ready to forgive those who come to Him and ask. And He will make clear which direction you should go in your walk with Him. Why? Because He, like you, wants you to live your best life in Him.

Thank You, Lord, for forgiving my numerous sins.
Show me which way to go and how to live a good life in You.

PRAYER JAR INSPIRATION:
With God's help, my soul will only live in goodness!

Day 321

NEVER TOO LATE

Cast your burden on the Lord, *and he will sustain you;*
he will never permit the righteous to be moved.

Psalm 55:22 esv

Do you have relational issues that go back to childhood?

It's hard to recover from childhood relational traumas. As a little one, you simply didn't have the tools necessary to mend the heartbreak caused by others, especially adults.

Now here you are, an adult yourself, having to make adult decisions. But the lingering pain caused long ago by people has left its mark.

It's not too late to heal. You may never see that person again. (Or you might.) But the truth is, God can bring complete and total healing to your heart and give you the tools you need, not only to forgive but to live in freedom. You don't have to repeat the patterns learned as a child. You can walk in liberty from now on, completely healed from the past.

I'm so glad I don't have to worry about the pain of yesterday, Jesus. I don't have to repeat the patterns taught to me as a child. You've set me free, and I'm so grateful. Amen.

PRAYER JAR INSPIRATION:
I can live in the freedom of Christ.

Day 322

LIVING IMAGE

He is the exact living image [the essential manifestation] of the unseen God [the visible representation of the invisible], the firstborn [the preeminent one, the sovereign, and the originator] of all creation. . . . And He Himself existed and is before all things, and in Him all things hold together. [His is the controlling, cohesive force of the universe.]

Colossians 1:15, 17 AMP

When the world and everything in it seems like it's falling apart, God's followers need not become uneasy or discouraged. Because Jesus is with us. He's holding everything together—from our frail bodies to the entire universe.

And Jesus has not left us without the knowledge of who God is. All we must do is look at the Son, the living image of the holy Father. When we read about Jesus in the Word, we perceive that He is love personified. That He has not left us alone, but His Spirit remains with us. That He longs for us to be His companion, follower, and replica, a sensitive soul with empathy for the lost, hurt, broken, and afraid.

In the knowledge of all these things—in the fact that Jesus, love personified, is continually and constantly with us, showing us how to live as He lived—we find our hope, security, and peace.

Firstborn of my Father God, work and dwell within me. Hold me together. Be my living hope.

PRAYER JAR INSPIRATION:

Jesus, thank You for the hope I find in Your presence within and without.

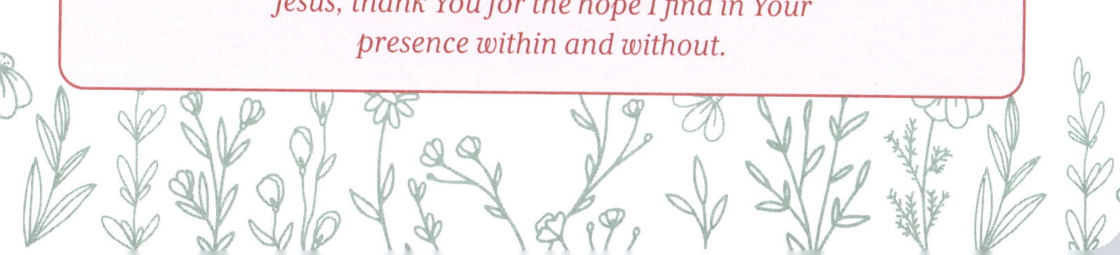

Day 323

HOPE IN GOD

Turn to me and have mercy, for I am alone and in deep distress. My problems go from bad to worse. Oh, save me from them all! Feel my pain and see my trouble. Forgive all my sins. . . . May integrity and honesty protect me, for I put my hope in you.

PSALM 25:16–18, 21 NLT

When the world feels like it's caving in on you, when you feel as if you're all alone, when all you want to do is sit down and cry, go to God. Tell Him exactly how you feel. Tell Him everything that's going on in your world, knowing that Jesus can feel your pain. He can understand your trouble. He can sympathize with your struggles—because He Himself has been there.

Yet, there's one thing Jesus never knew: sin. That's why He could die to save you from yours. So don't hold back. Put it all out there for God. If you must, wallow in your pain for a little bit. But when you rise up, remember who is on your side: God—the Creator, protector, refuge, All-Powerful. . . Put your hope in Him, and you will find strength to face your troubles. . .and the relief of forgiven sins!

To You I turn, Lord. Hear my prayer! Save me quickly! Forgive all! Be my hope!

PRAYER JAR INSPIRATION:

My forgiveness and hope are found in my God!

Day 324

BETTER TO BE PATIENT

It is better to be patient than powerful. It is better to win control over yourself than over whole cities.

Proverbs 16:32 GNT

We live in a world filled with people who have different personalities and different belief systems. What's perfectly acceptable and normal to one person might be taboo to another. It's hard to know how to communicate effectively with so many different perspectives at play.

This is particularly hard when you're thrown into a situation where you have no choice but to play nice with one another. Maybe you've been placed on a team at work with someone who rubs you the wrong way. You're doing your best, but the other person sure doesn't make it easy.

Relational issues can reach the boiling point if we don't respond kindly. But God can bring healing even in the toughest work-related relationship if you ask Him to be at the center of it.

Show me how to be patient with others, Jesus.
It's not easy, so I'll need Your help for sure. Amen.

PRAYER JAR INSPIRATION:

It is better to be patient than powerful.

Day 325

INDEPENDENTLY GODLY

Teach those who are rich in this world not to be proud and not to trust in their money, which is so unreliable. Their trust should be in God, who richly gives us all we need for our enjoyment. Tell them to use their money to do good. They should be rich in good works and generous to those in need, always being ready to share with others.

1 Timothy 6:17–18 NLT

Some women think they can only really live, can only really enjoy their lives, if they have enough money in the bank to allow them to spend as they please. They believe they will only be truly happy if they can keep up with the Joneses, take a nice vacation, have the bigger house, or buy that darling outfit they saw advertised online.

If thoughts like these start wending their way through your head, you can be sure danger lies ahead.

Money is an uncertain commodity. If you trust in that today, you will fall tomorrow. Instead of trusting in money, bank on the only thing that is certain: God. He'll supply all you need—and leave you enough left over to share with others.

Strive to be godly, not wealthy.

In You I trust, Lord. Not in the almighty dollar.
Show me today who You would have me spend Your love on.

PRAYER JAR INSPIRATION:

I trust and hope in the God of plenty.

Day 326

HEALING OF THE INNER SOUL

The Lord will sustain, refresh, and strengthen him on his bed of languishing; all his bed You [O Lord] will turn, change, and transform in his illness. I said, Lord, be merciful and gracious to me; heal my inner self, for I have sinned against You.

Psalm 41:3–4 AMPC

Sin is an offense against God. Anything you do that's contrary to His plan is harmful not only to yourself and others but to Him. And when you harm God, your soul feels it, prompting you to cry out to the Father of forgiveness.

Sometimes, your soul sickness can even lead to physical maladies. So when you find yourself feeling unwell—spiritually or physically—cry out to God. Ask Him to transform your illness, to touch You with His love, care, mercy, and forgiveness. Then rest easy, knowing that God loves to bring transformation and healing, love and compassion, mercy and forgiveness into your life and soul.

Lord of mercy, forgive me for harming You, myself, and others. Transform my weakness, my malady, with Your grace, mercy, and strength.

PRAYER JAR INSPIRATION:

Only God can transform me and heal my inner self!

Day 327

LOVER OF MY SOUL

"The Lord appeared to him from far away. I have loved you with an everlasting love; therefore I have continued my faithfulness to you."

Jeremiah 31:3 ESV

Romance movies have given us a somewhat unrealistic expectation of life. We imagine that Prince Charming will be waiting around the next corner, ready to make all things right.

Sometimes it works out like that, and we meet the perfect person to share life with. Other times things go catastrophically wrong and we feel we've been cheated of the fairy tale. The person we thought we could trust turns out to be a villain in the story, not a hero.

If you've been hurt in a romantic relationship—a marriage, a dating relationship, an engagement—you are certainly not alone. And perhaps (like many), you're tempted to back away from future possibilities because of past hurts.

That's understandable, but it's not always God's best for you. He wants you to lift your eyes and look forward, not back. Know that Jesus is always right there with His hand in yours. He's the lover of your soul!

Thank You for loving me through all my relationships, Jesus.

PRAYER JAR INSPIRATION:

I have the best relationship a person could ever ask for—with Jesus!

Day 328

WALKING IN THE WAY

This is what the LORD says—your Redeemer, the Holy One of Israel: "I am the LORD your God, who teaches you what is good for you and leads you along the paths you should follow. Oh, that you had listened to my commands! Then you would have had peace flowing like a gentle river and righteousness rolling over you like waves in the sea."

ISAIAH 48:17–18 NLT

Are you a woman who is walking in the Way of the Lord, looking to God for direction, following His teachings, obeying the Holy Spirit? Or are you a frazzled female who has lost every bit of peace she once knew and rarely opens her ears to God's voice?

If you want to know the right way to go, if you want your life to be filled with peace like a river and to have righteousness roll over you like a wave, look to God to lead you. Don't go off on your own but stay on the path outlined in His Word. Then you will gain all He has provided for you—and so much more!

I'm looking to You, Lord. Teach me what is good. Lead me along the right paths. Open my ears to Your voice, my heart to Your love. In Jesus' name, amen.

PRAYER JAR INSPIRATION:

The right way is God's Way.

Day 329

EXCEPT THE LORD

When it was time for my first defense, no one showed up to support me. Everyone abandoned me (may it not be held against them) except the Lord. He stood by me, strengthened me, and backed the truth I proclaimed with power so it may be heard by all the non-Jews. He rescued me.

2 Timothy 4:16–17 voice

Let's face it. People often disappoint us. We find ourselves counting on them for love and support, but just when we need them the most, they're nowhere to be found!

That's what happened to Paul. He had many friends in Rome, but as it turned out, they didn't support him when he was on trial for his life. Yet amazingly, despite their desertion, Paul knew fear was the motivating factor, so he offered God his forgiveness for them.

What's even more wonderful is that the Lord remained by his side through it all. God is a blessing within reach of all believers, even those riddled with fear.

Lord, may I be as merciful as You toward those who have wronged me. Thank You for Your continual mercy in my life and constant presence by my side!

PRAYER JAR INSPIRATION:

"I know the Lord will continue to rescue me. . .and carry me safely to His heavenly kingdom" (2 Timothy 4:18 voice).

Day 330

GO FIRST

Bear with each other and forgive one another if any of you has a grievance against someone. Forgive as the Lord forgave you.

COLOSSIANS 3:13 NIV

Sometimes relationships hit a wall because neither party is willing to apologize first. Maybe you've said things like, "Well, if she would just come to me and say she's sorry, I would forgive her and we could move on."

You've heard the phrase "Be the bigger person," no doubt. It does take courage (and humility) to be the first to say you're sorry. But when you do, you open the door to healing in the relationship. And isn't that more important than holding fiercely to your stubborn pride?

Be the first. Even if time has passed and it's awkward. Those first few words won't be easy, but they will be life-changing for both of you.

Pray about it and ask God to show you the perfect way to nudge the door open. When it comes to forgiveness, He's the pro!

It's not easy to humble myself, Lord, but with Your help, I can do it! Amen.

PRAYER JAR INSPIRATION:
When relationships are hard, I can be the bigger person.

Day 331

GOD'S CHART

"This Book of the Law shall not depart from your mouth, but you shall read [and meditate on] it day and night, so that you may be careful to do [everything] in accordance with all that is written in it; for then you will make your way prosperous, and then you will be successful."

JOSHUA 1:8 AMP

Henry Ward Beecher, an American preacher, said, "The Bible is God's chart for you to steer by, to keep you from the bottom of the sea, and to show you where the harbor is, and how to reach it without running on rocks or bars." Are you charting your course by the Word? Or are you too busy looking to the opinions of others, navigating by societal mores or religious traditions?

God wants you to sink yourself into His Word: To read it and meditate on it day and night. To navigate your life by its precepts and lessons. For only then will you prosper and succeed in all you do—perhaps not as the world sees prosperity and success but as God sees it, which is infinitely more stupendous and life changing.

Help me, Lord, to make time in my schedule to consult and meditate on Your Word. For Your Word is what I base my life on.

PRAYER JAR INSPIRATION:

God's Word is my hope and stay.

Day 332

HEARTFELT INTENT

May your silver rot right along with you, Simon! To think the Holy Spirit is some kind of magic that can be procured with money! You aren't even close to being ready for this kind of ministry; your heart is not right with God. You need to turn from your past, and you need to pray that the Lord will forgive the evil intent of your heart.

Acts 8:20–22 voice

Simon, a local sorcerer, had been amazing the people of Samaria for years. Everyone there referred to him as "the Great One—the Power of God" (Acts 8:10 NLT). But when the apostle Philip preached the good news of Jesus Christ, many people—including Simon—were baptized and began to follow Philip instead, awed by the miracles he performed.

Then, when apostles Peter and John arrived in Samaria and prayed for the new believers to receive the Holy Spirit, they did! Simon, seeing this great power coming upon his fellow citizens, offered to give the apostles money so that he could have the power to pass on the Spirit as well. But Peter set him straight, telling him the Spirit is not some magic trick that can be bought.

God knows your heart. He knows when your intent is evil. But if you pray, He will forgive and help you turn your heart around.

Help me, Lord, to keep my heart's intent pure.

PRAYER JAR INSPIRATION:

May my heart's intentions always be good.

Day 333

CALM WATERS

Get rid of all bitterness, passion, and anger. No more shouting or insults, no more hateful feelings of any sort. Instead, be kind and tender-hearted to one another, and forgive one another, as God has forgiven you through Christ.

Ephesians 4:31–32 GNT

Politics. Religion. How to raise children. These can be very divisive topics. And there are hot seasons where tempers are flaring on both sides of the aisle. No doubt you've read stories of twentysomethings who ended relationships with their parents over differing political affiliations.

Even inside the church, people disagree. There are dozens of theological viewpoints over hot-button topics. Maybe you've even witnessed a fight or two inside the walls of your church over doctrinal issues or music choices.

People fight. And every single person wishes that every other single person believed the way they believe.

When it comes to disagreements, there's a simple way to put an end to strife. Agree to disagree. Say to your friend or loved one: "We don't agree on this, but I still love you and will *always* love you, no matter what." These words will be healing balm.

I will do my best to keep the waters calm, Lord. Amen.

PRAYER JAR INSPIRATION:

Just because others overreact doesn't mean I have to.

Day 334

THE POWER OF GOD'S WORD

"The rain and snow come down from the heavens and stay on the ground to water the earth. They cause the grain to grow, producing seed for the farmer and bread for the hungry. It is the same with my word. I send it out, and it always produces fruit. It will accomplish all I want it to, and it will prosper everywhere I send it."

Isaiah 55:10–11 NLT

God's Word has great power. Wherever He sends it, it accomplishes what He desires.

And you have access to that Word 24–7. Night and day, day and night, you can read His Word. Follow it. Pray it back to Him. Meditate on it. Study it. Love it. Rest on it. Hope in it. Be empowered and encouraged by it. Write it on your heart and etch it into your mind.

No matter how many times you read the Bible, you can still find a new meaning to ponder, a new direction to take, a new vision to see. For God's Word is alive in power, in fruitfulness, in prosperity.

Today, open God's Word. Thank Him for giving you access to it. Then allow it, word by word, to direct your love and your life.

I open my heart, mind, soul, and spirit to Your Word today, Lord. May it take root within and produce heavenly fruit without.

PRAYER JAR INSPIRATION:

Oh, Word of God, grow deep within me.

Day 335

GOD HEARS YOUR PRAYER

Come with great power, O God, and rescue me! Defend me with your might. Listen to my prayer, O God. Pay attention to my plea. . . . I took my troubles to the Lord*; I cried out to him, and he answered my prayer.*

Psalm 54:1–2; 120:1 NLT

Know this, woman of God: The Lord hears your prayers. His eyes are constantly watching you. He even sends angels so that you won't trip. But if and when you do, His ears are open to your pleas. All you have to do is come to Him and pray for forgiveness.

If you do, you can be sure that even if you can't find the words, God will know what you are trying to say, what you are asking, what your soul and heart are feeling, what your spirit is craving, and what you need.

So do not fear that the Lord doesn't hear. He is open to you, 24–7. All you need to do is lift up your heart and soul to Him. Give Him your plea for forgiveness, your request for guidance. And you will receive all!

Hear my prayer, Lord, as I bring my sins, my soul, and my troubles to You.

PRAYER JAR INSPIRATION:

My God hears my prayers!

Day 336

STOP!

"The Lord will fight for you; you need only to be still."

Exodus 14:14 NIV

You're always on the go, moving a hundred miles an hour. And the troubles that plague you? Well, you drown them out with activity. Go, go, go. Rush, rush, rush. Before long, you can barely remember the things that were troubling you.

When you buzz along at lightning speed, there's no time to do the deep intense work on your heart to heal. So you pretend. You just keep going. No one can tell the difference if you keep that smile plastered on your face.

Only God wants you to stop. He needs you to stop so that He can do a deep work. It won't be easy. It will take time. But once you've done the hard work, you won't have to pretend anymore. You won't have to fill the hours with distractions. You can settle in. . .and just be.

I'm ready to stop running from the pain, Jesus. Ready to stop pretending. Slow me down so I can heal, I pray. Amen.

PRAYER JAR INSPIRATION:

Faster isn't always better. More isn't always more.

Day 337

LESSONS IN THE WORD

Such things were written in the Scriptures long ago to teach us. And the Scriptures give us hope and encouragement as we wait patiently for God's promises to be fulfilled. May God, who gives this patience and encouragement, help you live in complete harmony with each other, as is fitting for followers of Christ Jesus.

ROMANS 15:4–5 NLT

Although the stories in the Bible took place in ancient days and in places we may never have visited, the people in them were pretty much the same as the people you meet today. Humankind has not changed so drastically that we cannot imagine ourselves in the same scenarios as many of our Bible heroes and take heed of the lessons they learned.

For example, when you need to be brave, look to Esther, who was made queen for such a time as hers (Esther 4:14). When you're full of sorrow, look to Hannah, who poured her heart out to God (1 Samuel 1:15). And if you're not sure what pathway to take, take a cue from the things Jesus did, and do that (John 13:15).

Thank You, Lord, for the gift and guidance of Your Word.

PRAYER JAR INSPIRATION:
Today I will scour God's lesson book, my source of hope and encouragement.

Day 338

A NATIONAL REQUEST

Do not hold the sins of our ancestors against us, but send Your compassion to meet us quickly, God. We are in deep despair. Help us, O God who saves us, to the honor and glory of Your name. Pull us up, deliver us, and forgive our sins, for Your name's sake. Don't give these people any reason to ask, "Where is their God?"

Psalm 79:8–10 voice

There may come a time when we feel compelled to pray for our entire nation. A time when we feel as if we are being punished for the sins of those before us. A time when we wonder how we, a supposedly God-fearing nation, might appear in the eyes of outsiders as the enemy tramples us.

When our nation is under attack, we may experience shock, despair, and fear. We feel beaten down and unable to look anywhere but up. For we know that is where our help comes from.

Today, pray for your nation. Pray not only for its leaders but for the common person who is just trying to live a godly life in the midst of societal upheaval. Pray that God's compassion, deliverance, and forgiveness shines down upon you and lifts you—and your nation—up.

Lord, we've really messed things up. I pray You would, in Your compassion, deliver and forgive our nation.

PRAYER JAR INSPIRATION:

God, forgive this nation. Deliver us for Your name's sake!

Day 339

SEASONS OF REST

The Lord is my shepherd, I lack nothing. He makes me lie down in green pastures, he leads me beside quiet waters, he refreshes my soul. He guides me along the right paths for his name's sake.

Psalm 23:1–3 niv

We don't always feel like slowing down. Sometimes slowing down forces us to confront the issues we've been avoiding.

Maybe the psalmist understood this when he penned the phrase "He makes me lie down in green pastures."

Why do you suppose God had to "make" him lie down? Interesting question, right? Until we slow down, we don't have the headspace (or the heart space) to do the hard work that we need to do to heal. Busy people aren't healing on the go, after all.

Still people. Quiet people. These are healing people.

So slow down. Lie in green pastures. Rest. Reflect. Do the hard work on the inside, not just the outside. And watch as God heals you from the inside out, a true green-pasture healing.

I will be still whenever You call me to lie down, Jesus. I won't fight You on this because I know You have my well-being at heart. Amen.

PRAYER JAR INSPIRATION:
What a good, good Father, to call us to seasons of rest.

Day 340

SHINING LIGHT

Jesus shouted to the crowds, "If you trust me, you are trusting not only me, but also God who sent me. For when you see me, you are seeing the one who sent me. I have come as a light to shine in this dark world, so that all who put their trust in me will no longer remain in the dark."

John 12:44–46 nlt

No one enjoys stumbling around in the dark. It's too easy to stub our toes or trip over a piece of furniture and break something—including ourselves! Yet that's what happens when we stop opening up the Word and letting Jesus' light shine, not just on us but on any situation we may find ourselves in.

Jesus told crowds of people that when they trusted in Him, they were also trusting in Father God. For He, Jesus, was the manifestation of God Himself! He also told them that He was the light who had come to shine in this dark, dark world and that if they trusted in Him, they'd no longer be stumbling around in the dark.

Looking for a way in, up, or out? Open up the Word. Allow it to shine into your life and show you the way.

Lord, I trust in You and Your Word to show me the way through the darkness—to You.

PRAYER JAR INSPIRATION:

Jesus is the light of my life!

Day 341

BOLDLY TO THE THRONE

This High Priest of ours understands our weaknesses, for he faced all of the same testings we do, yet he did not sin. So let us come boldly to the throne of our gracious God. There we will receive his mercy, and we will find grace to help us when we need it most.

Hebrews 4:15–16 NLT

How wonderful that Jesus came to save us! That He is our High Priest who totally understands what we're going through—who knows and is ready to supply whatever we need, whenever we need it!

So, when you need help, when you stumble, when you are weak, head to the throne of God's grace. Do so with all boldness, knowing you will find the mercy, grace, and love you require—just when you need it the most.

Thank You, Lord, for understanding me and making allowances for my weakness. May I run to You when I need Your mercy. In Jesus' name, amen.

PRAYER JAR INSPIRATION:

Because of Jesus' love and grace, I receive all the mercy and grace I need, just when I need it!

Day 342

GIANT TIME-OUT

Jonah was in the belly of the fish three days and three nights.

JONAH 1:17 NIV

Jonah probably didn't anticipate landing in the belly of a huge fish. But there's no denying his own actions led him there. God instructed him to go to Nineveh. Jonah (not so graciously) declined and ran in the opposite direction, boarding a ship to Tarshish.

And that's when the trouble began. A storm hit. The boat rocked. The men panicked. And everyone agreed in unison that Jonah was to blame.

So off the boat he went, straight into the waters. And from there? Swallowed whole by a giant fish.

In the belly of the fish, Jonah had one thing he hadn't allowed himself before: time. Time to think. Time to repent. Time to pray. Time to figure out a new plan.

Maybe you've landed in the belly of a giant fish too. Don't waste the opportunity. Let God do the hard work while you're in there.

I won't make You put me in time-out, Lord!
Hopefully I will learn my lessons the first time! Amen.

PRAYER JAR INSPIRATION:

Repentance is key. I need to let God work in my heart.

Day 343

THE BEST PATHWAY

You are my hiding place; you protect me from trouble. You surround me with songs of victory. The Lord says, "I will guide you along the best pathway for your life. I will advise you and watch over you."

Psalm 32:7–8 NLT

When you need a place to hide out until the dust settles, God is the ultimate hiding place for you. For in Him, you not only find refuge from trouble but are surrounded with songs and shouts of victory. There you can find a new direction from God, who is committed to leading you along the best road for your life here on earth.

Yes, God is here to give you all the advice you need. But you need to actually follow it. God doesn't want you to be like a stubborn mule that needs coaxing or goading or the horse that won't be led unless someone puts a bridle on it and pulls with all his might.

God promises that when you trust in Him and follow the plan He gives you, you'll be surrounded by unfailing love. So run to God. Bask in His songs of victory!

Thank You, Lord, for watching over me as I grow in trust and obedience.

PRAYER JAR INSPIRATION:

I trust God's advice and guidance, for I know He'll put me on the best pathway for my life.

Day 344

WHITE AS SNOW

Come on now, let's walk and talk; let's work this out. Your wrongdoings are bloodred, but they can turn as white as snow. Your sins are red like crimson, but they can be made clean again like new wool.

Isaiah 1:18 voice

Jesus has a knack for transformation. So once you've turned from your former ways, confessed your missteps to God, and asked for His mercy and forgiveness, you must accept that you've been cleansed. He's done something for you that you could've never accomplished yourself. And now, the stain of your mistake has been wiped away. You are now white as snow.

So let the weight of your burden slide off your shoulders. Leave it at the bottom of the cross. Know you've been relieved of your wrongs. Although you may still have to suffer whatever consequences your error caused, you are fully cleansed in God's eyes! Do you see yourself cleansed in your own eyes?

Help me, Lord Jesus, to understand that because of Your sacrifice for me, You made me squeaky clean the moment I confessed my sins and turned to You! For that I praise and thank You!

PRAYER JAR INSPIRATION:

Jesus' forgiveness makes me white as snow!

Day 345

GOOD THINGS WILL COME

The end of a matter is better than its beginning, and patience is better than pride.

Ecclesiastes 7:8 niv

Wouldn't it be amazing if a broken bone could heal overnight? And wouldn't it be wonderful if a deep gash in your arm could be mended in an instant?

These things take time, and often lots of it!

God created us to heal naturally, but He deliberately chose a slower method. Why do you suppose that is? Why intentionally make us wait for healing?

The process of a bone mending is just that. . .a process. Sure, God could have set it all on warp speed, but it's mesmerizing to think about the immune system springing into action to bring about inflammation, which triggers the surrounding tissues, marrow, and blood to respond. It's all a chain reaction that leads to new bone forming at the point of the break.

Healing takes time. And it's never a good idea to rush the process. So don't push yourself to make everything perfect today. Good things come to those who wait.

I will trust Your process, Lord. Amen.

PRAYER JAR INSPIRATION:

Good things are coming—all in God's good timing.

Day 346

THE GOD WHO SEES YOU

The angel of the Lord found her by a spring of water in the wilderness, the spring on the way to Shur. And he said, "Hagar, servant of Sarai, where have you come from and where are you going?"

Genesis 16:7–8 ESV

God had promised the aging Sarah and Abraham a child. After patiently waiting for years and still no baby, Sarah gave her maid Hagar to Abraham, thinking they'd gain a child that way. Hagar *did* get pregnant. But then she lorded it over Sarah. And when Sarah began mistreating Hagar in return, the maid ran away.

Hagar hadn't even been looking for God's direction. But He'd been keeping watch over her. So God asked Hagar where she was coming from and where she was going to. After Hagar admitted she was running away from Sarah, God told her to go right back and submit to Sarah's authority. Then He promised her a son.

Just as God saw Hagar, He sees you. And if you keep your ears open, you can hear His directive. Your job is to follow it, even if that means retracing your steps.

"God Who Sees" (Genesis 16:13 HCSB) me no matter where I am, lead where You would have me go.

PRAYER JAR INSPIRATION:

Father God has His eyes on me. He will not let me stray.

Day 347

INTIMATE WITH GOD

No longer will people have to teach each other or encourage their family members and say, "You must know the Eternal." For all of them will know Me intimately themselves—from the least to the greatest of society. I will be merciful when they fail and forgive their wrongs. I will never call to mind or mention their sins again.

Jeremiah 31:34 voice

Jesus came into this world especially for you. He knew you couldn't keep God's laws. So Jesus did what nobody else could: He sacrificed His life so that you could live in an intimate relationship with God.

Perhaps you don't feel as close to God as you'd like. If so, take this opportunity to start your journey! First, immerse yourself in God's Word. Take His promises to heart. Learn of the overwhelming love Jesus has for you. Then, know that when you get things wrong, God will make them right—in your relationships, your life plans, your hopes, and your dreams. Know that He not only forgives but forgets your missteps. Simply believe!

I want to be closer to You, Lord, to experience You more when I'm in Your Word. Lead me the way You want me to go. Help me know I have received Your forgiveness. Amen.

PRAYER JAR INSPIRATION:

Jesus is my intimate Lord and friend— my passageway to God's presence!

Day 348

A SPECIAL PLACE

He says, "Be still, and know that I am God; I will be exalted among the nations, I will be exalted in the earth."

Psalm 46:10 NIV

When you've had a hard day, you just want to get home, put on your pj's, and kick up your feet. There's something about slowing down that makes everything better.

God always intended healing to come in the quiet, slow spaces. Maybe that's why He instructs us to meet Him in our prayer closet, a place set apart, away from others. It's so much easier to get His perspective when the loud voices around us have quieted down.

Where do you meet with God? Do you have a special location? Maybe it's time to create a set-apart place where you can have your quiet time with Him.

A favorite chair. The back patio. Your recliner. The bathtub. Any and all of these places will do. Just create a mindset that things will slow down in that space so that you can focus on Him.

I want to be where You are, Jesus. Meet me in our special place. Amen.

PRAYER JAR INSPIRATION:

My favorite place to meet with Jesus is _____.

Day 349

WHERE YOUR STRENGTH LIES

The Lord God, the Holy One of Israel has said this, "In returning [to Me] and rest you shall be saved, in quietness and confident trust is your strength."

Isaiah 30:15 AMP

Speaking through Isaiah, God told the people of Judah that sorrow awaited them because they made plans contrary to His and alliances that were not directed by His Spirit. Without consulting God, they went to Egypt for help, putting their trust in Pharaoh's protection instead of God's! God told them that doing so would only lead them to humiliation and disgrace.

Things were so bad that God's people not only refused to heed His instructions but also told His prophets, "Don't tell us what is right. Tell us nice things. Tell us lies. . . . Stop telling us about your 'Holy One of Israel'" (Isaiah 30:10–11 NLT).

Want to be on the right side of God? Follow His path; turn to Him for advice. Then you will find the rest and salvation you're seeking. And you'll find your strength by settling down and trusting in Him and His Spirit, completely depending on Him for your present and future.

I trust in You, Lord. Be my strength.

PRAYER JAR INSPIRATION:

You, Lord, are my hope, my confidence, my strength, my way.

Day 350

MOST BLESSED WOMAN

[Most] blessed is the man who believes in, trusts in, and relies on the Lord, and whose hope and confidence the Lord is. For he shall be like a tree planted by the waters that spreads out its roots by the river; and it shall not see and fear when heat comes; but its leaf shall be green. It shall not be anxious and full of care in the year of drought, nor shall it cease yielding fruit.

JEREMIAH 17:7–8 AMPC

God wants you to trust in Him for *everything*. He wants your hope and confidence to be in Him. So on those days that you feel like no one—not even God—can forgive you, think again.

After confessing your missteps to God, don't allow your shame to obscure His forgiveness. Instead, claim it! For when you do, you'll find yourself opening up to Him about everything that's going on in your life. You'll feel closer than ever to your Lord of forgiveness. And you'll begin to see your life prosper. Even when circumstances turn sour, you'll neither fear nor become anxious but find yourself at peace with the God who loves you more than you'll ever know.

Thank You, Lord, for forgiving me and loving me beyond all others.

PRAYER JAR INSPIRATION:

My hope and confidence are in my Lord!

Day 351

SOMETHING BETTER

Therefore, since we are surrounded by so great a cloud of witnesses, let us also lay aside every weight, and sin which clings so closely, and let us run with endurance the race that is set before us.

Hebrews 12:1 esv

When you're running a race, you have a destination in mind. You're doing everything you can to get to the finish line and win the prize. Nothing can slow you down. Your eye is fixed on the goal in front of you.

Unfortunately, life has a way of creating interruptions, and we don't always reach our goals. We make plans, and they fizzle. We set our sights on a job opportunity, and it falls through. We face disappointment when we fall short.

Today God wants to heal you from those disappointments. Who cares if things didn't go exactly as planned? You serve a heavenly Father who has His very best in mind for you.

Go ahead and make goals. But don't beat yourself up when you don't hit them. Trust Him to give you something even better!

I will keep running, Jesus. But if I fall short, I won't beat myself up. Amen.

PRAYER JAR INSPIRATION:

Disappointment isn't a reason to give up. I trust that God has something better in store for me.

Day 352

THE LORD'S PRESENCE

Whether it was two days or a month or a year that the cloud [of the Lord's presence] lingered over the tabernacle, staying above it, the Israelites remained camped and did not set out; but when it was lifted, they set out. At the command of the Lord they camped, and at the command of the Lord they journeyed on.

Numbers 9:22–23 amp

The cloud of God represented His presence among His people, a presence that was with them night and day. As long as the cloud lingered over the ark of God, the people stayed put. But when the cloud lifted, they set out, following wherever He led.

God's presence, His Spirit, continues on. By that Spirit, God continues to direct His people, instructing their hearts when they can rest and when He would have them move on.

Today, pray to Father God that He would direct you—that He would lead you where He would have you go. Pray that He would not allow your mind to have the final say but that His Spirit—the companion He left with you to guide, comfort, and strengthen—would have the last word.

Spirit of God, instruct my heart in the way You would have me go. Give me patience if Your will and way is for me to rest, and give me courage when You would have me set out.

PRAYER JAR INSPIRATION:

I hope in and follow the divine presence, the Holy Spirit that directs my heart's way.

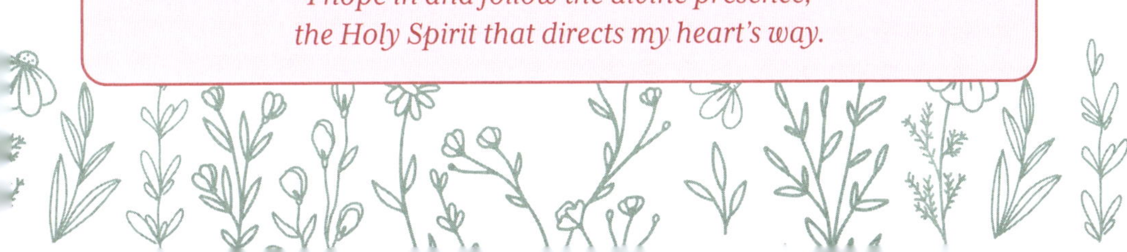

Day 353

TURN AROUND

God fulfilled what He foretold. . . , that His Christ (the Messiah) should undergo ill treatment and be afflicted and suffer. So repent (change your mind and purpose); turn around and return [to God], that your sins may be erased (blotted out, wiped clean), that times of refreshing (of recovering from the effects of heat, of reviving with fresh air) may come from the presence of the Lord.

Acts 3:18–19 AMPC

God's intense, profound, and abundant love for you prompted Him to allow His Son to be sacrificed on your behalf so that your sins could be forgiven. There's no way you can repay that sacrifice—but what you *can* do is walk God's way the best you can and confess your missteps along the way.

Yet there's one more box to check, one more task to take up: to turn from your old path. To change the way you've been living your life. To perhaps even rethink your goals. If you don't have any goals, perhaps turning around means living more intentionally for God.

The point is that once you've been forgiven, repentance is necessary. From what path might you need to turn?

Help me, Lord, to turn from the path that caused me to stumble. I want to walk more closely with You.

PRAYER JAR INSPIRATION:

Lord, show me how to turn around my life for You.

Day 354

QUIET AND CONCENTRATED

Be still before the Lord and wait patiently for him; fret not yourself over the one who prospers in his way, over the man who carries out evil devices!

Psalm 37:7 esv

Hurry! Go, go, go! Get in the car and buzz your way there, slapping on lipstick on the way. Eat that sandwich in the driver's seat. Make that business call from the car. There's no time to stop—not when you live on the edge.

Maybe you can relate. Perhaps this is how you live: late to every important (and unimportant) event. And when you come tearing into the parking lot, your heart is racing, you have mayonnaise on your chin, and you can't find your phone—even though you just made a call.

This lifestyle is way too common in the twenty-first century, but oh the troubles that come from it: Health challenges. Emotional traumas. And worst of all, when you're always late, there's no time for God.

This might be the hardest thing you've ever had to do, but today God is asking you to slow down that train. He has work for you to do, but it's quiet, concentrated work that requires stillness.

It's not going to be easy, but I will slow down, Lord! Amen.

PRAYER JAR INSPIRATION:

Hurry leads to worry.

Day 355

YOUR FAITHFUL LORD

"I have loved you with an everlasting love; therefore with lovingkindness I have drawn you and continued My faithfulness to you." . . . "There is [confident] hope for your future," says the Lord.

Jeremiah 31:3, 17 amp

God has loved, is loving, and always will love you. His love for you is everlasting. And it's because He loves you that He has drawn you to Himself so that you can play your part in His plan and further His kingdom by loving and drawing others to His light.

God would have it that you need nothing more than His love to content you—that you need not desire anything more than Him to find true joy. All afflictions you face are temporary, all woes are passing, all fears are fleeting. When you keep this in mind, you will find peace in the present and have confident hope for your future.

Don't waste your time and energy on worry, fears, or angst. Instead, live in the present with the Lord whose love and hope for you will never ever end.

The fact that You will always love me touches something deep within me, Lord. Because of You and Your everlasting love, I am content and filled with joy.

PRAYER JAR INSPIRATION:

I am a woman confident of God's love and filled with hope for my future.

Day 356

HIGH-POWERED DEFENSE LAWYER

I am writing these things to help you avoid sin. If, however, any believer does sin, we have a high-powered defense lawyer—Jesus the Anointed, the righteous—arguing on our behalf before the Father. It was through His sacrificial death that our sins were atoned. But He did not stop there—He died for the sins of the whole world.

1 John 2:1–2 voice

The disciple John wrote to early Christians, hoping his letter would help them stay away from sin. Even so, he also told them that if they said they didn't sin, they were lying!

But John then reminded them that whenever they fell short, they'd have a wonderfully powerful advocate to represent them before the Father: Jesus, the one who never sinned.

How blessed can we be? Jesus not only died on our behalf to restore our relationship with our Creator, He *continues* to defend us, even today!

Today and every day, remember that Jesus, your sinless Savior, has died for your sins and continues to defend you before God the Father when you mess up. Praise Him!

Thank You, Jesus, for continually rescuing me!

PRAYER JAR INSPIRATION:

My life is blessed by Jesus!

Day 357

POWER DOWN

Be angry, and do not sin; ponder in your own hearts on your beds, and be silent.

Psalm 4:4 esv

It's hard to quiet yourself long enough to heal when notifications are going off on your phone, your smart watch, and your laptop. All that ding-ding-dinging is a terrible distraction.

Let's face it: Technology can be a wonderful thing, but with music playing, movies streaming, friends texting, and bosses emailing, it can get overwhelming. You can slip into sensory overload with so many devices vying for your attention all at once.

It's time for some stillness. Turn off the ringer on that phone. Power down the laptop. Shut off the TV show. Close your eyes and just. . .be.

Sure, you might not know what to do with all that stillness if you're used to go-go-going. But God can (and does) speak during the quiet times. Listen for His still, small voice. Watch as He begins to heal you as you rest from the chaos.

I will do my best to avoid the distractions today, Lord. I'll close myself off from the chaos and spend quiet, peaceful time with You. Amen.

PRAYER JAR INSPIRATION:

I will choose to have a "powered down" day.

Day 358

FAITH, LOVE, AND HOPE

We have heard of your faith in Christ Jesus and your love for all of God's people, which come from your confident hope of what God has reserved for you in heaven. You have had this expectation ever since you first heard the truth of the Good News.

COLOSSIANS 1:4–5 NLT

Wouldn't it be great for others to hear about your faith and love, about the trust you have in Jesus, about your affection for all believers—all of which is born out of your hope of what God has reserved for you in heaven?

At this point you may be wondering, *What are those heavenly rewards awaiting me?* Someday you will be transformed. You'll see God's face, walk down streets paved with gold, and nevermore feel pain or sorrow. One day you'll reside forever after in the light of the Lord's presence! Knowing these rewards are in your future is what will surely help you get through whatever may be happening in the moment.

Allow that future hope to ignite and sustain your present faith in Jesus and to fire up your affectionate love for all believers. And you will find yourself and your world transformed.

Help me, Lord, to focus on my future hope by building up my faith in You and my love for others in the present. In Jesus' name, amen.

PRAYER JAR INSPIRATION:

Faith, hope, and love are my present—and future—reward!

Day 359

PETER'S FEAR

When they saw the armed crowd take Jesus into custody,
the disciples fled. . . .Peter followed, at a safe distance, all the way
into the courtyard of the high priest, and he sat down with the guards
to warm himself at their fire. He hoped no one would notice.

Mark 14:50, 54 voice

For all his bravado on the night of Jesus' arrest, Peter was only human. Although he'd promised to stay by Jesus' side no matter what, he still turned tail and ran. Later, he followed at a safe distance, curious about Jesus' fate.

As Peter waited outside the high priest's courtyard, warming himself by a fire, someone recognized him as one of Jesus' followers. And Peter denied it. This happened three times. . .and all three times, Peter denied knowing Jesus. Suddenly, the cock crowed for the third time, just as Jesus had predicted (Mark 14:66–72), leaving Peter in tears.

We too may sin out of weakness or fear. We too may weep tears of shame. But we must remember: Jesus can work with us—where we are and as we are. He's there at every turn.

Forgive my weakness and fears, Lord.
Help me become stronger and take courage in You.

PRAYER JAR INSPIRATION:

Jesus meets me where I am, as I am!

Day 360

STORM-CALMER

He stilled the storm to a whisper; the waves of the sea were hushed.
They were glad when it grew calm, and he guided them to their desired haven.

Psalm 107:29–30 niv

Some days the troubles are so deep that you can't wade through them. Why do bad things always seem to compound—one on top of the other?

If you're having a day like this, take a deep breath. If you can, tuck yourself away from people for a few minutes (even if it's in the restroom at work). In that place, God can calm the storm. Make a list of what needs to be done and put those things in a workable order. (One reason we often feel overwhelmed is because we can't determine a path of action.)

Once you've started your list, map out individual strategies for the problems you're facing. Having a written plan will help a lot. And remember, God sees you—even in the restroom with tears rolling down your cheeks. He's keenly aware of what you're going through and already sees the solutions before you do. So trust Him. Even if it feels impossible. Lift your hands and say, "Jesus, please heal this situation and mend my heart as well."

You can calm the storms in my heart, even on the hardest day, Jesus. Amen.

PRAYER JAR INSPIRATION:

I can have God-breathed strategies in place for dealing with hard situations.

Day 361

A WEANED CHILD

Lord, my heart is not proud; my eyes are not haughty. I don't concern myself with matters too great or too awesome for me to grasp. Instead, I have calmed and quieted myself, like a weaned child who no longer cries for its mother's milk. Yes, like a weaned child is my soul within me. O Israel, put your hope in the Lord—now and always.

Psalm 131:1–3 NLT

God's message to us stands in stark contrast to the message we get from the world. Our society would have us be proud, strong, and ambitious women, always finding a way to get ahead no matter who we might step on along the way.

Yet our God wants us to be humble. To trust not in our own strength and power but in His. To be satisfied with and grateful for what He has given us—no more, no less. To put all our hope in Him, now and always. For only then can we find true contentment and be able to calm and quiet our souls within us.

Today and every day, walk God's way. And you will find rest for your body, spirit, and mind.

Because of You, Lord, I can find the peace and calm I crave.

PRAYER JAR INSPIRATION:
My hope rests in the Lord—now and always.

Day 362

ATTENTION PLEASE!

Saul was [not only] consenting to [Stephen's] death [he was pleased and entirely approving]. . . . Saul shamefully treated and laid waste the church continuously [with cruelty and violence]; and entering house after house, he dragged out men and women and committed them to prison.

Acts 8:1, 3 ampc

Before he became the apostle Paul, Saul of Tarsus was a "fuming, raging, hateful man who wanted to kill every last one of the Lord's disciples" (Acts 9:1 voice). But then Jesus got Saul's attention by literally stopping him in his tracks.

One day, when Saul was traveling to Damascus, a light from heaven flashed around him, bringing him to the ground. He then heard Jesus saying, "Saul, Saul, why are you attacking Me?" (Acts 9:4 voice). Jesus ordered Saul to get up, go into the city, and wait for further instructions. Now blinded, Saul was led by his speechless traveling companions into Damascus.

When we've gone too far, when our malicious missteps are too much for the Lord, He calls our attention to our mistake.

To what might the Lord be drawing your attention?

Draw attention to areas in my life that aren't pleasing to You, Lord. Show me how to change my ways.

PRAYER JAR INSPIRATION:

Lord, show me where I may be walking out of Your will.

Day 363

PACE YOURSELF

Surely there is a future, and your hope will not be cut off.

Proverbs 23:18 ESV

Maybe you're a real go-getter, always racing toward the goal. You don't think about pacing yourself until your body breaks down or you end up plowing over someone on your way to the goal.

When it comes to healing, God wants you to pace yourself. It might sound disingenuous to say, "Lower your expectations" but if they're too high—if you're expecting instant gratification or healing—then you're bound to be disappointed every time.

Adjust those expectations. Pace your healing so you don't end up disappointed time and time again. "Good things come to those who wait" isn't just a platitude; it's truth. If everything came easily, you wouldn't be as grateful.

Today, take a close look at some of your current expectations. Are they a bit lofty? Are you expecting too much too fast? Are you constantly disappointed (by yourself and others) because of these unmanaged expectations? Pace yourself, friend. Good things will come. . .in time.

With Your help, I can manage my expectations. Amen.

PRAYER JAR INSPIRATION:

I can learn to pace myself with God's help.

Day 364

NO WORRIES TODAY

"Do not worry or be anxious (perpetually uneasy, distracted), saying, 'What are we going to eat?' or 'What are we going to drink?' or 'What are we going to wear?' . . . But first and most importantly seek (aim at, strive after) His kingdom and His righteousness [His way of doing and being right—the attitude and character of God], and all these things will be given to you also."

MATTHEW 6:31, 33 AMP

It's exhausting trying to get through your day when your mind is focused on what you might need for tomorrow! That kind of fretting can only lead to stress.

Jesus has a better idea. Instead of worrying about what you will eat, drink, or wear tomorrow, seek out God—how He would have you live, what He would have you do today. Make Him your priority. . .because God knows exactly what you need and has you *more* than covered regarding the material side of things.

So, precious daughter of God, put aside your worries about tomorrow. Seek out your Father today, knowing He will never let you down.

Help me, Lord, to put aside any worries about tomorrow and to seek You and Your way of doing things today. In Jesus' name, amen.

PRAYER JAR INSPIRATION:

Undistracted by tomorrow's needs, I can focus on God today!

Day 365

GOD'S TRUTH

I would have despaired had I not believed that I would see the goodness of the Lord *in the land of the living. Wait for and confidently expect the* Lord*; be strong and let your heart take courage; yes, wait for and confidently expect the* Lord.

Psalm 27:13–14 amp

Psalm 27:13–14 are some of the most uplifting and courage-inducing Bible verses you can find. For they tell you God will bring good into your life. All you need to do is expect it, to wait for it, knowing with confidence that God will come through in His good time.

Take these verses to heart. Commit them to memory so that when trouble comes or discouragement knocks at your door, you'll be ready. Allow these verses to give you the assurance you need to begin looking for and expecting the good things God will be bringing your way. Remind yourself that all you need to do is *wait with confidence* for Him to come through for you.

Woman, wait. Expect God to move. You will see God's goodness. In the meantime, wait. Expect God to move.

Lord, thank You for Your goodness. As I wait for You to come through once again, I will be strong. My heart will take courage.

PRAYER JAR INSPIRATION:

God's truth will keep me strong and courageous.

SCRIPTURE INDEX

OLD TESTAMENT

Genesis

3:21....Day 65
16:7–8....Day 346
21:6–7....Day 87
28:16....Day 298
32:9, 11–12....Day 14
37:5–7....Day 134
45:4–5....Day 280
50:20–21....Day 283

Exodus

14:13–14....Day 253
14:14....Day 336
34:6–7....Day 221

Numbers

5:6....Day 62
9:22–23....Day 352

Deuteronomy

31:6....Day 160
33:26–27, 29....Day 256

Joshua

1:5–6....Day 12
1:8....Day 331
1:9–11....Day 238

Judges

4:8–9....Day 235

Ruth

2:11–12....Day 156

1 Samuel

1:15–16....Day 2
17:45....Day 137

1 Kings

8:23–24....Day 302
8:35–36....Day 305
8:39–40....Day 308

2 Kings

4:22–23....Day 244
20:4–5....Day 143

1 Chronicles

16:11–12, 27....Day 18
28:20....Day 105
29:12–13....Day 24

2 Chronicles

7:14....Day 278

Nehemiah

2:17....Day 73

Esther

8:11, 15–16....Day 84

Job

1:22....Day 88

17:9 .... Day 288
34:4 .... Day 40
42:1–3, 5–6 .... Day 311

Psalm

3:5 .... Day 146
4:4 .... Day 357
4:8 .... Day 52
6:2 .... Day 148
9:2–3, 9–10 .... Day 177
9:10 .... Day 182
16:7 .... Day 207
16:8–9, 11 .... Day 223
18:32–33 .... Day 169
19:11–13 .... Day 290
23:1–3 .... Day 339
23:1–4 .... Day 192
23:4–6 .... Day 216
25:1–2, 6 .... Day 314
25:7–8, 11 .... Day 211
25:7–9 .... Day 317
25:11–13 .... Day 320
25:16–18, 21 .... Day 323
27:13–14 .... Day 365
30:5 .... Day 95
30:11–12 .... Day 72
31:19 .... Day 126
32:1–2 .... Day 299
32:3–4 .... Day 11
32:7–8 .... Day 343
33:11 .... Day 127
33:16–17 .... Day 163
33:18, 20–22 .... Day 93
34:4 .... Day 79
34:4, 7, 17 .... Day 180
34:8–10 .... Day 144
34:12–15 .... Day 247
34:18 .... Day 234
37:7 .... Day 354
37:7, 34 .... Day 186
37:23–24 .... Day 189
41:3–4 .... Day 326
42:5 .... Day 78
43:5 .... Day 111
44:21 .... Day 10
46:1–2 .... Day 6
46:4 .... Day 16
46:10 .... Day 348
46:10–11 .... Day 123
48:14 .... Day 207
51:8 .... Day 252
51:17 .... Day 121, 243, 258
54:1–2 .... Day 335
54:4 .... Day 94
55:22 .... Day 321
55:22–23 .... Day 53

59:10, 16 ....Day 30
68:3–4, 19–20 ....Day 90
68:5–6, 35 ....Day 226
79:8–10.....................Day 338
86:5..........................Day 224
91:1–2......................Day 147
91:4–6......................Day 203
92:12–14...................Day 165
94:17–19............ Days 41, 51
103:2–4....................Day 116
103:10–11................Day 236
103:12–14................Day 239
107:28–30................Day 132
107:29–30................Day 360
108:1, 4, 12–13 ....Day 162
116:16......................Day 188
119:81–82, 114, 147,
130...........................Day 204
120:1........................Day 335
121:1–2......................Day 76
130:1–3....................Day 208
131:1–3....................Day 361
138:1–2....................Day 193
138:3...........................Day 3
143:8........................Day 207
145:13–16................Day 171
147:3...............Days 194, 231
147:3, 11 ....Day 39

Proverbs

3:5–6...........................Day 89
3:8............................Day 151
3:24..............................Day 1
4:20–22....................Day 110
4:23..........................Day 267
4:25..........................Day 139
10:11–12....................Day 54
12:16........................Day 312
14:32........................Day 319
16:20........................Day 129
16:32........................Day 324
17:22................ Days 74, 246
18:10..........................Day 15
18:14.............. Days 249, 273
23:18........................Day 363
24:13–14..................Day 228
25:11–12..................Day 103
25:26........................Day 113
29:25..........................Day 61

Ecclesiastes

3:4............................Day 261
4:9–12......................Day 104
5:7............................Day 106
7:8................. Days 124, 345

Song of Solomon

2:11..........................Day 282

8:3, 6–7 .... Day 187

Isaiah

1:17–18 .... Day 257
1:18 .... Day 344
26:3 .... Day 114
30:15 .... Days 259, 349
30:20–21 .... Day 198
33:2 .... Day 175
35:4 .... Day 85
40:8 .... Day 166
40:10–11 .... Day 183
40:31 .... Day 157
41:10, 13 .... Day 108
43:1–2 .... Day 96
43:16, 18–19 .... Day 138
43:18–19 .... Day 291
43:25 .... Day 251
44:4 .... Day 97
46:3–4 .... Day 117
48:17–18 .... Day 328
49:9 .... Day 125
50:4 .... Day 136
55:6–7 .... Days 205, 263
55:10–11 .... Day 334
58:10–11 .... Day 201
59:19 .... Day 49

Jeremiah

14:22 .... Day 168
17:7–8 .... Day 350
17:9–10 .... Day 56
17:14 .... Days 68, 240
30:17 .... Day 237
31:3 .... Day 327
31:3, 17 .... Day 355
31:34 .... Day 347
32:17–19 .... Day 174

Lamentations

3:21–23 .... Day 48
3:22–24 .... Day 135

Daniel

10:17, 19 .... Day 72

Joel

2:13 .... Day 44
2:21–23 .... Day 274

Jonah

1:17 .... Day 342
4:1–2 .... Day 242

Micah

7:18–19 .... Day 269

Habakkuk

2:3 .... Day 195
3:2 .... Day 86

3:17–18 .... Day 81

Zephaniah

3:16–17 .... Day 262

Zechariah

2:5, 10 .... Day 153

Malachi

3:6 .... Day 225

NEW TESTAMENT

Matthew

4:24 .... Day 152
6:14–15 .... Days 29, 272
6:31, 33 .... Day 364
6:34 .... Day 115
7:9–11 .... Day 141
9:20–21 .... Day 304
11:28 .... Day 4
11:28–29 .... Day 120
11:28–30 .... Day 13
12:34–36 .... Day 287
13:24–26 .... Day 173
17:20 .... Days 27, 209
18:20 .... Day 155
26:34 .... Day 47

Mark

10:50–52 .... Day 301
11:25 .... Days 60, 130
14:6, 8–9 .... Day 250
14:50, 54 .... Day 359

Luke

1:37 .... Day 17
6:19 .... Day 92
6:27–28, 37 .... Day 199
6:37–38 .... Day 20
8:43–44 .... Day 140
9:16–17 .... Day 295
10:34 .... Day 98
12:57 .... Day 91
15:17–19 .... Day 57
15:31–32 .... Day 196
18:9 .... Day 59
23:33–34 .... Days 202, 233

John

1:14 .... Day 145
3:16 .... Day 178
3:16–17 .... Day 230
8:7 .... Day 50
8:44 .... Day 43
10:10 .... Day 276
12:44–46 .... Day 340

14:1 .... Days 200, 214
14:27 .... Day 265
15:9–11 .... Day 75
16:13 .... Day 109
16:24 .... Day 217

Acts

3:5–6 .... Day 313
3:18–19 .... Day 353
5:3–4 .... Day 284
8:1, 3 .... Day 362
8:20–22 .... Day 332
13:23 .... Day 58
13:38–39 .... Day 35
16:25–26 .... Day 307
26:17–18 .... Day 227

Romans

3:22–23 .... Day 63
3:23 .... Day 170
3:23–24 .... Day 32
5:5 .... Day 42
8:28 .... Day 222
10:9 .... Day 179
12:2 .... Day 215
12:9–10 .... Day 26
12:17–18 .... Day 23
12:18 .... Day 315
13:10 .... Day 71
15:4–5 .... Day 337

1 Corinthians

2:9 .... Day 264
6:19–20 .... Day 164
10:13 .... Day 70
13:1 .... Day 45
13:4–7 .... Day 260
13:7 .... Day 181
13:13 .... Days 184, 197
14:33 .... Day 28

2 Corinthians

1:3–4 .... Day 5
1:8–9 .... Day 150
1:10–11 .... Day 316
3:17 .... Days 218, 306
4:17–18 .... Day 219
10:3–5 .... Day 82
10:5 .... Day 122
10:18 .... Day 167
12:9 .... Day 21

Galatians

2:16 .... Day 80
2:20 .... Day 25
5:16 .... Day 296
5:16–17 .... Day 255
5:16–18 .... Day 293
6:7, 9 .... Day 277

Ephesians

1:7–10 .... Day 248
2:4–7 .... Day 275
2:8–9 .... Day 212
2:8–10 .... Day 286
4:2 .... Day 190
4:15 .... Day 128
4:30, 32 .... Day 66
4:31–32 .... Day 333
5:11 .... Day 37

Philippians

1:6 .... Day 297
3:13–14 .... Days 142, 210
4:4, 12 .... Day 229
4:8 .... Day 34
4:8–9 .... Day 271
4:19 .... Day 161

Colossians

1:4–5 .... Day 358
1:12–14 .... Day 266
1:15, 17 .... Day 322
2:13–14 .... Day 245
3:1–2 .... Day 310
3:2 .... Day 19
3:9–10 .... Day 31
3:12 .... Day 22
3:12–14 .... Day 8
3:13 .... Day 330
3:15 .... Day 268

1 Thessalonians

2:4 .... Day 64
4:11–12 .... Day 67
5:8–10 .... Day 159
5:16–18 .... Day 100
5:22 .... Day 46

1 Timothy

6:12 .... Day 107
6:17–18 .... Day 325

2 Timothy

1:6–7 .... Day 102
2:24–25 .... Day 69
3:16 .... Day 7
4:16–17 .... Days 33, 329

Philemon

1:22 .... Day 292

Hebrews

4:7 .... Day 279
4:12 .... Day 119
4:15–16 .... Day 341
8:12 .... Day 294
10:16–18 .... Day 254
11:1–2 .... Day 206
11:8 .... Day 241

11:31 .... Day 154
12:1 .... Day 351
12:1–2 .... Day 55
12:2 .... Day 131
13:8 .... Day 225

James

1:12 .... Day 309
5:13 .... Day 220
5:13–15 .... Day 38
5:16 .... Day 133

1 Peter

2:4–5 .... Day 112
2:16 .... Day 303
2:24 .... Day 191
3:9 .... Day 289
3:15 .... Day 99
4:10 .... Day 83
5:10 .... Days 9, 285

1 John

1:7 .... Day 77
1:8–10 .... Day 281
1:9 .... Day 318
2:1–2 .... Day 356
4:1 .... Day 185
4:8, 16 .... Day 36
4:18 .... Day 101
5:3 .... Day 158

2 John

12 .... Day 232

3 John

2 .... Day 270

Jude

3 .... Day 176

Revelation

2:19 .... Day 149
4:11 .... Day 118
21:3–4 .... Day 213
21:5 .... Day 300